THE ECSTATIC AND THE ARCHAIC

The word 'archaic' derives from the Greek *arkhaios*, which in turn is related to the word *archē*, meaning 'principle', 'origin', or 'cause'; the notion of ecstasy, or *ekstasis*, implies standing outside or beyond oneself, a self-transcendence. How these two concepts are articulated and co-implicated constitutes the core question underlying this edited collection, which examines both the present day and antiquity in order to trace the insistent presence of the ecstatic amid the archaic.

Presented in three parts, the contributors to this diverse book take the concept of the archaic in an entirely new direction. Part I, 'Ecstasy and the psychological', covers topics including Jung, Freud, ancient psychotherapy, desire, and theatre. Part II, 'Ecstatic-archaic history', considers Ludwig Klages, Orestes and Dionysus. Finally, Part III, 'Ancient ecstatic in other worlds', examines Luo Guanzhong's *Three Kingdoms* and Enki at Eridu. The collection offers a distinctive contextualisation of the dimension of the archaic in relation to the ecstatic experience.

The Ecstatic and the Archaic will appeal to readers interested in the relationship between ancient and postmodern worlds, and in how the past manifests itself in the present. It will be of great interest to academics and students of Jungian and post-Jungian ideas, classical religions and the history of ideas, as well as practitioners of analytical psychology and psychoanalysis.

Paul Bishop is William Jacks Chair of Modern Languages at the University of Glasgow, UK. His previous publications include *On the Blissful Islands*, *Analytical Psychology and German Classical Aesthetics*, volumes one and two, and, as editor, *The Archaic: The Past in the Present* and *Jung in Contexts: A Reader* (all Routledge).

Leslie Gardner is Fellow at the Department of Psychosocial Studies, University of Essex, UK, and author of *Rhetorical Investigations: G.B. Vico and C.G. Jung* and co-editor of *House: The Wounded Healer on Television* (both Routledge). Gardner co-founded the International Association of Jungian Studies and established the *International Journal of Jungian Studies*.

THE ECSTATIC AND THE ARCHAIC

An Analytical Psychological Inquiry

Edited by Paul Bishop and Leslie Gardner

Routledge
Taylor & Francis Group

LONDON AND NEW YORK

First published 2018
by Routledge
2 Park Square, Milton Park, Abingdon, Oxon OX14 4RN

and by Routledge
711 Third Avenue, New York, NY 10017

Routledge is an imprint of the Taylor & Francis Group, an informa business

British Library Cataloguing in Publication Data
A catalogue record for this book is available from the British Library

Library of Congress Cataloging in Publication Data
Names: Bishop, Paul, 1967- editor. | Gardner, Leslie, 1949- editor.
Title: The ecstatic and the archaic : an analytical psychological inquiry / [edited by] Paul Bishop and Leslie Gardner.
Description: Abingdon, Oxon ; New York, NY : Routledge, 2018. | Includes bibliographical references and index.
Identifiers: LCCN 2017050157 (print) | LCCN 2017054737 (ebook) | ISBN 9780203733332 (Master e-book) | ISBN 9781138300538 (hardback : alk. paper) | ISBN 9781138300545 (pbk. : alk. paper)
Subjects: LCSH: Psychoanalysis and religion. | Ecstasy. | Jungian psychology.
Classification: LCC BF175.4.R44 (ebook) | LCC BF175.4.R44 E37 2018 (print) | DDC 150.19/54—dc23
LC record available at https://lccn.loc.gov/2017050157

ISBN: 978-1-138-30053-8 (hbk)
ISBN: 978-1-138-30054-5 (pbk)
ISBN: 978-0-203-73333-2 (ebk)

Typeset in Bembo
by Swales & Willis Ltd, Exeter, Devon, UK

CONTENTS

CONTRIBUTORS

Paul Bishop is William Jacks Chair of Modern Languages in the School of Modern Languages and Cultures at the University of Glasgow. He edited *The Archaic: The Past in the Present* (2012) for Routledge, and his most recent publications include *On the Blissful Islands with Nietzsche & Jung* (Routledge, 2016) and *Ludwig Klages and the Philosophy of Life: A Vitalist Toolkit* (Routledge, 2017).

Alan Cardew is a Senior Fellow at the University of Essex, a Member of the Athens Institute for Education and Research, and a Member of the *Foro di Studi Avanzati* in Rome. At Essex he was Director of the Centre for Interdisciplinary Studies in the Humanities and Director of the Enlightenment. He has written on Heidegger, Jung, Cassirer, and Nietzsche, and his recent publications have been on the idea of the *protrepticus* and the sublimity of origins.

Terence Dawson spent the larger part of his academic career in Singapore. Now retired, he continues to pursue his interest in the relation of Jungian theory to literature and the other arts. He is an Associate Editor of the *International Journal of Jungian Studies*, the co-editor with Polly Young-Eisendrath of *The Cambridge Companion to Jung* (2nd edn, Cambridge University Press, 2008), and the author of *The Effective Protagonist in the Nineteenth-Century British Novel* (Ashgate, 2004), as well as of wide-ranging articles on English and European literature.

Leslie Gardner is a Fellow in the Department of Psychosocial and Psychoanalytic Studies, University of Essex, where she obtained her Ph.D. She published *Rhetorical Investigations: G.B. Vico and C.G. Jung* (Routledge, 2010); and has published chapters in several volumes, most recently in *Jung and the Question of Science*, edited by Raya A. Jones (Routledge, 2014) and in a forthcoming film handbook edited by Luke Hockley. She co-edited (with Luke Hockley) *House: The Wounded Healer on Television* (Routledge, 2013) and (with Fran Gray) *Feminist Views from Somewhere*

(Routledge, 2017), and she has convened conferences on '(Dis)enchantment' and 'Ecstatic archaic thought and analytical psychology' in London. She co-founded the *International Journal of Jungian Studies* with Renos Papadopoulos.

Raya A. Jones is a Reader in the School of Social Sciences, Cardiff University. She was a member of the Executive Committee of the International Association for Jungian Studies (2003–2009) and chaired the IAJS Second International Conference in 2009. She is the author of *Personhood and Social Robotics* (Routledge, 2016), *Jung, Psychology, Postmodernity* (Routledge, 2007) and *The Child–School Interface* (Cassell, 1995), editor of *Jung and the Question of Science* (Routledge, 2014), *Body, Mind and Healing after Jung* (Routledge, 2010), and co-editor of *Jungian and Dialogical Perspectives* (Palgrave Macmillan, 2011), *Cultures and Identities in Transitions* (Routledge 2010) and *Education and Imagination* (Routledge, 2008). She has published numerous journal articles on Jungian and postmodern approaches to the self.

Catriona Miller is a Senior Lecturer at Glasgow Caledonian University where she teaches television script writers and media students. She publishes in the field of film and television studies, with a particular interest in Horror, Cult TV and Science Fiction genres from a Jungian perspective. She is currently working on a joint book *The Heroine's Journey: Female Individuation on Screen* for Routledge.

Ben Pestell holds a Ph.D. from the University of Essex on divine contact and mythical thought in the *Oresteia* of Aeschylus. He serves on the executive committee of the Centre for Myth Studies at Essex. He is co-editor of *Translating Myth* (Legenda, 2016), and has published on Aeschylus and contemporary classical reception.

Mark Saban is a senior analyst with the Independent Group of Analytical Psychologists. He recently co-edited (with Andrew Samuels and Emilia Kiehl) *Analysis and Activism: Social and Political Contributions of Jungian Psychology* (Routledge, 2016). Recent papers include 'Jung, Winnicott and the divided psyche', *Journal of Analytical Psychology* (61(3), June 2016; and 'Two in one or one in two? Pushing off from Jung with Wolfgang Giegerich', in *Journal of Analytical Psychology* (60(5), November 2015).

Richard Seaford is Emeritus Professor of Ancient Greek at the Unversity of Exeter. He is the author of numerous papers and books on Greek drama, Greek religion, Greek philosophy, Greek society, and on the interrelation between them, most notably *Money and the Early Greek Mind: Homer, Philosophy, Tragedy* (Cambridge University Press, 2004).

Yulia Ustinova is Associate Professor at the Department of General History, Ben-Gurion University of Negev, Israel. Her current research is entitled 'Mania: Alteration of consciousness and insanity in Greek culture', and her publications on Greek religion and culture include *The Supreme Gods of the Bosporan Kingdom: Celestial Aphrodite and the Most High God* (Brill, 1999) and *Caves and the Ancient Greek Mind: Descending Underground in the Search for Ultimate Truth* (Oxford University Press, 2009).

PREFACE

Leslie Gardner

In this volume, we look both to contemporary times, and back to the ancients, to trace the insistent presence of the ecstatic, as it presents itself in – what is deemed to be – an archaic frame of mind. This self-aware state of being transports the mind and emotion out of their ordinary and sensible states. Psychologists, classicists, philosophers, and literary theorists have focused on such ancient thought and its bearing on contemporary analytical psychology to explore in this volume its tenacious and compelling hold.

Walter Benjamin associated intoxication with that 'ecstatic component [which] lives in every revolutionary act', adding that this component 'is identical with the anarchic'.[1] As Michael Löwy points out in his discussion of Benjamin's essay 'Surrealism' (included in *One-Way Street and Other Writings*), intoxication is 'an expression of the magical relationship between the ancients and the cosmos'.[2] Löwy proposes that Benjamin implies that 'the experience (*Erfahrung*) and the *Rausch* that once characterized that ritual relationship with the world disappear in modern society.' The notorious concept of 'profane illumination' is Benjamin's alternate phrase for the ubiquitous experience of transcendence in a mystical world without God.[3]

Exploring the ecstatic state in the same geographical frame as Benjamin's were such psychoanalysts as C.G. Jung, who looked to ancient constructs to try and evoke that supra-rational and distinctly human mode. They found the ecstatic-archaic mind still in evidence in the modern world, despite wondering at its diminished power. And as Richard Seaford has also reminded us, there is a vital connection between how the ecstatic state played out in ancient classical times and in psychological contemporary applications.

The papers given at the original colloquium in London at the Freud Museum have been expanded and substantially revised for publication. While building on an earlier volume edited by Paul Bishop (*The Archaic: The Past in the Present*,

Routledge, 2012), this new collection takes the concept of the archaic in an entirely new direction, and offers a distinctive contextualisation of the dimension of the archaic in relation to the ecstatic experience. We want to thank our excellent editor at Routledge, Susannah Frearson, and her attentive colleagues for all their help.

Notes

1 W. Benjamin, 'Surrealism', in *One-Way Street and Other Writings*, tr. E. Jephcott and K. Shorter, London: Verso, 1985, pp. 225–239 (p. 236).
2 M. Löwy, 'The Young Benjamin'. Available online from: https://www.jacobinmag.com/2016/01/walter-benjamin-anarchism-surrealism-marxism-theses/. Accessed 4 May 2017.
3 Benjamin, 'Surrealism', in *One-Way Street and Other Writings*, p. 227. Cf. M. Cohen, *Profane Illumination: Walter Benjamin and the Paris of the Surrealist Revolution*, Berkeley and Los Angeles, CA and London: University of California Press, 1993.

INTRODUCTION

Paul Bishop

This volume has its origin in a conference held on 15–16 July 2016 at the Freud Museum, London, in a room right above Freud's study with its ancient statues and sculptures. In some ways, the very title of this conference—'Ecstatic Ancient/ Archaic Thought and Analytical Psychology: An Inquiry'—was an act of defiance, because its subject is exactly counterposed to the dominant discourse in the arts and humanities. According to this discourse, which describes itself as postmodern but might equally well be described as 'sophistical', what we are talking about does not exist. On this account, there is no origin, no *Ursprung*, no *archē*; instead, as good Foucauldians reading our Nietzsche, we have to talk about 'provenance' (*Herkunft*) and 'point of emergence' (*Entstehung*). And equally there is no 'ecstasy' or *ekstasis*, for there is nothing outside the self, indeed there is nothing outside the text (*il n'y a pas de hors-texte*); indeed, there isn't even a text, there is only a structure, a *tissu*, a web, a network. (And there certainly isn't a canon; although, in a way, there is, for the new canonicity resides precisely in the denial of canonicity, and in the destruction, ridicule, or avoidance of the canon.)

Nor is there any ecstatic in the more circumscribed sense of its sexual or erotic dimension, because in the study of sexualities, in gender studies, in LGBT studies—all of which have, rightly, established themselves over recent years as valid areas of scholarship and contributed vital insights—everything is collapsed into 'discourse'. So we should forget the Kama Sutra, forget the troubadours, forget Petrarch; forget the Marquis de Sade, forget Leopold von Sacher-Masoch, forget Foucault (who knew a thing or two about sexuality, thanks to his experiences in the bathhouses of San Francisco . . .); and above all forget *cherchez la femme*, because (according to Jacques Lacan) *la femme n'existe pas*.

And yet the thesis informing the conference and subsequently this volume—which does not claim to be definitive, but deliberately describes itself as *an inquiry*—is that, however much we might want to or try to, we cannot escape the archaic dimension of existence, nor can we remain oblivious to its ecstatic manifestation. On the one hand, the ecstatic-archaic manifests itself through something that can be called *Grenzerlebnisse*, *Grenzsituationen*, oder *Grenzerfahrungen*, and which derives from the experience of what Karl Jaspers (1883–1969) called a *Grenzsituation*.[1] 'Limit situations' is a term is used by Jaspers to describe situations in which the human individual comes up against the limitations of his or her being—ultimately, his or her mortality. On the other hand, the ecstatic-archaic is something one can encounter in a more everyday experiential way as well, as the introductory blurb to Joseph Campbell's *Myths To Live By* suggests: 'The latest incarnation of Oedipus, the continued romance of Beauty and The Beast, stands this afternoon on the corner of 42nd Street and Fifth Avenue, waiting for the traffic light to change.'[2]

The ecstatic dimension of the archaic is clearly brought out in the experience explored by the cultural critic Jonathan Meades towards the end of the first episode of the three-part documentary series *Magnetic North*, first broadcast on BBC Four in 2008, when he visits the famous chalk cliffs on the island of Rügen—famous not least because of their depiction in a famous painting by the German Romantic artist Caspar David Friedrich (1774–1840), his *Chalk Cliffs on Rügen* (1818–1820). Its three figures gazing out to sea are, Meades suggests, not so much looking out towards a bright new dawn as turning away from the immensity of the forest behind them: 'What Friedrich's painting does not reveal is the forest behind him, behind the figures staring transfixedly at the sea and at a limitless world.' As Meades goes on to explain: 'For Friedrich, as for the Brothers Grimm, forests were places of real and metaphorical darkness which mankind had ceased to dwell in and worship in; which mankind had escaped from, but which still exerted a morbid attraction.' For Meades, the forest was a location of the primitive, the primordial, or the archaic—and it is still is today. 'The fear that overtook me', he says,

> was primal; it went beyond that German conditioning, even though I was in Germany. Brain and body were united in foreboding; it was sufficient to persuade me that another memory might exist—an atavistic memory. I was the distant legatee of some distant, woad-smeared forebear's fear of the forest.

At this point, Meades turns directly to the camera and tells us:

> In places like this, reason does not sleep: it is concussed by a heavy blow. So I wouldn't have been surprised to see berserker warriors, in bloody furs and skin, or knots in wood mutating into witches' faces, or fabulous stags with shining bez tines, or enchanting wood sprites whose kiss is fatal. This place seemed to contain [he emphasises] an inventory of horrible possibilities.[3]

While the postmodernists deny the very idea of the archaic and show disdain for its ecstatic manifestations, there is nevertheless a strong tradition of scholarship that investigates the archaic and the ecstatic, the latter used here in the sense of 'rapture, beauty, adoration, wonder, awe, mystery, sense of the unknown, desire for the unknown'.[4] In 2012, a collection of papers was published under the title *The Archaic: The Past in Present*, building on work undertaken on Jung by contributors to *The Journal of Analytical Psychology*, on Schelling (1775–1854), on Martin Heidegger (1889–1976), and on Ernesto Grassi (1902–1991), in order to try and revive interest in the archaic as a valid category in the field of scholarly inquiry.[5] Yet an exploration of the ecstatic dimension of the archaic remained, as Leslie Gardner, the organiser of the London conference had realized, a desideratum in the field of 'Archaic Studies'.

Now the philosophical investigation of the ecstatic goes back as least as far as Plotinus in his celebrated *Ennead* (VI.9) on 'The Good or the One', which famously concludes with its description of the contemplative life as 'the flight of the lone to the Alone'.[6] In the final section of this text, Plotinus describes the moment of union with the divine in the following ecstatic terms:

> [The seer] was as if carried away or possessed by a god, in a quiet solitude and a state of calm, not turning away anywhere in his being and not busy about himself, altogether at rest and having become a kind of rest. He had no thought of beauties, but had already run up beyond beauty and gone beyond the choir of virtues, like a man who enters into the sanctuary and leaves behind the statues in the outer shrine; these become again the first things he looks at when he comes out of the sanctuary, after his contemplation within and intercourse there, not with a statue or image but with the Divine itself; they are secondary objects of contemplation. But that other, perhaps, was not a contemplation but another kind of seeing, a being out of oneself [*ekstasis*] and simplifying and giving oneself over and pressing towards contact and rest and a sustained thought leading to adaptation, if one is going to contemplate what is in the sanctuary.[7]

In this text, as Richard Harder remarks, Plotinus 'approaches the suprarational kernel of the experience of union above all by the means of a spiritual eroticism derived from Plato, but given new weight', for 'here the passion aroused is repeatedly assuaged by references to how the ecstasy is "calm", "still"'.[8]

In more recent times, the archaic and its ecstatic inflection have been investigated by numerous writers and thinkers, almost all of whom fall outside—or have been pushed outside—the mainstream of academic enquiry. In one way or another, all these thinkers tried to follow an injunction found in Nietzsche's unpublished fragments from 1881:

> *Stop feeling oneself to be such a fantasized ego!* Learn step by step to *throw away one's supposed individuality!* Discover the errors of the ego! Gain insight into *egoism as an error!* Understand that its opposite is not altruism! That would mean showing love towards *other apparent* individuals! No! Go **beyond** "you" and "me"! **Experience cosmically!**[9]

For instance, this sense of the cosmic or the archaic was explored at the beginning of the twentieth century by the Canadian psychiatrist Richard Maurice Bucke (1837–1902) in his account of various case studies (including Bucke's own), entitled *Cosmic Consciousness: A Study in the Evolution of the Human Mind* (1905).[10] Bucke's study introduced the notion of 'cosmic consciousness', a term derived from Edward Carpenter (in turn, one of the case studies in this book), but it also drew on Bucke's own, all-too-brief 'mystical' experience in London in 1872. (Perhaps there is something about London hotels that invites mystical experiences; after all, Swedenborg had his own mystical experience, referred to as his 'vision of vocation, in London in April 1745.)[11] In *Civilisation: Its Cause and Cure* (1889; 1920), Carpenter had argued in an almost proto-Klagesian manner that civilisation is a kind of disease through which human societies pass but, in *Cosmic Consciousness*, Bucke distinguished between the perceptual mind (sense impressions), the receptual mind (simple consciousness), the conceptual mind (self consciousness), and the intuitional mind (a mind in which 'sensation, simple consciousness and self consciousness are supplemented and crowned with cosmic consciousness')[12]. The historical figures considered in his study included Gautama Buddha, Jesus Christ, St Paul of Tarsus, Plotinus, the prophet Mohammed, Dante, Bartolomé de Las Casas, St John of the Cross, Francis Bacon, Jakob Böhme, William Blake, Honoré de Balzac, and Walt Whitman.

Very often those thinkers who are interested in theorizing the archaic pay close attention to the world of myth.[13] But what *is* myth? In his 'Prolegomena' to *Essays on the Science of Mythology* (1941), co-authored with Carl Jung, the Hungarian classicist Karl Kerényi (1897–1973) draws on the work of the anthropologist Bronisław Malinowski (1884–1942) to argue that myth is not 'an explanation put forward to satisfy curiosity', but rather 'the rearising of a primordial [i.e., archetypal] reality in narrative form'.[14] Drawing attention, as many other thinkers have done, to the importance of the German *gründen*, i.e., to 'found', to 'ground', or to 'establish', Kerényi claims that 'mythology gives a ground, lays a foundation', inasmuch as 'it does not answer the question "why?" but "whence?"'. Kerényi specifically draws on the Greek notion of the *arkhai* to explicate this notion of a ground:

> They form the ground or foundation of the world, since everything rests on them. They are the *arkhai* to which everything individual and particular goes back and out of which it is made, while they remain ageless, inexhaustible, invincible in timeless primordiality, in a past that proves imperishable because of its eternally repeated rebirths.[15]

Granted that these *arkhai* exist, then 'this return to the origins and to primordiality is a basic feature of every mythology', Kerényi argues, and mythology is 'the direct unquestioning return to the *arkhai*, a spontaneous regression to the "ground"'. Or put in terms of ancient Greek thought: 'behind the "Why?" stands the "Whence?", behind the *aiton* the *arkhē*'.[16]

Kerényi goes on to distinguish two dimensions to this origin, which are nevertheless linked—one metaphysical, one political:

'Origin' means two things in mythology. As the content of a story or mythologem it is the 'giving of grounds' (*Begründung*); as the content of an act it is the 'founding' (*Gründung*) of a city or the world.[17] In either case it means man's return to his own origins and consequently the emergence of something original, so far as it is accessible to him, in the form of primordial images, mythologems, ceremonies.[18]

And Kerényi's point is that mythology, whichever form it comes in, is still alive and relevant for us today:

> The ideal *primary* mythology [hovers] as it were between the *one* origin and the fixed monadic version of it. Living mythology, on the other hand, expands in infinite and yet shapely multiplicity, rather like the plant-world in comparison with Goethe's 'primal plant'. We must always keep our eyes on both: the historical Many and the unitive principle that is nearest to the origin.[19]

A similar sense of the persistence of the archaic informs *The Ever-Present Origin* (*Ursprung und Gegenwart*) (1949; 1953),[20] a two-volume work by the Hispanist linguist and philosopher, Jean Gebser (1905–1973).

In this study, Gebser undertook to trace the emergence of various structures of consciousness in history, in a manner entirely separate from yet not dissimilar to the more well-known account offered by the Neo-Kantian philosopher Ernst Cassirer (1874–1945) in his famous study of 'symbolic forms'.[21] Whereas Cassirer distinguished between language, mythical thought, and science as his major symbolic categories, Gebser distinguishes between (1) the archaic, (2) the magic, (3) the mythical, (4) the mental, and (5) the integral structures. As Ed Mahood notes in his online introduction to the thought of Gebser, 'the term "archaic" [. . .] is derived from the Greek *arche*, meaning inception or origin', he defines this 'origin (or *Ursprung*, in the original German)' both as 'the source from which all springs' and as 'that which is behind and which underlies consciousness'.[22] As Gebser portrays the archaic structure, in it consciousness is, in the words of Georg Feuerstein (1947–2012), no more than 'a dimly lit mist devoid of shadows'.[23] In the archaic, 'the human being was totally immersed in the world unable to extricate himself or herself from that world', for he or she was fundamentally 'identical with that world'.[24]

Yet Gebser's argument is not purely an historical one but concerns the present moment. As he noted at the end of the first volume, 'this spiritual present [. . .] elevates wholeness to transparency and frees us from our transient age, for this age of ours is not the present but partiality and flight, indeed, almost a conclusion', and 'only someone who knows of origin has present—living and dying in the whole, in integrity'.[25]

And as he sought to demonstrate at the beginning of the second volume, the persistence of the archaic present can be tracked across a variety of different manifestations: in the natural sciences (in mathematics, physics, and biology), in the sciences of the mind (psychology and philosophy), in the social sciences (law, sociology, and economics), as well as in the so-called 'dual sciences' (including psychosomatic medicine and parapsychology), the arts (music, architecture, painting, literature)—and crucially in our daily lives.[26] Gebser's warnings about the mutation in public consciousness, factory and office life as self-imposed falsifications of time, and the achievements necessary to become an individual are as urgent as, if not more so than, at the time of their writing in the 1950s:

> Origin is present. Anyone who is able to perceive this spiritual state of affairs has already overcome the confusion of our epoch and maintains the greater and more decisive reality of the whole: that unique entirety and integrity which is always both origin and present.[27]

Yet Gebser was by no means alone in emphasizing the existential dimension of an appreciation of the archaic.

In *Saving the Appearances: A Study in Idolatry* (1957), Owen Barfield (1898–1997) undertook, in less than 200 pages, an exploration of three millennia of human history—or, more precisely, human consciousness. In it Barfield, a disciple of Rudolf Steiner (1861–1925), propounded the case that not only do human consciousness and language evolve simultaneously, but that this evolution of consciousness is inseparable from the evolution of nature, arguing in effect for the interactivity of matter and mind. Barfield deserves a place in the history of modern reflection on the archaic, inasmuch as he proposes the notion of 'original participation'—the essence of which is that 'there stands behind the phenomena, *and the other side of them from me*, a represented which is of the same nature as me'—investigates language as having its source in such participation—'and, in doing so, indicates the direction in which we must look for a true understanding of those mysterious "roots"'; he argues that while it seems that Pan has 'shut up shop', he has, in fact, 'not retired from business' but has 'merely gone indoors'—'he has not only gone indoors; he has hardly shut the door, before we begin to hear him moving about inside'.[28]

Finally, at the very intersection—or, as critics would doubtless prefer, fringe—of academic and popular discourse, one finds the figure of Terence McKenna (1946–2000) and his study with a self-explicatory title called *The Archaic Revival: Speculations on Psychedelic Mushrooms, the Amazon, Virtual Reality, UFOs, Evolution, Shamanism, the Rebirth of the Goddess, and the End of History* (1991).[29] Although we might look askance at McKenna's accounts of his experiences with, say, tryptamine hallucinogens, his remarks can sometimes throw new light on Heraclitus—'the experience always reminds me of the twenty-fourth fragment of Heraclitus: "The Aeon is a child at play with colored balls"'[30]—as well as Jung's experiences as they are recounted in his *Red Book*: 'One not only becomes the Aeon at play with colored balls but meets entities as well.' McKenna explains, 'I describe them as self-transforming machine elves [. . .] dynamically contorting topological nodules that are somehow distinct from the surrounding background, which is itself undergoing a continuous transformation', and he adds that these 'tryptamine Munchkins', these 'hyper-dimensional machine-elf entities' are like 'fractal reflections of some previously hidden and suddenly autonomous part of one's own psyche'.[31] On reading these sentences, it is hard not to think of the mandalas and the Kabeiroi in the *Red Book* . . .

Yet all these accounts of the archaic in a cosmic sense nevertheless neglect, it could be argued, to take full account of a particular dimension of the archaic, and one that is easily misunderstood—its ecstatic quality. Precisely this dimension, however, is explored by a comparatively neglected thinker in the German intellectual tradition, Ludwig Klages (1872–1956).[32] Between 1900 and 1912, in fragmentary texts written at this time which he subsequently edited himself and published in 1944 as his own literary *Nachlass* under the title *Rhythms and Runes* (*Rhythmen und Runen*), Klages was already developing a theory of the ecstatic that would later inform his mature philosophical system.[33] In one fragmentary text from this period, entitled 'Life as a Retrospective', Klages describes the relation of the individual living being to the past in a way that builds up to a quotation from a work by one of his favourite writers, the German Romantic poet Joseph Eichendorff (1788–1857):

> What *is alive* in the individual being is related to the distance, which is to say: to the past. Every glance into the distance is a glance into the past, even a glance in a spatial sense; for what emerges as an image out of the distance will already have passed: space itself is the phenomenal form of time. This is only apparently contradicted by the exhilarated feelings of excitement, expectation, yearning, youthful intuitive anticipation of future vital plenitude, the exhilaration of spring and the promise of happiness, which glows and smiles at us from everything we love; in short, precisely that distant shudder which Eichendorff caught in these luminous verses:
>
> > The distance speaks, intoxicated,
> > Of a future, of a great happiness.
> > [*Es reden trunken die Ferne*
> > *Wie von künftigem, großem Glück.*][34]

Having reached an ecstatic high-point with this quotation from Eichendorff (a text which has, memorably, been set to music by Schumann),[35] and using these lines as a starting-point, Klages analyses what he has just described as the main contours to the ecstatic as he understands it:

> For these are all ecstasies coming into being, syntheses that are being prepared for a move from Now to Once, by means of which the past that flames up in the Now consumes the intellectual ghost of the Future. In the powerful accord with the 'Here-and-Now' the Past which is emerging to existence gleams and now entices as the 'Future'. These are explosive moments in which the ray of time, released from space, drowns, and it is the nuptial celebration of the universe with the individual being which time had surrounded as a glowing ring. In these verses by Eichendorff what we see aflame

is not just some distant sunset, but the entire horizon of the starry nocturnal firmament! In the form of intoxicated anticipations, what bursts forth out of the Now and Here is a spark which, igniting, falls into the There and Once. This is how the ecstasy of a wanderer is born.[36]

In line with this way of thinking, the papers in this collection are offered as a tentative first step in a new area of enquiry—into the relationship between the ecstatic and the archaic.

Moving between the theoretical and the clinical, between Western and Eastern, between the past and the present, and between pro-archaic and the anti-archaic, these papers from contributors across the globe might be regarded as a series, in the words of Thomas Merton, of 'raids on the unspeakable'[37]—unspeakable, that is, in both senses of the word as it is used in English. For the archaic and the ecstatic share the quality of being beyond articulation; as well as referring to an experience of something that might be inconceivably excellent—or utterly abysmal. Both the archaic and the ecstatic cry out for rehabilitation in our safe, sterile, box-ticking environment of the endless reinforcement of mindless platitudes and *idées reçues*. Or perhaps they simply cry out: depending on where one stands, a shriek, a sob, or a gentle sigh . . .

****

The chapters in this volume are intentionally broad in thematic scope and in methodological approach; the purpose of the volume is, after all, to conduct an inquiry. While nearly all the chapters draw to a greater or lesser extent on the thought of C.G. Jung, they are by no means 'Jungian' in their assumptions or interpretative framework. Indeed, some contributors explicitly question Jung's approach, while others still find in him a resource that can explain the archaic, the ecstatic, and the interrelation between the two.

Part I contains chapters examining ecstasy in its psychological dimension and function. In the *Republic*, Socrates tells Glaucon: 'We know that when someone's desires incline strongly to some one thing, they are therefore weaker with respect to the rest, like a stream that has been channeled off in that other direction.'[38] In 'The stream of desire and Jung's concept of psychic energy', Raya A. Jones examines how C.G. Jung's theory of psychic energy differs from Freud's notion of libido in ways that bring Jung close to field physics and gestalt psychology as well as to Bergson, but nevertheless carries vestiges of the hydraulic metaphor. Although neither Freud nor Jung cites Plato's analogy of the stream when articulating their respective theories, there is nevertheless a striking confluence in terms of the central image both thinkers use. At the same time, there are also significant differences across the ancient and modern uses of this image, differences reflecting the post-Enlightenment machine metaphor of the human individual, as Jones explores in her chapter.

In 'The characters speak because they want to speak: Jung, Dionysus, theatre and therapy', Mark Saban explores how Jung's early work on the differentiation and personification of the complexes revealed a psychological scene in which multiple figures—autonomous and personified—dynamically play out their interrelations on the intra-psychic stage. This highly dramatic (and dramatising) perspective on the psyche led Jung directly toward the development of what he called the 'transcendent function', a concept enacted in the improvisations and personifications of active imagination. In his chapter, Saban investigates the Dionysian (and, in this sense, ecstatic) implication of a psychological model whose aim to bring opposites together manages to combine both the paradoxical and the theatrical.

Yulia Ustinova's chapter, 'Ancient psychotherapy? Fifth-century BCE Athenian intellectuals and the cure of disturbed minds', takes as its starting-point the fact that the treatment of abnormal behaviour advocated in Hippocratic medicine was focused on the body of the patient; consequently, mental afflictions were attributed mainly to humoral misbalance or trauma. In fact, Hippocratic therapy was largely based on purgation of the body, using procedures which ensued from time-honoured techniques of purification. Madness and purification remained intertwined, and the innovation offered by scientific medicine was, she argues, in the realm of theory rather than practice. Actual innovation in practical terms came from the experts in the use of words, who recognized their healing power and began to elaborate methods of 'speaking therapy.' Now these methods may have been rooted, Ustinova suggests, in the age-long appreciation of compassionate conversation and the power of persuasion, and even in the ancient belief in the magic power of the words. On the other hand, she notes, therapy by persuasion involved close interaction with the ideas of contemporary thinkers on illness of the soul as ignorance, to be treated by education and wise words—a method developed by the Sophists, in particular by Gorgias and Antiphon. Ustinova explores the evidence which attests to the practical interest of the ancient thinkers in the subject which would be defined today as psychology and psychotherapy, as well as discussing the place of Gorgias' and Antiphon's ideas and activities in the fifth-century intellectual milieu, putting an emphasis on their dialogue with medicine and drama.

For his part, Alan Cardew starts with the questions: what can account for Freud's anxieties about visiting Rome and Athens, and Jung's physical inability to travel to Rome 'the smoking and fiery hearth of ancient culture'? Was the greatness of the classical ideal as developed by German classicists from Winckelmann to Nietzsche, Cardew asks, simply too imposing to be faced? The fact that Freud used a passage from Virgil as an epigraph for *The Interpretation of Dreams*: '*Flectere si nequeo superos, Acheronta movebo*' ('If I cannot move the higher powers, I will move the infernal regions'), prompts the further question: could the unconscious, with all its repressed desires, condensations, displacements and defensive obscurity, be something of a refuge from that terrible, high ideal? In 'Antiquity and anxiety: Freud, Jung, and the impossibility of the archaic', Cardew considers psychoanalysis from the position of late antiquity. In particular, he examines psychoanalysis from the perspective of Neoplatonism, which appears to possess the same central concerns: the importance of dreams, therapy, and the understanding and deliberate development of the psyche. His rich and wide-ranging discussion leads him to ponder these further questions: would such a late classical analysis be more bearable than one based on the forbidding principles of German classicism? And what are the implications for the status within psychoanalytic discourse of the status of the archaic?

If Alan Cardew suggests that the archaic may well be an impossibility, then the following chapter by Paul Bishop—which opens Part II, examining ecstatic-archaic history—explores a different set of options. This chapter, entitled 'I must get out (of myself) more often? Jung, Klages, and the ecstatic-archaic', proposes the view that we cannot escape the archaic, and by the same token nor can we remain oblivious to its ecstatic manifestation. While postmodernism denies the very idea of the archaic and shows disdain for its ecstatic manifestations, there is (as discussed above) a steadily growing literature on the archaic, and a growing appreciation of the role it plays in a diverse range of thinkers from Plotinus to Terence McKenna, including Ludwig Klages and C.G. Jung. Both Klages and Jung orient their discussion of the ecstatic and the archaic around the figure of Nietzsche, and this chapter proposes to examine some of the ways in which they do so. It argues that Klages and Jung stand as exponents of the importance of cultivating and nurturing a cultural memory (Assmann), and both of them warn us that, if we do not cultivate this cultural memory, what is not so much repressed as forgotten can and maybe will return in dangerous forms. For the archaic in general and in its ecstatic form in particular is a genuine case of something that is, in the parlance of postmodernism, 'always already' there: and it is something that we, quite literally, ignore at our peril.

Returning to the archaic and ecstatic dimensions of the theatre, Ben Pestell's chapter, 'Ecstatic atoms: The question of Oresteian individuation', begins by asking: should we see the protagonists of Greek tragedies as psychologised characters (as in 2015's acclaimed production of the *Oresteia* at the Almeida Theatre in London) or personified forces? In his study of Greek tragedy and the emotions, the Irish classical scholar W.B. Stanford (1910–1984) argued that fear is felt, not in the head, but as physical manifestations in the body. Yet Aeschylus's trilogy, the *Oresteia*, invites a different view, in which Phobos is not only palpably felt but—in Orestes' experience—also exists as a psychological experience, inducing a madness. Pestell proposes that the 'talking cure' of the persuasive language employed by Aeschylus's Athena activates an inherent property of the mythical method, as defined by the French anthropologist and ethnologist, Claude Lévi-Strauss (1908–2009): the dialectical powers of myth are able to overcome contradictions and trauma. By arguing that the work of Freud, Jung and others deploys a word magic that has remained latent throughout the history of human verbalisation, Pestell concludes that Athena unites the individual and society in a cure which supports the defence of Jungian individuation against the charge of solipsism.

In 'Monetised psyche and Dionysiac ecstasy', the classicist Richard Seaford engages with a Jungian approach to the philosophical thought of the ancient Greek world. His chapter is the response of a non-Jungian Hellenist to the strengths and weaknesses of Edward Edinger's Jungian account of early Greek philosophy. The first strength of this account, Seaford argues, is the claim that ideas from the remote past are relevant to understanding our own psyches. (Might this approach be enhanced by an encounter with the evolutionary psychology of Merlin Donald?)

Second, whereas most scholars of early Greek thought treat it as the purely intellectual activity of 'philosophy', i.e., the use of reason to understand the world, Edinger's entirely justified rejection of this assumption opens up possibilities well beyond the reach of the scholars, who are curiously uninterested in preconceptions. And third, Edinger asks the question that is almost never asked (and never properly answered) by scholars: given that the world around us is obviously multiple, why do the earliest (Presocratic) 'philosophers' concur in imagining that it is in fact composed of a single substance?

Edinger's answer is that this Presocratic monism is a projection of the 'unity of the psychic Self'. In fact, for Edinger, Greek metaphysics is always a 'projection of the reality of the psyche, which lies behind sensible, concrete existence'. Greek metaphysics varies greatly. For instance, Heraclitus maintains everything is constantly changing; whereas, for his contemporary, Parmenides, all change is an illusion, and what truly exists is invariant in time and space. For Edinger, Heraclitean metaphysics represents the constantly changing ego, whereas Parmenidean metaphysics represents the transpersonal Self, which transcends time. Now Edinger is right to assume that metaphysics (in this early period, at least) derives neither from observation nor from reason, but from preconception. Yet when the Greeks imagined the world as ruled by Zeus (with beard, sceptre and throne), this is, Seaford suggests, a projection not of the psyche but of social omnipotence (monarchy). In order to be effective, social omnipotence must be introjected (into the psyche) as well as projected (onto the cosmos). Whereas Edinger's approach is characterised by a ruthlessly one-sided exclusion of history and society, Seaford undertakes to show that, with the revolutionary new (impersonal, all-pervasive) omnipotence of money, this introjection-cum-projection provides a way of understanding Heraclitus (the first extant account of the soul as unified consciousness), Parmenides, and early Greek 'philosophy' generally.

In the final section, which considers the ancient ecstatic in other worlds, two chapters shift the discussion in a different direction, thematically and geographically. In 'History, philosophy, and myth in Luo Guanzhong's *Three Kingdoms*', Terence Dawson examines the notion of 'One China [i.e., One Nation]' as an archetype with reference to one of the best-known classics of Chinese literature. Ostensibly, *Three Kingdoms*, aka *Romance of Three Kingdoms*, is a prose epic of the late fourteenth century CE attributed to Luo Guanzhong, a fictionalised history spanning the collapse of the Han Dynasty, the turbulent period of the Three Kingdoms, and the reunification of China by the Jin (i.e., events set between 184 and 280 CE). Beneath the history, however, is a powerful moral novel based on the ideas of (or ascribed to) Confucius (*c.* 510 BCE). Dawson delves into the tangled relationship between the concerns of these three very different time periods and shows how they imply that the Chinese view of history rests on moral psychology; and, at the same time, to explore the differences between the fundamental assumptions of the Asian or Chinese mind from those of the Graeco-Christian West. On the surface, the characters of the novel have no notion of what Freud or Jung would call the 'unconscious'. And yet, in much the same way as Jung claims that a dream effectively challenges the whole being of the dreamer, Dawson argues that the 'novel' challenges the reader to integrate the moral values that lie at its heart.

Finally, we embark on a journey to the Sumerian Underworld, viewed from a Jungian perspective. In 'Enki at Eridu: God of directed thinking', Catriona Miller takes us through the story of Inanna and Enki, in which the goddess Inanna visits the god at his temple Eridu, described as being in the *abzu* (an underworld, watery abyss). After a good meal, the now-drunk Enki gives Inanna a large number of the *mē* (skills and attributes of civilisation) in his keeping. The following morning, regretting his largesse, Enki tries to get them back, but Inanna escapes to her own city of Uruk and gives them to her own people. Some critics, notably Samuel Noah Kramer, have suggested that this myth was inscribed as early as 2000 BCE and the ideas were no doubt current centuries earlier. As such, it considerably pre-dates the Greco-Roman mythology more usually discussed in relation to psychoanalysis and analytical psychology.

By exploring the key Sumerian concepts of the *abzu* and the *mē* in relation to the foundation of consciousness and Jung's model of the psyche, Miller reminds us how Jung, in 'Archetypes of the Collective Unconscious' (1934; 1954), reflects—with reference to Heraclitus[39]—that 'when our natural inheritance has been dissipated, then the spirit too . . . has descended from its fiery heights'.[40] When spirit becomes heavy, Jung writes, it 'turns to water', and 'with Luciferian presumption the intellect usurps the seat where once the spirit was enthroned'. Here is the source of the accusation that Jung is an 'irrationalist', when he argues that 'the spirit may legitimately claim the *patria potestas*'—the 'power of a father'. or the power exercised in Roman family law by the male head of a family over his children—'over the soul', but not so 'the earth-born intellect', for this is 'man's sword or hammer, and not a creator of spiritual worlds, a father of the soul'. On this point, Jung refers to the work of two contemporary thinkers, the German phenomenologist and philosophical anthropologist, Max Scheler (1874–1928)—and Ludwig Klages. These thinkers were, Jung observes, 'moderate enough in their attempts to rehabilitate the spirit, for both were children of the age in which the spirit was no longer above but down below, no longer fire but water' (§32).

Therefore, Jung says, striking a distinctly Gnostic note, 'the way of the soul in search of its lost father' is—like Sophia, the feminine figure of Wisdom, seeking Bythos (= Depth or Profundity), the supreme being (§33)—something that 'leads to the water, to the dark mirror that reposes at its bottom' (§33). This way of the soul, Jung says, one that 'leads to the water', water in this context being 'no figure of speech, but a living symbol of the dark psyche' (§33). Might the 'dark psyche' be the same as what we call the archaic?

In *Symbols of Transformation* (1952), Jung's 'remastering' of the 'track' he had originally published as *Transformations and Symbols of Libido* (1911–1912), Jung pursues in remarkable detail the dangers and the rewards of this descent to the depths. With good reason, one might describe §553 of volume 5 in the *Collected Works* as containing the essence of Jung's analytical psychology.[41] This passage contains more material than we have time or space to analyse here: the image of the rising and setting sun—'the sun, rising triumphant, tears himself from the enveloping womb of the sea, and leaving behind him the noonday zenith and all its glorious works, sinks down again into the maternal depths, into all-enfolding and all-regenerating night'; the reference to the Mothers of Goethe's *Faust*, Part Two—'always he imagines his worst enemy within himself—a deadly longing for the abyss, a longing to drown in his own source, to be sucked down to the realm of the Mothers'; and the allusion to the legend of Theseus and Peirithous—'if, like Peirithous, he tarries too long in this abode of rest and peace, he is overcome by apathy, and the poison of the serpent paralyses him for all time' (§553).

In this passage, Jung drives home the existential implications of his message. 'The mind shies away', he writes, 'but life wants to flow down into the depths', and so 'the daimon throws us down' and 'makes us traitors to our ideals and cherished convictions—traitors to the selves we thought we were' (§553). Jung contrasts this situation, which he describes as 'an *unwilling* sacrifice', with what happens when the sacrifice is *voluntary*: then 'things go very differently'. An *involuntary* sacrifice involves 'an overthrow, a "transvaluation of all values", the destruction of all we held sacred'; it is, despite that Nietzschean echo, something essentially negative. By contrast, a *voluntary* sacrifice brings 'transformation and conservation' (§553). Striking an elegiac note, Jung writes that 'everything grows old, all beauty fades, all heat cools, all brightness dims, and every truth becomes stale and trite'; thanks to 'the working of time', all things 'age, sicken, crumble to dust'—*unless, that is, 'they change'* (§553). Here, then, lies the confluence of the archaic and the ecstatic, inasmuch as Jung is convinced that 'the invisible spark that generated them is potent enough for infinite generation' (§553). The ecstatic, or ἔκστασις, literally 'a standing-outside-of-oneself', *is* this moment of change when something not just quantitatively, but qualitatively, new can happen.

On this account, our experience of the archaic is the act of descent—'And let those that go down the sunset way do so with open eyes', Jung warns, 'for it is a sacrifice which daunts even the gods' (§553)—while the moment of ascent represents the ecstatic, a moment in which, as Jung promises us, 'the vanishing shapes are shaped anew', in which truth 'suffers change and bears new witness in new images, in new tongues' (§553). The editors and contributors to this volume hope that its readers will find in the pages that follow inspiration for new thinking and, indeed, new possibilities for change.

Notes

1 For further discussion, see R.J. Kozljanič, 'Jaspers Periechontologie—lebensphilosophisch betrachtet', *Jahrbuch für Lebensphilosophie*, 1, 2005, 151–191; and 'Grenzerfahrungen bei Jaspers und Klages', *Hestia: Jahrbuch der Klages-Gesellschaft* 22, 2004–2007, 149–162.
2 J. Campbell, *Myths to Live By*, New York: Bantam, 1973.
3 J. Meades (presenter), *Magnetic North*, Episode 1, broadcast BBC Four, 21 February 2008, 21:00.
4 A. Machen, *Hieroglyphics: A Note upon Ecstasy in Literature*, London: Grant Richards, 1902, p. 11.
5 See P. Bishop (ed.), *The Archaic: The Past in the Present*, London and New York: Routledge, 2012. See also P. Bishop, 'Just A Moment? Or, the Archaic as an Expression of the Eternal

in Time', in A. Yiassemides (ed.), *Time and the Psyche: Jungian Perspectives*, London and New York: Routledge, 2017, pp. 87–105.

6 See *The Essential Plotinus: Representative Treatises from the Enneads*, ed. and tr. Elmer O'Brien, Indianapolis, IN: Hackett, 1964, pp. 72–89 (p. 88). Plotinus' striking phrase served, of course, as the inspiration for the retitling of a groundbreaking study by Henry Corbin (1903–1978) of Islamic mysticism, *Creative Imagination in the Sūfism of Ibn' Arabī* [1958], Princeton, NJ: Princeton University Press, 1968, as *Alone with the Alone: Creative Imagination in the Sūfism of Ibn' Arabī*, Princeton, NJ: Princeton University Press, 1977.

7 Plotinus, *Enneads VI. 6–9* 9, tr. A.A. Armstrong, Cambridge, MA, and London: Harvard University Press; Heinemann, 1988, p. 343.

8 R. Harder, 'Zu Plotins Leben, Wirkung und Lehre', in Plotinus, *Ausgewählte Schriften*, ed. W. Marg, Stuttgart: Reclam, 1973, pp. 245–268 (p. 144).

9 F. Nietzsche, *Kritische Studienausgabe*, ed. Giorgio Colli and Mazzino Montinari, Munich/ Berlin and New York: dtv; de Gruyter, 1988, vol. 9, 11(7), p. 443.

10 R. Bucke, *Cosmic Consciousness: A Study in the Evolution of the Human Mind*, Philadelphia, PA: Innes, 1901.

11 E. Benz, *Emanuel Swedenborg: Visionary Savant in the Age of Reason*, tr. N. Goodrick-Clarke, West Chester, PA: Swedenborg Foundation, 2002, pp. 261–271. According to Benz, 'Swedenborg's religious self-consciousness was wholly sustained by his London vision of vocation', since it was 'the decisive, precisely dateable event of his life, giving all his subsequent action a higher meaning and sanction' as well as 'the starting point of his mission, in which two elements of his vocation are linked: the revelation of the inner sense of Scripture and the opening of his vision into the spiritual world' (p. 270).

12 Bucke, *Cosmic Consciousness*, p. 13.

13 For an overview of different approaches to myth, see R.A. Segal, *Myth: A Very Short Introduction*, Oxford and New York: Oxford University Press, 2004.

14 See K. Kerényi, 'Prolegomena', in C.G. Jung and K. Kerényi, *Essays on a Science of Mythology* [1941], trans R.F.C. Hull, New York: Princeton University Press, 1969, pp. 1–24 (§3 [p. 6]), citing Malinowski, 'Myth in Primitive Psychology' [1926], in *Magic, Science and Religion and other Essays*, Garden City, NY: Doubleday, 1948, pp. 72–123.

15 Kerényi, 'Prolegomena', §4 (p. 7).

16 Kerényi, 'Prolegomena', §4 (p. 7); cf. Aristotle, *Metaphysics*, Λ 2, 1013a: 'We call an origin [*arkhē*] that part of a thing from which one would start first, e.g. a line or a road has an origin in either of the contrary directions ... Therefore the nature of a thing is an origin, and so are the elements of a thing, and thought and choice, and substance, and that for the sake of which—for the good and the beautiful are the origin both of the knowledge and of the movement of many things' (Aristotle, *Complete Works*, ed. J. Barnes, 2 vols, Princeton, NJ: Princeton University Press, 1984, vol. 1, pp. 1599–1600).

17 Compare with Klages's remarks about the decline of the city in ancient times: 'Anyone who has got used to understanding so-called world history in terms of the wisdom of emblems, will consider as the most momentous turning-point in the destiny of all settled peoples the lowering of the walls around the city and the castle, because this brought about the domination of mobility over the stationary centre, the deracination of women and the siderailing of men into the tangential, mistaken trajectory of something lacking in rest and return and therefore irremediably destructive—"progress"!' (*Der Geist als Widersacher der Seele*, in L. Klages, *Sämtliche Werke*, ed. E. Frauchinger et al., 9 vols, Bonn: Bouvier, 1964–1992, vol. 2, p. 1344).

18 Kerényi, 'Prolegomena', §6 (p. 14). Cf. §5: 'With the construction of a new world in miniature, an image of the macrocosm, mythological fundamentalism is translated into action: it becomes a founding (*Gründung*). Cities built in periods that knew a living mythology, and claiming to be images of the cosmos, are *founded* just as the cosmogonic mythologems *give ground for* the world' (p. 10).

19 Kerényi, 'Prolegomena', §7 (p. 24).

20 J. Gebser, *The Ever-Present Origin*, vol. 1, *Foundations of the Aperspectival World: A Contribution to the Awakening of Consciousness*, vol. 2, *Manifestations of the Aperspectival World: An Attempt at the Concretion of the Spiritual*, 2 vols in 1, Athens: Ohio University Press, 1985.

21 See E. Cassirer, *Philosophy of Symbolic Forms* [1923–1929], tr. R. Manheim, 3 vols, New Haven, CT and London: Yale University Press, 1955–1957, consisting of vol. 1, *Language*, vol. 2, *Mythical Thought*, and vol. 3, *The Phenomenology of Knowledge*. There are significant areas of intersection between Cassirer's approach and Jung's; see P. Bishop, 'Speaking of Symbols: Affinities between Cassirer's and Jung's Theories of Language', in C. Hamlin and J.M. Krois (eds), *Symbolic Forms and Cultural Studies: Ernst Cassirer's Theory of Culture*, New Haven, CT and London: Yale University Press, 2004, pp. 127–157; 'Cassirer and Jung on Mythology, Imagination, and the Symbol', in *The Way of the World: A Festschrift for R.H. Stephenson* [Cultural Studies and the Symbolic, vol. 4], ed. P. Bishop (Leeds: Maney, 2011), pp. 69–92; 'Das Goethe'sche Symbol als Instrument der morphologischen Wandlung in Philosophie und Psychologie: Cassirer, Jung und Klages', in J. Maatsch (ed.), *Morphologie und Moderne: Goethes 'anschauliches Denken' in den Geistes- und Kulturwissenschaften seit 1800*, Berlin and Boston, MA: de Gruyter, 2014, pp. 157–175.
22 E. Mahood, Jr., 'The Primordial and the Present: The Ever-Present Origin—An Overview of the Work of Jean Gebser'. Available online from: www.gaiamind.org/Gebser.html. Accessed 15 August 2016.
23 G. Feuerstein, *Structures of Consciousness: The Genius of Jean Gebser: An Introduction and Critique*, Lower Lake, CA: Integral Publishing, 1987, p. 57.
24 A. Mickunas, 'An Introduction to the Philosophy of Jean Gebser', in *Integrative Explorations: Journal of Culture and Consciousness* 4 (1), January 1997, 8–20 (p. 9).
25 Gebser, *The Ever-Present Origin*, p. 273.
26 For a list of the major characteristics of the ever-present origin or the aperspectival world, see Gebser, *The Ever-Present Origin*, pp. 361–362.
27 Gebser, *The Ever-Present Origin*, p. 281.
28 G.B. Tennyson (ed.), *A Barfield Reader: Selections from the Writings of Owen Barfield*, Edinburgh: Floris Books, 1999, pp. 96, 110, 115 and 117.
29 T. McKenna, *The Archaic Revival: Speculations on Psychedelic Mushrooms, the Amazon, Virtual Reality, UFOs, Evolution, Shamanism, the Rebirth of the Goddess, and the End of History*, New York: HarperCollins, 1991.
30 See Heraclitus, Diels-Kranz 22 B 52: 'Eternity is a child at play, playing draughts: the kingdom is a child's' (J. Barnes, *Early Greek Philosophy*, Harmondsworth: Penguin, 1987, p. 102).
31 McKenna, 'Tryptamine Hallucinogens and Consciousness' [1983], in *The Archaic Revival*, pp. 34–47 (pp. 36–37).
32 For an introduction to the life and thought of Klages, see P. Bishop, *Ludwig Klages and the Philosophy of Life: A Vitalist Toolkit*, New York and London: Routledge, 2017.
33 See, for instance, the text entitled 'Ecstasy', in L. Klages, *Rhythmen und Runen: Nachlass herausgegeben von ihm selbst*, Leipzig: Barth, 1944, pp. 269–270.
34 Klages, *Rhythmen und Runen*, p. 294.
35 See R. Schumann, *Eichendorff-Liederkreis* (Op. 39), §6.
36 Klages, *Rhythmen und Runen*, p. 294.
37 T. Merton, *Raids on the Unspeakable*, New York: New Directions, 1966.
38 Plato, *Republic*, 485d; in *The Republic of Plato*, ed. and tr. A. Bloom, New York: Basic Books, 1991, p. 165. If this is the case, Socrates concludes, then 'when in someone they have flowed toward learning and all that's like it, I suppose they would be concerned with the pleasure of the soul itself with respect to itself and would forsake those pleasures that come through the body—if he isn't a counterfeit but a true philosopher' (485d; p. 165).
39 See Heraclitus, Diels-Kranz fragment 22 B66: 'Fire will come and judge and convict all things' (Barnes, *Early Greek Philosophy*, p. 104).
40 C.G. Jung, 'Archetypes of the Collective Unconscious', in *The Archetypes and the Collective Unconscious* [*Collected Works*, vol. 9/i], tr. R.F.C. Hull, Princeton, NJ: Princeton University Press, 1968, §1–§86 (pp. 1–41), here: §32 (p. 16).
41 C.G. Jung, *Symbols of Transformation* [*Collected Works*, vol. 5], tr. R.F.C. Hull, Princeton, NJ: Princeton University Press, 1967. I am grateful to Peter Kingsley for drawing this passage to my attention.

PART I
Ecstasy and the psychological

1

THE STREAM OF DESIRE AND JUNG'S CONCEPT OF PSYCHIC ENERGY

Raya A. Jones

> Whether energy is God or God is energy concerns me very little, for how, in any case, can I know such things? But to give appropriate psychological explanations—this I must be able to do.
>
> *(C. G. Jung)*[1]

It is a remarkable quality of Jung's legacy that it appeals across diverse disciplines, but I put the above statement upfront as a reminder that as a therapist Jung was concerned first and foremost with explaining the kind of phenomena that clinicians confront in their patients. If a concept of energy or libido does the job, so to speak, that's more important than whether the concept is metaphysically sound or not. Nevertheless, Jung did attempt to articulate a cogent theory of what precisely psychic energy might be. His theorising about psychic energy took off in the 1912 monograph, *Psychology of the Unconscious*, which four decades later was lightly revised as *Symbols of Transformation*.[2] Seeking the appropriate psychological explanation for patients' symptoms, he argued that the Freudian notion of libido as sexual energy is inapplicable to dementia praecox since the illness is associated with the generation of a fantasy world rather than with heightened sexuality. This argument set him on a line of theorising that has culminated in the theory of the archetypes. The assumption of psychic energy runs throughout Jung's psychology in general. His differentiation between introverts and extroverts is based on it, and it is central for his theory of the autonomous complexes and how complexes form around archetypal nuclei (summarised in Jung's 1928 essay *On Psychic Energy*).[3]

Jung's attempt to clarify a concept of psychic energy was one of several theories of mental energy that were bandied about in the first half of the last century, not only in depth psychology but also in general psychology. Elsewhere I have compared Jung's revision of libido with the concept of energy underpinning the field theory that the gestalt psychologist Kurt Lewin articulated in the 1930s.[4]

In *The Energies of Men*, first published in 1932, William McDougall regarded a concept of energy as indispensable: 'In view of the purposive nature of human activity, [we] must postulate some energy which conforms to laws not wholly identical with the laws of energy stated by the physical sciences.'[5] Contesting the terminology of 'psychic' energy, he proposed a concept of 'hormic' energy (defined as an urge or impulse towards a goal) as a means to forging connections between processes of the body and processes of the mind within a unified science of psychology—a science that in McDougall's view had no room for psychoanalytical doctrines. And then, as if suddenly in mid-century, the whole discourse of energies vanished. Concepts of mental energy have become obsolete in the wake of the cognitive revolution.

A roughly parallel trajectory can be tracked in the history of the idea within analytical psychology. By the 1980s, Samuels queried whether analytical psychology needs a concept of energy, though he conceded that 'the notion of energy, even if taken nowadays purely as a metaphor, helps to explain differences in perception'.[6] However, in contradistinction to the academic debates about mental energy early on, Jung's concept of psychic energy has seldom been examined or debated in Jungian circles despite its original centrality. First published in 1948, Esther Harding's book, *Psychic Energy*—with a preface by Jung—is a tour-de-force of symbolism and symbols' signification;[7] but it does not contain any definition of psychic energy. A similar observation could be made about John Beebe's recent book, *Energies and Patterns in Psychological Type*.[8] Beebe uses the word 'energy' liberally but in a common-sense way, as an everyday concept that requires no explanation. His theoretical investment is in the concept of psychological types. 'Psychic energy' continues to be acknowledged in textbooks as something that Jung said,[9] and is the topic of scholarly publications that attempt to clarify what Jung meant and to locate his idea historically,[10] but at best we can offer fresh insights into what he was saying and why he was saying it. As a scientific or quasi-scientific explanation, this construct has lost its vitality.

This chapter revisits Jung's concept from another direction. Instead of examining its place in the intellectual history of modern psychology, I want to tease out an ancient image—the stream of desire—that Jung both inherits and resists when he strives to improve upon the Freudian concept: 'By libido I mean *psychic energy*. Psychic energy is the *intensity* of a psychic process, its *psychological value* [. . .] Neither do I understand libido as a psychic *force*, a misconception that has led many critics astray,' says Jung.[11] We should not be misled by the linearity of terminological succession. Jung's *psychological value* is not a synonym for Freud's *libido* but its antonym, as will be seen.

The ancient stream

There is an obvious association, a kind of continuity, between the Freudian libido and the stream-of-desire image. Dictionaries tell us that the word *libido* originates in the Latin for desire or lust; and there is an etymological connection to the English word 'love'. The imaginative association between a stream and desire is explicit in the *Dhammapada*, where it carries a moral message: 'When the thirty-six streams of desire that run towards pleasure are strong, their powerful waves carry away that man'; 'Go beyond the stream [. . .] go with all your soul: leave desires behind.'[12] In historical parallel, in *Republic*, Plato deploys an almost identical image: 'anyone whose predilection tends strongly in a single direction has correspondingly less desire for other things, like a stream whose flow has been diverted into another channel.'[13] The same imagery flows on into psychoanalytical theory. Freud speaks of 'a collateral filling of subsidiary channels when the main current of the instinctual stream has been blocked by "repression"'.[14] Likewise in Jung's works we find assertions such as:

> Just as the libido may be compared to a steady stream pouring its waters into the world of reality, so a resistance [to sexual desire] [. . .] resembles, not a rock that juts up from the river-bed and causes the stream to flow around it, but a flowing back towards the source. Part of the psyche really wants the external object, but another part of it strives back to the subjective world, where the airy and lightly built palaces of fantasy beckon.[15]

In the 1928 essay on psychic energy and elsewhere, Jung devoted considerable space to libidinal flow—he talks of regression, progression, and canalisation and transformation—which he offers as an explanation for a variety of response patterns, including fantasies.

Neither Freud nor Jung mentioned Plato's stream analogy apropos of libido (to my knowledge). Instead, in the 1920 Preface to the fourth edition of *Three Essays on the Theory of Sexuality*, Freud cites a 1915 article that compared his own theory with Plato's Eros, and reflects 'how closely the enlarged sexuality of psycho-analysis coincides with the Eros of the divine Plato'.[16] Ever since, some scholars seem inclined to fuse Plato's hydraulic metaphor with Eros and to discuss both the *Republic* and the *Symposium* as postulating a primordial energy source. According to Jon Moline:

> The parts of the psyche are like channels or tubes into which the flow of a single stream is divided. The total flowage is constant, so that what goes into one tube or channel is lost to the others [. . .] Both the *Republic* and the *Symposium* suggest that this single source is *eros*, a primordial energy source powering not simply the stereotypically erotic activities, but all human activities whatsoever.[17]

Similarly, Henry Teloh took the stream analogy in the *Republic* as pivotal for understanding Plato's conception of the soul as psychic energy.[18] Commenting on Teloh's paper, M.L. Osborne contends that such interpretation is not borne out by Plato's argument in the same context.[19] I concur with Osborne.

Arguably, it is Freud who has made it possible to link Plato's stream analogy and some concept of Eros (Plato in fact presents several concepts through the various speakers in the *Symposium*). It is Freud—not Plato—who upheld Eros, equated with sexual excitation, as universally the strongest motivating force. This claim seemed justified in view of how evolution, human biology, and energy were understood circa 1900, but it was not possible to make in Plato's time. It seems anachronistic to attribute to Plato an understanding of the Greek love-god as psychic energy. The ancients did not have the mechanistic concept of energy that underpins Freudian thinking, and by extension empowers Jung's departure from Freud. The pitfalls of reading Plato through a Freudian lens may serve as a cautionary tale for seeking continuities between Jung and the classics.

Bridging Jung and ancient thought

One obvious way to bridge analytical psychology and the study of ancient thought is to approach the topic from the standpoint of Jung scholarship; that is, 'Jung' being one's subject matter. It is possible to scour the *Collected Works* for citations and to analyse how Jung brings those to bear on his theory building; or to interrogate the Jungian corpus for 'influences', whether acknowledged or not. As Henri Bergson averred, 'even today, we shall philosophize in the manner of the Greeks, we shall rediscover, without needing to know them, such and such of their general conclusions.'[20] However, this strategy might not take us very far regarding the topic of psychic energy.

In the 1928 essay,[21] Jung lists the following in a single sentence—and in this order—as concepts that are similar to his own but only of limited overlap:

- Schopenhauer's Will
- Aristotle's *horme*
- Plato's Eros
- Empedocles' 'love and hate of the elements'
- Bergson's *élan vital*.

The order of the list perhaps represents a descending order of similarity. In *Symbols of Transformation*, Jung quotes Schopenhauer at length by way of supporting why he himself insists that energy is not a force.[22] Schopenhauer distinguished Will from its phenomenal appearances, reasoning that the abstract concept of force is derived from sense perception.[23] But unless we delve into Schopenhauer's system of thought, this comparison can backfire, so to speak. Schopenhauer's concept does not imply freedom to control one's behaviour (or willpower). Bergson is at the bottom of Jung's list perhaps because Jung repeatedly fended off his own critics who accused him of vitalism; hence he was not keen to associate his concept with *élan vital*. In the present context, the main point is that the Greeks are merely sandwiched between the two modern philosophers.

The link that Jung ultimately makes—or the bridge he builds—is across modernity and so-called 'primitive' mentality. A few paragraphs before the aforementioned list, he states that 'energy is an immediate, a priori, intuitive idea', concludes in a related footnote that 'therefore the idea of it is as old as humanity' and proceeds to discuss the Melanesian concept of *mana* as reported by anthropologists of the era.[24] The final part of 'On Psychic Energy' is dedicated to examples of equivalent concepts among tribal societies all over the world.

A second strategy to bridge Jung and the ancients is to take the classics as our subject matter and revisit them through a Jungian lens, though here lies the epistemological risk demonstrated in the case of reading Plato through Freud. If we take 'ancient thought' to mean also traditions from the Far East and what Jung called 'primitive' mentality, we can see a version of this strategy in his own work—the way he revisits those in order to demonstrate manifestations of the psychological principles he has already postulated.

The final strategy is where the troll under the bridge comes into the picture, trying to stop us from crossing. Asking what Jung and the ancients have and do not have in common brings to the fore discontinuities and contingent tensions as well as similarities or continuities of thought. Jung's theorising about psychic energy, especially in the 1928 essay, focalises a few sites of tension that characterise modern psychology in general. One site, which he identifies himself, is comprised of tensions between causal-mechanistic and functional explanations in psychology (more about this in the next section); and, placed in the same site, tensions between qualitative and quantitative concepts. Another site is implicated by Jung's distinction between 'pure' and the 'concrete' concepts of psychic energy. It focalises tensions associated with the traditional debate of whether psychology is a science or an art. Jung presents his pure/concrete distinction as a matter of convenience: strictly speaking the pure concept does not permit us to think of energy as if it were a causal factor; but when we wish to apply it, especially in clinical practice, it is convenient to speak in concrete terms, such as saying that someone's fantasies or emotional reactions and so forth are caused by libidinal regression or progression. Jung moves at ease from one mode to the other, but this makes his 1928 essay on the whole appear to be inconsistent.

A third site of tensions arises from Jung's claim that the intuitive notion of energy is as old as humanity itself. His case for revising the libido concept in the 1912 monograph involved lengthy and quite dense accounts of myths of the sun god, fire, and related etymologies, which was slightly streamlined in the 1952 revision. He relates these to bodily sensations of rhythm. The final section of the 1928 essay lists at length examples of 'primitive' concepts of power, typically attributed to spirits. Comparable views can be found also in Eastern mysticism—notions of cosmic energy that flows through mind and body and everything. Indeed, since about the 1960s, Jung's exposition of psychic energy has become eclipsed by popularised extrapolations from Oriental mysticism. Jung himself seems to orient us in that direction in his accounts of intuitive precursors of the modern concept of energy, and indirectly to reinforce the orientation with the *unus mundus* premise he extrapolated from medieval alchemy. Ultimately the invocation of those (or any) cosmologies is incommensurable with his definition of energy as *psychological value*— a concept that refers to the meaning that something has for someone. Remember that whether energy is God or God is energy concerned him very little. In terms of a psychological explanation, the tensions that come to light at this juncture gravitate towards the ancient metaphysical problem of universals. It is a problematic throughout modern psychology, but in the context of Jungianism, it manifests in a tendency to abstract psychological universals, such as archetypes, from an aggregate of particular instances (myths, fairy tales, patients' dreams, etc.) that at best share a family resemblance; and then to concretise the abstract construct as if it were a causal factor, saying that these instances occur because of the archetypal configuration.

Enter the machine

What Jung and the ancients do not have in common can be conveyed, again, with the aid of Bergson, namely that 'ancient science applied to *concepts*, while modern science seeks *laws*'.[25] Unlike the *Dhammapada*, which instructs how to live virtuously, both Freud and Jung inform us why we live as we do, vice and virtue alike. In modernity, the stream analogy merges into a mechanistic metaphor of energy as a motivating force. The stream becomes steam power. Concepts of mental energy, libido and so forth, were invented so as to account for how the psyche works. It is (or was) commonly assumed that some form of energy powers the intrapsychic machinery in accordance with natural laws; and those laws have to be discovered and articulated. Consequently, debates during the first half of the last century centred on what is the appropriate conceptualisation.

Jung entered the intellectual arena with a contention that previous definitions (not only Freud's) were mistaken because they confused energy with a substance:

> The idea of energy is not that of substance moved in space, it is a concept abstracted from relations of movement. The concept, therefore, is founded not on the substances themselves but on their relations, whereas the moving substance itself is the basis of the mechanistic view.[26]

Jung thus pitches two approaches against each other. According to the causal-mechanistic view (which he contests), energy is synonymous with a force or a drive. It is conceptualised as substance-like, a 'thing' that causes movements in the psyche. We may imagine, for instance, the water that makes the watermill turn (my metaphor). This posits the existence of energy as a precondition for psychological phenomena, just as water must exist before the watermill can do its work. In opposition to the causal-mechanistic view, Jung articulates what he calls the 'energic' or interchangeably the 'final' view, which removes the arrow of causality. It puts the phenomena first, arguing that intrapsychic movements (which already exist) can be expressed in terms of an energy quantum. By analogy, we are looking at the energy that the watermill produces by virtue of its operation (while the causal-mechanistic position confuses the force of the flowing water for the energy that the watermill produces). The word 'final' has connotations of the teleological, which Jung himself contested. The epistemological position that he endorses is best called a functional approach.[27] Such an approach identifies how something functions within the whole of the person's psychological processes. It does not necessarily oppose the machine metaphor, for we may compare it to describing the function of a cog in a machine, i.e., how this element is necessary for the machine's *capacity for doing its work* (to paraphrase the commonplace definition of energy in physics).

The energic/final/functional approach does not eliminate the epistemological necessity of explaining how movements in the psyche are caused. Jung does not reject causal explanations per se, but objects to regarding energy as a causal factor. He brings together causality and functionality, for instance, when attributing the formation of symbols to a situation where a conflict between two mutually incompatible subjective states generates psychological tension that is eventually transcended through the formation of a new symbol:

> The confrontation of the two positions generates a tension charged with energy and creates a living thing, a third thing [. . .] a movement out of the suspension between opposites, a living birth that leads to a new level of being, a new situation.[28]

The new symbol constitutes a new object—not merely a token for something repressed (contra Freud), but something with its own meaning or aura of meaningfulness. Its energy quantum is its psychological value, evident in the intensity and direction of affect, for '*psychological value* [. . .] does not imply an assignment of value, whether moral, aesthetic, or intellectual; the psychological value is already implicit in its *determining* power, which expresses itself in definite psychic effects'.[29]

Conclusion

We cannot step into the same stream twice. As seen, some scholars who step into Plato's stream analogy after Freud see reflections of Eros there and are inclined to redefine Plato's Eros as a primordial energy source powering human activities. How should we step into the stream after Jung? His reformulation of the libido does not write off the stream analogy, but alters its application. Jung's 1928 essay labours towards a concept of dynamism as an abstract property of the psyche in the sense that 'flow' is a property of a stream. With Freud, we would see libido like seeing the 'behaviour' of water when standing outside a stream: libido is channelled, blocked, diverted, or dispersed unequally across various channels. Following Jung, we may imagine ourselves like a grain of sand carried by its torrent, experiencing it from within, and should ask what it 'feels like' to be caught in the turbulence.

Jung insists that his own task, what he must be able to do, is to give an appropriate psychological explanation. However, explanatory constructs in psychology come and go like intellectual fashions, though every new fashion is heralded as a scientific paradigm shift and therefore as progress. Walter Benjamin has given a vivid characterisation of the concept of progress in his meditation on a painting by Paul Klee ('Angelus Novus'). Describing it as showing an angel 'looking as though he is about to move away from something he is fixedly contemplating,' Benjamin mused:

But a storm is blowing in from Paradise; it has got caught in his wings with such a violence that the angel can no longer close them. The storm irresistibly propels him into the future to which his back is turned, while the pile of debris before him grows skyward. This storm is what we call progress.[30]

In a way, Jung is like this angel when theorising about psychic energy. He sees the debris of previous concepts, which he deconstructs and finds deficient, and cannot see the future—the cognitive revolution in psychology of the second half of the twentieth century, which has rendered concepts of mental energy obsolete and has redefined psychological explanations based on such concepts as inappropriate. However, Jung is fixated on the past not only like Benjamin's angel of history, but also in that he looks to the very far distance, our evolutionary past, and finds the intuitive notion of energy as old as humanity itself.

Jung neither endorsed nor challenged the primitive and ancient cosmologies he identified as precursors of the modern 'energy' construct. Instead, he asks why human beings have these notions at all, what psychological function these might serve. Jung ends his essay on psychic energy thus:

The most universal incidence of the primitive concept of energy is a clear expression of the fact that even at early levels of human consciousness man felt the need to represent the sensed dynamism of psychic events in a concrete way. If, therefore, in our psychology we lay stress on the energic point of view, this is in accord with the psychic facts which have been graven on the mind of man since primordial times.[31]

Rhetorically this 'final word' performs an interesting manoeuvre that undermines the thrust of the first part of the same essay. The essay began with an intense effort to establish the correct logical way of conceptualising psychic energy by eliminating rival theories as mistaken. Jung even contrives to specify psychic parallels of the laws of thermodynamics (which arguably does not really 'work'). But he ends up persuading us that in any permutation such notions capture something that is intuited from bodily lived experience. In other words, the scientific concept is just one of many historically contingent manifestations of something that is timeless within our psyche.

Notes

1 C.G. Jung, *Collected Works*, ed. Sir H. Read, M. Fordham, G. Adler, and W. McGuire, 20 vols, London: Routledge & Kegan Paul, 1953–1983, vol. 8, *The Structure and Dynamics of the Psyche*, §678.

2 C.G. Jung, *Psychology of the Unconscious*, London: Kegan Paul, Trench, Trubner & Co. 1919; revised *Symbols of Transformation* [*Collected Works*, vol. 5].

3 C.G. Jung, 'On Psychic Energy', in *Collected Works*, vol. 8, §1–§130.

4 R.A. Jones, 'Psychological Value and Symbol Formation', *Theory & Psychology*, 2001, vol. 11, 233–254; and R.A. Jones, *Jung, Psychology, Postmodernity*, London: Routledge, 2007.

5 W. McDougall, *The Energies of Men*, 8th edn, London: Methuen 1950, p. 10.

6 A. Samuels, *Jung and the Post-Jungians*, London: Routledge & Kegan Paul, 1985, p. 114.

7 E. Harding, *Psychic Energy*, 2nd edn, Princeton, NJ: Princeton University Press, 1963.

8 J. Beebe, *Energies and Patterns in Psychological Type*, London: Routledge, 2016.

9 See, for example, M. Stein, *Jung's Map of the Soul*, Chicago, IL: Open Court, 1998.

10 See, for example, C. Kerslake, 'Rebirth through Incest: On Deleuze's Early Jungianism', *Angelaki*, 2004, vol. 9, 135–156; S. Shamdasani, *Jung and the Making of Modern Psychology*, Cambridge: Cambridge University Press, 2003; D.I. Tresan, 'This New Science of Ours: A More or Less Systematic History of Consciousness: Part 1', *Journal of Analytical Psychology*, 2004, vol. 49, 193–216; and my own works (op. cit.).

11 Jung, *Collected Works*, vol. 6, *Psychological Types*, §778.

12 J. Mascaró, *The Dhammapada*, Harmondsworth: Penguin, 1973, §339, §383.

13 Plato, *Republic*, 485d; in Plato, *Republic*, trans. R. Waterfield, Oxford: Oxford University Press, 1993, §485d/p.205

14 S. Freud, 'Three Essays on the Theory of Sexuality', in *On Sexuality: Three Essays on Sexuality and Other Works* [The Pelican Freud Library, vol. 7], ed. A. Richards, Harmondsworth: Penguin, 1991 pp. 33–170 (p. 156).

15 Jung, *Collected Works*, vol. 6, *Psychological Types*, §253.

16 Freud, 'Three Essays on the Theory of Sexuality', p. 43.

17 J. Moline, *Plato's Theory of Understanding*, Madison, WI: University of Wisconsin Press, 1981, pp. 77–78.

18 H. Teloh, 'Human Nature, Psychic Energy, and Self-actualization in Plato's *Republic*', *The Southern Journal of Philosophy*, 1976, vol. 14, 345–358.

19 M.L. Osborne, 'On the Image of the Soul as a Stream in Plato's *Republic*', *The Southern Journal of Philosophy*, 1976, vol. 14, 359–363.

20 H. Bergson, *Creative Evolution*, Mineola, NY: Dover, 1911, p. 316.

21 Jung, *Collected Works*, vol. 8, *The Structure and Dynamics of the Psyche*, §55.

22 Jung, *Collected Works*, vol. 5, *Symbols of Transformation*, §197.

23 A. Schopenhauer, *The World as Will and Idea*, London: Kegan Paul, 1922.

24 Jung, *Collected Works*, vol. 8, §52.

25 Bergson, *Creative Evolution*, p. 333.

26 Jung, *Collected Works*, vol. 8, *On the Nature and Dynamics of the Psyche*, §3.

27 See Jones, 'Psychological Value and Symbol Formation', pp. 239ff.

28 Jung, *Collected Works*, vol. 8, *On the Nature and Dynamics of the Psyche*, §189.

29 Jung, *Collected Works*, vol. 6, *Psychological Types*, §778.

30 W. Benjamin, *Selected Writings*, vol. 4: *1938–1940*, ed. H. Eiland and M.W. Jennings, Cambridge, MA: Harvard University Press, 2003, pp. 392–393.

31 Jung, *Collected Works*, vol. 8, *On the Nature and Dynamics of the Psyche*, §130.

2

THE CHARACTERS SPEAK BECAUSE THEY WANT TO SPEAK

Jung, Dionysus, theatre, and therapy

Mark Saban

In this chapter I intend to think of psychoanalysis, and particularly Jung's analytical psychology, in conjunction with the idea of theatre, and with the god of theatre—Dionysus. There is a theatrical aspect to psychotherapy, and perhaps a therapeutic aspect to theatre, that have been, for various reasons, articulated only rarely.[1]

The motifs of possession, spirits, the dead, ghosts and trance (all of them motifs that cluster around the Dionysiac) have haunted and interpenetrated the idea of theatre (and particularly with that of the actor) throughout its history. Joseph Roach (in the invaluable *The Player's Passion* [1985]) shows how Renaissance ideas about the actor's ability to affect the audience through a kind of possession by spirits goes back at least as far as Plato.[2] In effect, the spirit moves the actor who, in the authenticity of his transport, moves the audience. It is not hard to see a continuity between this approach and that of Franz Anton Mesmer (1734–1815), exerting hypnotic control by means of the spiritual '*fluidium*'. Mesmer (whom Henri Ellenberger identifies as the crucial early figure in the rise of the dynamic psychiatries)[3] expertly utilised theatre and showmanship in his cures.

An example of the living overlap between theatre and spirit-possession in modern culture can be found in Jonathan Pryce's memorable performance as Hamlet in the 1980 production of Shakespeare's tragedy at the Royal Court theatre; Pryce performed his ghostly father's lines as though undergoing 'some kind of possession'. As Pryce describes it, 'Hamlet becomes taken over by his father's spirit, who tells him everything he needs to hear', and Pryce researched the part by watching documentaries on Haitian voodoo that featured possession by gods.[4] He had taken on the role of Hamlet in the wake of the sudden violent death of his father:

It took me a long time to process how I'd reacted to his death, the violence of it, the sense of something unfulfilled or incomplete. One day I became convinced that he'd appeared to me: only for a moment, but clearly I'd wanted to conjure him back into being.[5]

Stories like this place theatre in a liminal tension with the notion of being visited by, or possessed by, those spirits or gods who have something they need to communicate. We can see a different face of this tension in Daniel Day Lewis's traumatic experience of playing Hamlet in 1989 when, so the story goes, the uncanny manifestation of his own dead father (poet laureate Cecil Day Lewis) led him to leave the stage, mid-performance, never to return.[6]

Freud, hysteria, and the theatre

The overt theatricality of the weekly spectacle stage-managed by Jean-Martin Charcot (1825–1893) at the Salpêtrière, whereby hysterics rehearsed their supposed symptoms before an invited audience, has received much attention.[7] Such displays look back to Mesmer's public displays of healing. Freud himself attended such events in 1885–1886, and indeed prominently displayed on the wall of his consulting room a reproduction of André Brouillet's famous painting of Charcot's dramatic demonstration of a hypnotised female hysteric.

Given that Freud and his psychoanalysis dealt primarily at first with patients suffering with hysteria, and that its characteristic technique grew out of hypnosis, we might expect something of this theatricality to have survived into those early accounts of psychoanalytic cases. However, although a dramatic quality certainly persists in the 'talking-cure' developed by Breuer and Freud (and written up in their *Studies on Hysteria*, published in 1895), it has a quite different character from the extraverted histrionics of Mesmer or Charcot. This difference is well captured in the term 'private theatre', coined by the very first psychoanalytic patient, Anna O., for the daydreamed scenes that she recounted to Breuer.[8] Freud and Breuer branded their new approach to hysteria the 'cathartic method' (*kathartische Methode*), a name that summoned up echoes of Greek tragedy, or rather Aristotle's treatise on tragedy. These echoes were to become much louder when, in *The Interpretation of Dreams* or *Die Traumdeutung* (1900), Freud plucked the figure of Oedipus from Sophocles' tragedy and placed him at the centre of the psychoanalytic stage.[9] In the meantime, the catharsis exemplified in the *Studies on Hysteria* was the supposed curative consequence of the patient's re-living (repeating, re-enacting), before an audience of one, the traumatic events or feelings that were the original cause of the hysteria. As Rachel Bowlby puts it, this theatre is 'no longer like [Charcot's] real one, with symptoms induced to appear, but an analogical one in which they spontaneously perform for one last time'.[10]

Jung's inner stage

Carl Gustav Jung developed his own distinct approach to depth psychology, and to the theatrical nature of that psychology, via a different route from that of Freud. His doctoral dissertation was an account of a medium who, as Sonu Shamdasani puts it, 'would become different personalities, and [Jung] could call up these personalities by suggestion', so that 'dead relatives appeared, and she became completely transformed into these figures'.[11] This exposure to the tendency of the unconscious to dissociate into different, personified, autonomous figures was later to find scientific articulation during Jung's work during his early years at the Burghölzli psychiatric hospital. Jung's word-association experiments led to the identification and differentiation of the psychological feeling-toned complexes.

I would maintain that this work on word-association, and particularly Jung's emphasis upon the self-presentation of these complexes *as persons*, laid the foundation for his entire mature psychology. Given the context of this chapter, it would perhaps be more evocative to suggest that his early work *set the stage* on which his mature psychology would subsequently play itself out. For it seems to me that the psychic model he fashioned, or which fashioned itself through him, enables us to vision the event we call 'psychic life' as an essentially *theatrical* event in which multiple figures—autonomous and personified—dynamically play out their interrelated roles before, and for, multiple inner witnesses. The dramatic (and dramatising) perspective on the psyche that emerged from this new complex-psychology paved the way for what Jung was to articulate as the 'transcendent function'—a concept that itself was primarily exemplified, according to Jung, in the dynamic improvisations and personifications of what came to be called 'Active Imagination'.

From an archetypal perspective, to evoke the theatre is to evoke Dionysus, and my hope in this chapter is to illustrate some ways in which an awareness of the Dionysian can shed light upon its psychological complexities, and in turn, the complexities of Jung's model of the psyche. After all, it is well known that Dionysus manifests as the most paradoxical of gods, and his position as god of theatre is entirely consistent with this fact, since the event of theatre is a highly paradoxical event; a fact recognised since Diderot's *Paradoxe sur le comédien* of 1773.[12] The fact that the avowed *telos* of Jung's psychological model is that of bringing opposites together, a paradoxical goal if there ever was one, only lends more emphasis to the fact that the Dionysian is, in this context, a crucially relevant archetypal theme.

Jung's model of the psyche entails multiplicity. Like Frederic W.H. Myers (1843–1901), Pierre Janet (1859–1947), Théodore Flournoy (1854–1920), and William James (1842–1910)—and unlike Freud—Jung posits, alongside the ego-complex and its hegemonic (though blinkered) form of consciousness, numerous other complexes, each of which possess a certain autonomy, and even a kind of consciousness, of its own. So it is appropriate that, according to Jung, these complexes (refigured in his later theory as *archetypes*) tend to acquire a personified form—in other words, they show up, in fantasy, dream, or hallucination, *as persons*.[13] Most of us are familiar with the particular personifications that Jung made famous: the shadow, the animus, the anima, the hero, the wise old man, etc.

According to Jung, it is necessary to psychological life, and essential to what he describes as the process of individuation, that the ego should not only become aware of, but ultimately engage in dialogue with, these other figures. However, such a confrontation is not something that the ego tends to enjoy; indeed, it is the inveterate nature of the ego-complex to find itself in tension with, resistant to and even conflict with the other psychic complexes. This is why, Jung tells us, our dreams so often offer us scenes of discord, friction, and dispute—scenes which we (or at least our egos) can experience as a succession of attacks, humiliations, rejections, and abandonments. This is because dreams, or at least the dreams we best remember, frequently enact scenes in which the ego reveals an inability or unwillingness to engage with or even acknowledge the call of the inner other, in its myriad forms. Because of this, the therapeutic approach that Jung recommends (1934) is 'a dialectical procedure, a real coming to terms with them, often conducted [. . .] in dialogue form'.[14]

As Jung often reminds us, all psychologies are highly conditioned by the 'personal equation' of their creators. Given which, it comes as no surprise to discover that Jung himself was intimately acquainted with the experience of inner discord from his earliest years. In the opening chapters of his autobiography, he describes his own possession of (or should I say *by*) two personalities. Throughout his childhood, according to his *Memories, Dreams, Reflections* (1961), Jung was tossed to and fro between Personality No. 1 and Personality No. 2, possessed first by one and then by the other. Eventually, in the wake of his 'storm lantern' dream, he came to the realisation that in order to achieve psychic wholeness he needed to find a way to accommodate both of these personalities.[15] However, it was not until the traumatic break with Freud and the psychological crisis that played out in its wake, that the conflict between Jung's two personalities returned to centre stage and he started to deliberately explore, from the inside as it were, the lived implications of his dissociationist theory. The fruit of Jung's years of inner exploration and dialogue was the *Red Book* (published in 2009). In the original German edition of *Memories, Dreams, Reflections*, Jung uses the term '*die Auseinandersetzung mit dem Unbewussten*' to describe his experience during this time.[16] In the English translation, the word *Auseinandersetzung* was rendered as 'confrontation'—the confrontation with the unconscious—but it is a word that could also mean 'dialogue', 'discussion', 'involvement', or 'engagement' with the unconscious, and these alternative translations perhaps convey better the highly *reciprocal* nature of what Jung is describing. In the *Red Book* (or *Liber novus*), Jung's ego-complex finds itself in various dramatic settings, many of which entail conversation and debate with the figures it meets. So Jung is never 'confronted' by something called 'the unconscious'. Rather, what happens is far more specific: Jung finds himself speaking and being spoken to by various autonomous and personified consciousnesses of which his ego has hitherto been unconscious.

That there is something intrinsically dramatic, not to say theatrical, about Jung's psychodynamic model, was obvious to many, not least Jung himself. Not only did he analyse dream structure in the literary terms of classical drama, uncovering in dreams moments of exposition, lysis, and culmination (*peripeteia*), and described the theatre as a 'psychotherapeutic institute where complexes are staged' but more interestingly, for our purposes, he also drew a more direct parallel between dream as event and theatre as event: 'A dream is a theatre in which the dreamer is himself the scene, the player, the prompter, the producer, the author, the public, and the critic.'[17]

Ostensibly, Jung is utilising this metaphor to show us how the dream functions 'on the subjective level' by which he means to suggest that everything in the dream is a portrait of the inner dynamics of the dreamer's psyche. However, Jung is simultaneously, by implication, pointing out the dynamic complexity of the theatrical model: the unique, living event of theatre is envisaged here as the dramatic interaction of a multiplicity of persons and energies, and therefore by extension, not only dream, but psyche itself exists as a similarly complex interaction involving a similar multiplicity of inner personalities.

As we have seen, it was during the difficult period following his split with Freud that Jung first found himself confronted by inner pressures that led him to the brink of questioning his own sanity. Eventually, despite strong resistance from the ego (expressed in the form of a powerful sense of shame and humiliation), he eventually bowed to what he experienced as inner necessity. Deliberately loosening the controlling grip of his (Personality No. 1) ego, he (re)opened himself to the voices of a multiplicity of personified inner others (Personality No. 2). It is worth noting here that the cluster of terms I have found myself using here (madness, loosening, multiplicity) are precisely the terms most often to be found in the vicinity of Dionysus and the Dionysian.

Jung's experience at that time, leading up to and during the writing of the *Red Book*, has been described by various Jungian scholars as Dionysian. In a recent study entitled *Remembering Dionysus* (2016), Susan Rowland pays particular attention to the *Red Book*'s fragmentary qualities.[18] For her, whether we regard the work from a literary perspective or a psychological perspective, what we find imaged there is dismemberment. In one of the myths of Dionysus, the god is torn to pieces by the Titans, but is later reborn. In other myths, it is the god himself who brings about the dismemberment of his enemies. His female followers, the wild maenads, are described as tearing apart both animals and men. Images of rending, splitting, and subsequent re-membering are characteristic of the complex of motifs that constellate around Dionysus in both his mythology and his rituals. Images and motifs of this kind when approached psychologically seem to speak of dissociation and madness, and indeed these themes too are native to the world of the Dionysian. There is much to be said with regard to the psychology of the Dionysian, but my focus here is the Dionysian as it reveals itself in theatre. As a radically decentred form that often features the conflictual interplay of multiple consciousness, theatre carries the metaphor of dismemberment in a direction all its own.

Rowland herself brings together the themes of dismemberment and of theatre in the *Red Book* when she draws attention to the fact that it is Jung himself who emphasises the dramatic aspect of his writing—describing it with the term 'mystery play'.[19] Indeed, she goes so far as to suggest that the *Red Book* 'seeks to be a mystery play for our time, re-incarnating the Dionysian spirit in the textures of living'.[20] Nietzsche's *Also Sprach Zarathustra*, a work that is undoubtedly a stylistic influence upon Jung's *Red Book*, also shares this highly psychological Dionysian quality. As Graham Parkes puts it, Nietzsche's book is 'a play of images constituting a consummate picture of the most comprehensive soul, of psyche in totality', so that

> it is possible, and enlightening, to read the entire text as a complex image of a single soul—Zarathustra's—and to understand as the major theme the Dionysiac dissolution of the unitary I through multiple overflowings into a plurality of persons [. . .].[21]

When it comes to the *Red Book*, James Hillman (1926–2011) has particularly emphasised its Dionysian theatrical dimension. In a dialogue conducted with Sonu Shamdasani on the subject of the *Red Book*, Hillman begins by pointing out that, even in the pre-*Red Book* period of *Symbols and Transformations of the Libido* (*Wandlungen und Symbole der Libido*) (1911–1912), Jung was already in 1912 depicting the libido in mythical forms and that such a psychology should be described as 'psychodramatics'. 'It implies', Hillman argues, 'that we're in a different realm of a different God':

> We're in the realm of Dionysus who was the patron, the God, of the theater. And then we have to use another language altogether for doing psychology. We have to imagine it as a realm of Dionysian life. Of life force, of passion, of tragedy and comedy and not a clarification that you would get from an Apollonic or an Athenian or another perspective of what goes on.[22]

Hillman goes on to suggest that in the *Red Book*, we find

> break-ins of the unwanted forces of nature, passion, revelry, violence, and so on, that are supposed to be kept out of the *temenos* in a way—or at least brought in and held within the vessel—this would be the reappearance of the Dionysian, which is there authentically in the psychodramatics of engaging with the other persons

concluding that 'it's a theater' and that '[Jung's] thought develops in this work as an interplay between characters': 'They stage positions and also are tremendously cultural and historical.'[23]

Psychotherapeutically, Hillman suggests, the implications of such an approach are profound. A step beyond the Freudian, Jung's multiple, dramatic model of the psyche is crucial because it enables us to see the ego as merely one complex among many. The ego is 'a member of the dramatis personae':

He's in the cast [. . .] one among others. Now isn't that a huge insight just to begin with? Isn't that a huge relief for the egocentric human being of our time, who goes to his therapy and tries to work out his problems, when this says you're one among others. There are a lot of people in your house. You don't live alone.[24]

Acting imagination

The process or technique that grew out of the experiences described in Jung's *Red Book* became known as 'active imagination'. In his subsequent work with analysands, Jung liked to recommend it as a dynamic means of enabling a meeting with their unconscious inner other(s). At the age of 75, and writing his master-work *Mysterium coniunctionis* (1955–1956), Jung still considered the technique to be sufficiently important to warrant a lengthy description. Significantly, in this account, he chooses to use theatrical terminology to describe this means for bring-ing about a dialectical meeting of the conscious ego and the personified energies of the deep unconscious, which reveal themselves as autonomous figures that, as Wallace Stevens put it, 'speak because they want to speak'.[25]

Jung recommends that we catch a dream or fantasy image and fix it with our gaze until it begins to alter. Thus animated, it takes on its own autonomous life and so it is that a kind of drama begins to be played out. Now, as the images begin to flow, he says, we can either sit back and enjoy the drama as a mere entertainment *out there,* or we may start to see that 'the piece that is being played does not want merely to be watched impartially, it wants to compel [the imaginer's] *participation*': 'If [the imaginer] understands that his own drama is being performed on this inner stage, he cannot remain indifferent to the plot and its denouement.'[26] Later, Jung comes back to this image, when he talks about the way in which the reality of the psychic process is experienced by an individual: 'Although, to a certain extent, he looks on from outside, impartially, he is also an acting and suffering figure in the drama of the psyche.'[27] So long as you just stare at the pictures, Jung goes on, noth-ing transformative happens and nothing will happen. But:

> If you recognize your own involvement, you yourself must enter into the process with your personal reactions, just as if you were one of the fantasy figures, or rather, as if the drama being enacted before your eyes were real. It is a psychic fact that this fantasy is happening, and it is as real as you—as a psychic entity—are real.[28]

The evident care that Jung takes in this lengthy description within his *magnum opus* is a clear indicator of the central importance of such encounters within his psy-chology. They exemplify, according to him, the so-called 'transcendent function', whereby the opposites are brought together, a process for which the alchemical term is *mysterium coniunctionis* and constitutes both the essence and the culmination of individuation. And it is highly significant that, in order to explicate it, Jung chose the theatrical metaphor as the most appropriate parallel. For this process takes a form whereby one engages with an inner other, thus creating a relationship of tension and even conflict, and through this enactment, which is somehow simultaneously engagement and observation (one foot in/one foot out, actor/audience), we both meet and are met by something that is experienced as both utterly different and yet also, uncannily, our own inner other. This strange recognition brings about, or perhaps is even identical to, an inner movement of transformation.

Why Dionysus?

When I describe such an encounter as Dionysian, it is not purely because Dionysus is the god of theatre. It is rather because the theatrical is always already essentially Dionysian.

When we examine a cluster of themes, motifs, and actions that have been associated with the Greek god Dionysus, we can see that they tend to easily fall into oppositional binaries. When such binaries are held together in one place—the Dionysian—we are presented with a paradox:

- he is both very near and yet somehow very far;
- he is thoroughly masculine, and yet somehow effeminate;
- he takes one out of oneself, and yet leaves one more whole;
- he is always a stranger, and yet is not only authentically Greek, but has a place at the centre of Greek culture;
- he appears in the form of a mask, which emphasizes both presence and absence, hiding as much as it reveals;
- he has been aptly described as the 'image of indestructible life', and yet he is, according to Heraclitus, also Hades, god of the dead.[29]

If theatre is Dionysian, then it is so, because it holds together some of the impossible contradictions that characterise Dionysus—presence and absence, truth and lie, connection and detachment. If Jean-Paul Vernant (1914–2007) is right when he says that Dionysus is 'a god with whom man can only make contact face to face', then theatre is most certainly the prime locus for that encounter.[30] It manifests as the face-to-face meeting of the actor with the mask, of one actor with another actor, of actor and audience, and of audience with audience. Through masked fiction we are presented, face to face, with a truth in the shape of a lie.

There is something essentially Dionysian about the mutuality of this encounter. In Euripides' *Bacchae* (perhaps our richest theatrical and meta-theatrical source for the Dionysian), the young tyrant Pentheus first interrogates the stranger (Dionysus pretending to be one of his own followers) about his god. Pentheus asks him, 'How did you see him? In a dream, or face to face?' (468), to which the stranger replies obliquely: *horon horonta*, 'I saw him seeing me.' As Vernant remarks, this reply

> stresses that the god's epiphany [. . .] is based on the meeting of two gazes in which (as in the interplay of reflecting mirrors), by the grace of Dionysus, a total reversibility is established between the devotee who sees and the god who is seen, where each one is, in relation to the other, at once the one who sees and the one who makes himself seen.[31]

Intentionally or not, Vernant seems here to echo an idea found in the work of Maurice Merleau-Ponty (1908–1961). For Merleau-Ponty, reversibility is an important aspect of what he calls the *chiasm*, whereby 'every perception is doubled with a counter-perception', since it is 'an act with two faces, one that no longer knows who speaks and who listens'.[32]

Such ideas seem highly relevant to a model of psyche in which, as Jung emphasises, ego not only meets, and sees the autonomous other of the deep unconscious, but also crucially experiences what it is to be in turn met and seen by these autonomous others. As Marie-Louise von Franz (1915–1998) puts it, 'one sees oneself for a moment through the eyes of another, of something objective which views one from the outside, as it were.'[33] This is the discomfiting experience of seeing the unconscious seeing us.

But this is also highly pertinent to the realm of analysis, wherein both analyst and analysand are not only seen by each other, but also are seen to be seen. A relation of such complexity and subtlety has been perhaps best articulated in Merleau-Ponty's concept of *chiasm*. With the image/concept of *chiasm*, Merleau-Ponty seeks to avoid a reductive short-circuiting of what is a profoundly delicate and asymmetrical relation: a relation situated on the fault-line between self and other. It is intended, with the lightest step, to tread this fine line, the interface where the otherness of the other gets related back, in paradoxical fashion, to the self's own radical otherness, while at the same time allowing for the revelation that the common humanity felt between us is intimately bound up with its own shadow—unassimilable alterity. As Lisa Folkmarson Käll has put it:

> By taking perspective on us, others bring to light our limits and by contesting what we say about them, point to the limits of our own perspectives. I see myself limited by the other and, yet, I nevertheless need the other to give birth to me through dialogue and interaction. I need the other to strengthen and validate as well as doubt and contest my experience of the world and of myself.[34]

Theatre—and also analysis—exist on, and exist to reveal, that fault-line, one that holds us apart but also holds us together, because it holds apart our parts, our personae (in Dionysian dismemberment), while providing the space in which they can be held together, maintaining an essential wholeness.

So in Euripides' *Bacchae*, for example, Dionysus is evidently present in the figure, the role, the person of Dionysus, the stranger, a figure that disrupts, bringing chaos and catastrophe. But we need to remember that Dionysus is also present in the theatrical event as a whole, which, by presenting it in a form that can be met, though not thereby swallowed up or assimilated, nonetheless contains that chaos—or at least holds open a space, in which the chaos—our chaos—may be encountered, and not just undergone. At the end of a Greek tragedy, we, and our emotions, are left in a state of fruitful perturbation. This has nothing to do with the smug *schadenfreude* that comes from observing from a distance the safe and tidy packaging of catastrophe visited upon others. Rather it reflects the fact that in the theatrical event, it is we (audience and actors) who have together shared in, truly participated in, though without being overwhelmed by, this terrible undoing.

Theatre and analysis are both *ec-static* in that they point toward the need to stand outside or ourselves, or rather our ego-selves, thus opening up an awareness that we are more than (or is it less than?) we thought we were, and also more vitally and immediately connected to the Other (in the form of inner and outer others) than we knew or perhaps wanted to know. As Charles Segal puts it, 'in the tragic theatre, as in the Bacchic ecstasy'—and, I would add, in active imagination, and even in analysis—'the participant "stands outside" of himself: he temporarily relinquishes the safe limits of personal identity, in order to extend himself sympathetically to other dimensions of experience.'[35] And this is another Dionysian paradox: we lose ourselves in order to gain a deeper sense of ourselves.

Yet, however terrifying to ego the experience of such ecstatic states may be, it is nonetheless, in both theatre and analysis, somehow *contained*. In both events, what gets opened up is an *empty space* (in Peter Brook's sense) for the playing out of the rawest and most violent complexes and emotions in an atmosphere of improvisation and spontaneity, and yet this empty space, the container (and I mean the analytic third, not the analyst) somehow holds these forces in an elastic envelope that works, because it inhabits a world that is not the 'real world'; it is animated through a relationship that is not quite a 'real relationship'—although, for this very reason, it is felt to be more real in a more focused and more visible way than any number of so-called 'real' relationships.

Dionysus in analysis

The rites of Dionysus, as Richard Seaford has pointed out, are essentially to do with the transformation of individual identity.[36] Just as, for the Greeks and also for us today, the theatrical event constitutes a place of transformation and liberation, so too does the therapeutic event. As we have seen, for Jung the psychic dynamics whereby these goals, both of which make up individuation, are achieved, or rather find their achievement through us, may be envisioned most fully through the theatrical metaphor. On the empty stage of dream, or active imagination, our inner figures make their exits and their entrances. Through interminable agonistic encounters, the heroic ego meets, battles with, and is humiliated by its own others, and thus, learning through suffering, we, as 'acting and suffering figures in the drama of the psyche', but also as an audience that is passionately and intimately engaged with what it witnesses, become able to achieve insight on a level that transcends, or burrows beneath, the simply intellectual.

This is exemplified perhaps most clearly in analysis, where the patient—but also crucially (as Jung emphasised), the analyst—strut and fret their hour (or 50 minutes) upon the stage. I have already drawn attention to the ambiguity that surrounds the fictive truth or truthful fiction of what occurs on this analytic stage. But there is more to be said. In the mysterious events and processes we call transference and countertransference, we tend to find and engage with the very figures that we (unconsciously) need to find and engage with. In effect, we cast the analyst in the role or roles we need her to play, and insist upon hearing all her lines as making sense, possessing meaning, only within this, our own plot. Our ultimate task is to release ourselves from this singleness of plot by coming to recognise the true otherness of our dialogical partner, a recognition that is, paradoxically, precisely what will enable us to gain knowledge of ourselves. As Folkmarson Käll says, echoing Merleau-Ponty:

> I can neither know the other in the same way as I can know myself nor myself in the same way as the other knows me. There is thus a clear duality at the very heart of the relation between self and other and the issue at stake in understanding intersubjectivity is how to preserve the uniqueness of the other while at the same time bridging the gap between self and other.[37]

The encounter in 1913 that initiated the succession of highly developed meetings with inner others that we can read in the *Red Book* also marked Jung's first meeting with what he was later to describe as the 'anima', i.e., the inner feminine aspect of a man. As Jung describes it in his 1925 seminar, while questioning himself about the scientific status of his visions, he hears the voice of a woman telling him, 'that is art'.[38] On Jung's account, this comment, and the conversation that ensued, had a perfectly ordinary feel to it: 'A living woman could very well have come into the room and said that very thing to me.'[39] This was particularly the case since Jung, as he tells us in *Memories, Dreams, Reflections*, recognised the voice as that of 'a patient, a talented psychopath who had a strong transference to me'.[40] Jung thus associates the dialogue that plays out (once Jung has succeeded in offering her the use of his 'speech-centres') with that of a conversation taking place in analysis—and, specifically, one taking place in the context of an erotic transference. Interest in the identity of this female patient[41] has obscured the crucial point here: that Jung is identifying the dialogical relationship between his ego and his inner other not just with a clinical relationship but with the sort of highly reciprocal relationship that characterised his erotic bond with Sabina Spielrein, and very likely that with Maria Moltzer (and subsequently, of course, with Toni Wolff). Jung later emphasises the mutuality of the relationship with the anima by noting that he 'was like a patient in analysis with a ghost and a woman' (*Ich kam mir vor wie ein Patient in Analyse bei einem weiblichen Geist!*).[42] So although Jung has informed us that the woman's voice was that of a patient, in the dialogical experience that ensues it is Jung himself who somehow becomes the patient and the woman/ghost the analyst. At times during the Spielrein relationship, Jung himself had played the patient role in receipt not only of her penetrating analytical interpretations, but also of her love and support. (For example, in his letter to Spielrein of 4 December 1908, he writes: 'Give me at this moment something back of the love and patience and unselfishness that I was able to give to you during the time of your illness. Now I am the sick one. . ..')[43] This ambiguity with regard to the question of who here is the analyst and who the patient gains in focus when we re-place this mutual, dramatic model into its proper context: the clinical world of transference and countertransference from which, as we have seen, it partly derives.

Conclusion

We can now see how three different, but related, settings, all Dionysian in their own way, may be seen to illuminate each other. The first is the virtual world of the theatrical event, a world parallel to that of 'ordinary life'; a world of dynamic, complex, and reciprocal relationships between audience and actor, actor and role, actor and actor. Here unreality, fiction, and mimesis enable the unveiling of truth. The second is the virtual world of active imagination, another world parallel to 'ordinary life'; a world in which ego engages in reciprocal dramatic and dialogical relations with internal others—a virtual realm, that is nonetheless, Jung emphasises (or rather his internal other emphasises), a field of 'objective' psychic reality. And the third is the virtual world of analysis, yet another world parallel to 'ordinary life'—a world in which analyst and patient playfully though seriously co-discover/ co-create a subjective/objective reality by standing in for those others (inner/ outer) who need to be encountered or re-encountered. Here, by (re-)enacting those dramas that need enacting, each partner is (re)acquainted with those psychic parts that have been split off, forgotten, or never met and thus to come home to themselves and, to borrow Eliot's words, 'know the place for the first time'.[44]

It is crucial to remember that the actor is never a characterless nothing who simply pours himself into the role, or hides behind the mask, but is always a complex individual who brings to any role a unique and personal history and sensibility, such that what we see on stage is always an amalgam of both role and actor. In analysis too, as Jung suggests, it is the 'whole person' of the analyst that is engaged with the 'whole person' of the analysand; indeed, analysis is no more than the meeting of these two wholenesses, although the event of that meeting also somehow constitutes, or is constituted by, a third event. This event is transcendent in the sense that it cannot be reduced to a formula of person plus person, any more than theatre can be reduced to the formula of actor plus audience. So it is never accurate to portray the event of analysis as a one-sided projection from client onto the blank screen therapist—an event that adds up to merely a rehash or replay of old patterns, old plots. The living drama of analysis is far more complex, and far more interesting than that. That dynamic interaction possesses the potential for infinite novelty and spontaneity. It is truly an inter-play, and it plays between and within the rich events that we soberly describe with the terms 'transference' and 'countertransference', as if we knew what they were—processes in which both patient and analyst enact and improvise a bewildering array of roles in a bewildering array of dramatic genres, moving together and apart, forming anew ever-shifting compounds and amalgams.

The *Dionysian* aspect of all this, as in theatre, resides not just in the chaotic emotional maelstrom which this process can sometimes resemble, but also in the very container—the boundaries and structures—that, on a good day, can hold it. Dionysus—paradoxically—exists in the unstable tension between the two: chaos and container, just as the boundaries that always surround theatre are always in tension with the tragic destructive/creative energies unleashed within them. The essential power of theatre resides in this tension, as it does also in the power of psychotherapy.

Notes

1 In this chapter, I am focusing upon the relation between theatre and Jungian psychoanalysis. It is beyond my remit to explore the twin disciplines of Dramatherapy and Psychodrama, which of course play upon aspects of precisely the relation I am attempting to emphasise here. With regard to what seems to be a general reluctance to acknowledge the close relation between the therapeutic and the theatrical, one should not discount the prejudice against all things theatrical that has run through the entire history of Western culture; for further discussion, see J.A. Barish, *The Antitheatrical Prejudice*, Berkeley, CA: University of California Press, 1985.
2 See J.R. Roach, *The Player's Passion: Studies in the Science of Acting*, Newark, DE: University of Delaware Press, 1985.
3 H.F. Ellenberger, *The Discovery of the Unconscious: The History and Evolution of Dynamic Psychiatry*, New York: Basic Books, 2008, pp. 57–69.
4 For an interesting paper exploring the theatrical elements of Voodoo possession, see A. Metraux and J.H. Labadie, 'Dramatic Elements in Ritual Possession', *Diogenes* 3, 1955, 18–36. Another fruitful parallel in the spiritual practice of traditional cultures can be found in shamanism, and in *The Theatrical Event*, David Cole draws close parallels between the work of the shaman and that of the actor; see D. Cole, *The Theatrical Event: A Mythos, a Vocabulary, a Perspective*, Middletown, CT: Wesleyan University Press, 1975, pp. 12–57
5 From an interview in 2016 with Andrew Dickson; see A. Dickson, 'Voodoo Child: Jonathan Pryce on Channelling His Father's Death for Hamlet', *The Guardian*, 18 April 2016. Available online from: https://www.theguardian.com/stage/2016/apr/18/jonathan-pryce-hamlet-royal-court-1980. Accessed 19 March 2017.
6 In 2012, Day-Lewis revised earlier reports of his father's appearance to him by emphasising the metaphorical nature of the event. *The Guardian*, 29 October 2012. Available online from: https://www.theguardian.com/stage/2012/oct/29/daniel-day-lewis-hamlet-ghost. Accessed 2 April 2017.
7 See, for example, R. Justice-Malloy, 'Charcot and the Theatre of Hysteria', *Journal of Popular Culture* 28, 1995, 133–138.
8 S. Freud and J. Breuer, *Studies on Hysteria*, New York: Random House, 2001, p. 22.
9 S. Freud, *The Interpretation of Dreams*, London: Penguin, 1980, pp. 363–365.
10 R. Bowlby, *Freudian Mythologies: Greek Tragedy and Modern Identities*, Oxford: Oxford University Press, 2007, p. 49.
11 S. Shamdasani, 'Introduction', in C.G. Jung, *The Red Book: Liber novus*, ed. S. Shamdasani, tr. M. Kyburz, J. Peck, and S. Shamdasani, New York and London: Norton, 2009, pp. 193–221 (p. 195).
12 D. Diderot, *Paradoxe sur le comedien*, Cambridge; London: Cambridge University Press, 2002. English version: *The Paradox of Acting*, tr. Walter Herries Pollock, London: Chatto & Windus 1883

13 These ideas are developed in M. Saban, 'Jung, Winnicott and the Divided Psyche', *Journal of Analytical Psychology* 61, 2016, 329–349.

14 C.G. Jung, 'Archetypes of the Collective Unconscious' (1934; 1954), in *The Archetypes of the Collective Unconscious* [*Collected Works*, vol. 9/i], tr. R.F.C. Hull, London: Routledge, 1968, §1–§86 (pp. 3–41) and §84 (p. 40).

15 C.G. Jung, *Memories, Dreams, Reflections*, ed. A. Jaffé, New York: Vintage Books, 1989, pp. 87–89.

16 C.G. Jung, *Erinnerungen, Träume, Gedanken von C.G. Jung: Aufgezeichnet und herausgegeben von Aniela Jaffé*, Zurich and Düsseldorf: Walter-Verlag, 1962.

17 The reference to dream structure occurs in Jung's paper entitled 'On the Nature of Dreams' (1945; 1948), in *The Structure and Dynamics of the Psyche* [*Collected Works*, vol. 8], tr. R.F.C. Hull, London: Routledge, 1969, §530–569 (pp. 281–297) (§561–564 [pp. 294–250]). His comment on theatre is to be found in C.G. Jung, *Dream Analysis: Notes of the Seminar Given in 1928–30*, London: Routledge, 1990, p. 2; and the remark comparing the dream to the theatre occurs in 'General Aspects of Dream Psychology' 1916; 1948, in *The Structure and Dynamics of the Psyche*, §443–529, pp. 237–280), §509 (p. 266).

18 S. Rowland, *Remembering Dionysus: Revisioning Psychology and Literature in C.G. Jung and James Hillman*, Abingdon and New York: Routledge, 2016, pp. 71–88.

19 The term 'mystery play' occurs in Jung, *The Red Book*, p. 246; cf. Rowland, *Remembering Dionysus*, pp. 75–76.

20 Rowland, *Remembering Dionysus*, p. 76.

21 G. Parkes, *Composing the Soul: Reaches of Nietzsche's Psychology*, Chicago, IL: University of Chicago Press, 1996, p. 360.

22 J. Hillman and S. Shamdasani, *Lament of the Dead: Psychology After Jung's Red Book*, New York: Norton, 2013,. p. 33

23 Hillman and Shamdasani, *Lament of the Dead*, p. 34.

24 Hillman and Shamdasani, *Lament of the Dead*, p. 101. Here Hillman develops themes he touches on elsewhere in his work; for example, discussing the Dionysian, theatrical, approach to psyche, he suggests that 'the self divided is precisely where the self is authentically located [. . .] Authenticity is the perpetual dismemberment of being and not-being a self, a being that is always in many parts, like a dream with a full cast' (J. Hillman, *Healing Fiction*, Putnam, CT: Spring Publications, 2012, p. 39)

25 W. Stevens, *Selected Poems*, New York: Random House, 2011, p. 194. As the title of my chapter I have shamelessly stolen this phrase, not only from Stevens, but also from Mary Watkins who uses it as a chapter title in her important book *Invisible Guests*, which explores at great depth the ways in which inner others manifest in the lives of creative people such as novelists, but also in the creative lives of us all; see M. Watkins, *Invisible Guests*, New Orleans, LA: Spring Publications, 2000. Another book of hers, *Waking Dreams*, also makes an important contribution to the literature of Active Imagination in the Jungian tradition; see M. Watkins, *Waking Dreams*, New Orleans, LA: Spring Publications, 1976.

26 C.G. Jung, *Mysterium coniunctionis: An Inquiry into the Separation and Synthesis of Psychic Opposites in Alchemy* [*Collected Works*, vol. 14], tr. R.F.C. Hull, London: Routledge, 1955, §706.

27 Jung, *Mysterium coniunctionis*, §753.

28 Jung, *Mysterium coniunctionis*, §753.

29 For the phrase 'image of indestructible life', see the title of K. Kerényi, *Dionysos: Archetypal Image of Indestructible Life*, tr. R. Manheim, Princeton, NJ: Princeton University Press, 1966. For the Heraclitus quotation, see C.H. Kahn, *The Art and Thought of Heraclitus*, Cambridge and London: Cambridge University Press, 1981, p. 8 (Diels-Kranz, fragment 15). I refer here, not to the Dionysus of Nietzsche's *The Birth of Tragedy* (1872), who makes up half of a polar binary with Apollo, but rather the more complex and interesting Dionysus whom we actually find in ancient Greek culture in all its multiplicity. The later Nietzsche's Dionysus is paradoxical in precisely this way, that through a kind of

binary synthesis he becomes (for Nietzsche) a kind of dialectical unity contained in and transcending the tension between both Dionysus and Apollo.

30 J.-P.Vernant, *Myth and Society in Ancient Greece*, tr. J. Lloyd, New York: Zone Books, 1988, p. 202.
31 Vernant, *Myth and Society*, p. 393.
32 M. Merleau-Ponty, *The Visible and the Invisible*, ed. C. Lefort, tr. A. Lingis, Evanston, IL: Northwestern University Press, 1968, pp. 264-265.
33 M.-L. von Franz, 'The Hidden Source of Self-Knowledge', tr. K.E. Xippolitas and V. Brooks, in *Dreams: A Study of the Dreams of Jung, Descartes, Socrates, and Other Historical Figures*, Boston, MA and London: Shambhala Press, 1991, p. 7.
34 Quoted in A. Celenza, *Erotic Revelations: Clinical Applications and Perverse Scenarios*, London: Routledge, 2014, p. 22.
35 C. Segal, *Dionysiac Poetics and Euripides' 'Bacchae'*, Princeton, NJ: Princeton University Press, 1997, p. 215.
36 R. Seaford, *Dionysos*, Abingdon and New York: Routledge, 2006, p. 11.
37 L. Folkmarson Käll, 'Expressive Space: Encountering Self and Other' (2009). Available online from: https://philosophy.columbian.gwu.edu/sites/philosophy.columbian.gwu.edu/files/image/Kall_gwu_presentation.pdf (p. 21). Accessed 19 March 2017.
38 C.G. Jung, *Analytical Psychology: Notes of the Seminar Given in 1925*, London: Routledge, 1990, p. 42.
39 Jung, *Analytical Psychology: Notes of the Seminar Given in 1925*, p. 42.
40 Jung, *Memories, Dreams, Reflections*, p. 185.
41 Shamdasani has weighed up various suggestions in his study entitled *Jung Stripped Bare by His Biographers, Even*, London: Karnac, 2005.
42 Jung, *Memories, Dreams, Reflections*, p. 186; cf. Jung, *Erinnerungen, Träume, Gedanken*, p. 189.
43 Quoted in A. Carotenuto, *A Secret Symmetry: Sabina Spielrein between Jung and Freud*, New York: Pantheon, 1984, pp. 195–196.
44 T.S. Eliot, *Four Quartets*, Boston, MA: Houghton Mifflin Harcourt, 2014, p. 59, l. 242.

3

ANCIENT PSYCHOTHERAPY?

Fifth-century BCE Athenian intellectuals and the cure of disturbed minds

Yulia Ustinova

In antiquity, as in our time, insanity was notoriously difficult to treat.[1] In the Hippocratic tradition, health, mental health included, was construed in the framework of the so-called 'humoral theory', expounded in the *Nature of Man*: the body is healthy, when the quality-carrying bodily humours—blood, phlegm, bile and black bile—are balanced; their excess, shortage or blockage cause disease.[2] Hippocratic medicine almost did not recognise emotional and social factors as causes of mental afflictions, and explained all diseases, including psychological and psychiatric disorders, as resulting from physiological causes only.[3] Furthermore, in the Hippocratic literature, with its emphasis on fits of florid madness and lack of interest in borderline mental states,[4] moderate deviations from the norm are seldom noted. Following the basic principle of their science, Hippocratic physicians treated all mental ailments, acute and chronic, by physical means, and in order to restore the correct humoral balance, happily prescribed violent purgatives as part of a mad person's regimen.[5] The emphasis on purgation appears to have been shared by Greek physicians belonging to different traditions, and not limited to the Hippocratic school.[6] In traditional medicine as well, 'cleansing and purifications' were the first remedy to try, if attempts at persuasion did not help, and a person continued to behave strangely.[7] Both Hippocratic doctors and traditional healers prescribed drinking hellebore, although the drug was toxic, and could kill easily: one of the Hippocratic aphorisms predicts: 'Convulsion after hellebore, deadly'.[8] It is hard to imagine how these drugs could alleviate mental disease, unless they either served as shock therapy, or acted as placebo. In the words of Guido Majno (1922–2010), 'hellebore alone could claim a long chapter in the history of human error.'[9]

Thus, in treating mental illness, Hippocratic physicians rationalised the ancient idea of purification, which became purgation, while the actual practice remained basically unchanged. Catharsis was all-important, and as it lurked in the background of the therapy, torturing and harmful methods were applied, despite their dreadful consequences and ineffectiveness.[10] The resulting vacuum was filled in two very different ways: by means of ecstatic rites, on the one hand, and by 'talking cure', an innovative method introduced by experts on human psyche, sophists and dramatists, on the other hand.

Ecstatic rites

The Corybantic rites offer a most notable example of initiations which attracted mentally handicapped patients who tried to find relief from their affliction.[11] While their power to cause mental disorders was shared with other deities and demons, the Corybantes were believed to possess this gift *par excellence*.[12] They were considered to be capable of healing frenzy as well, and Aristophanes refers to this fact as common knowledge.[13] This evidence implies that Corybantism was, *inter alia*, a technique of healing mental disorders.[14] Both healers and mad people were called *korubantiôntes*, and probably gathered in private homes.[15] These people could belong to various social classes, including individuals of considerable social standing and wealth. The common manifestation of Corybantism was ecstatic dancing in the state of collective violent frenzy, which was easily transmitted from one participant to another.[16]

Evidence on the Corybantic initiations is sufficiently rich to allow an attempt at reconstruction of the central ceremony of this cult. These rites appear in Plato's dialogues on several occasions, and were well-known to the Athenian upper classes.[17] Plato examines the methods used by 'women who in rites administer Corybantic cures (*iamata*)' and bring people 'into a sound state of mind instead of frenzied condition'.[18] The rites involved deafening music as well as dancing, and produced a powerful effect on the participants: music resounded in their bodies, their heart rate increased and they wept from excitement.[19] This physical and mental condition is certainly not the normal baseline state and can be appropriately described as alteration of consciousness.

Corybantic treatment of mental disorders, *korubantismos*, was based on the idea that madness may be cured by means of madness: a cathartic paroxysm could release a person from possession by a daemon or a divinity.[20] The main Corybantic ceremony may be reconstructed as follows: after offering a sacrifice,[21] and perhaps cleansing by bathing,[22] the leader of the initiation, who was also the healer, drove the patient into a state of excitement.[23] The healer asked questions, gave orders, and sang incantations to intensify the suggestive influence on the patient. This procedure was called *thrônosis* ('chairing'), and it is described by Plato.[24] The patient sat on a chair, while other participants danced and sang, raising a great din around him and playing tambourines, flutes, and other musical instruments. As a result, the patient was driven to a frenzy, gradually losing consciousness of all but the whirling rhythm, and began dancing and singing, while other participants experienced ecstatic states of varying intensity. Afterwards the patient might return to their former pathological condition, but usually the new balanced state was maintained by means of participation in the rites. During the *thrônosis* ceremony, the psychological condition which caused the mental disorder was 'polarised', the result being an intensification of religious feelings leading to ecstasy—*mania*—during the rites, on the general background of normal behaviour: the frenzy attacks were regulated, and madness received 'telestic (ritual) orientation'.[25] Thus an ex-mad person became initiated or 'Corybanted', which is the literal translation of the word *kekorybantismenos*, appearing in a second-century inscription, probably from Erythrae (Asia Minor).[26] Other participants, once initiated in the same way, also returned to their normal tranquil state—until the next gathering. The majority of participants did not suffer from a particular mental ailment, and simply enjoyed the excitement caused by the ritual tunes. In fact, Aristotle discusses 'enthusiastic excitement' caused by ecstatic ritual music, which brings about cure and purification (*katharsis*), as well as feelings of relief and delight.[27]

Historical and anthropological parallels allow some insights into the composition, organisation, and ritual of Corybantic associations. In medieval and early modern Europe, periodic cure of patients suffering from epilepsy and psychiatric ailments by means of compulsive dances gave rise to annual dancing festivals, some of them surviving well into the twentieth century, such as the dancing processions of Esternach.[28] Modern anthropology is familiar with a great number of healing techniques similar to Corybantism, notably *zar* and *bori*, used in some regions of modern Africa and Arabia.[29] Cognitively, these healing techniques are based on the representativeness heuristic, which is attested cross-culturally and consists of the tendency to associate similar objects or phenomena, and believe that an effect is to resemble the cause. This way of thinking is prominent in the history of medicine. In the West, the best-known example is homeopathy, based on the 'law of similars', which remains popular notwithstanding its pseudo-scientific foundations.[30]

Most significantly, homeopathy and participation in possession cults are healing. Ecstatic possession is beneficial for people suffering from mental afflictions: observing such people during and after voodoo ceremonies in Haiti, the psychiatrist William Sargant (1907–1988) noted that they felt better, and did not suffer from any adverse effects. The primary condition for the success of this treatment was of course sincere faith in its fundamental validity.[31] Therapeutic methods used by native practitioners in their séances combining exorcism, persuasion, shock, suggestion, and hypnotic-like techniques have been found to be effective in the treatment of a variety of mental and other disorders.[32]

The exorcist him- or herself was usually someone who had formerly experienced possession, and in order to keep healthy must practice trancing.[33] Symptoms associated with spirit possession often include depression, guilt feelings, and dissociation, reported by patients who had suffered a period of acute or chronic stress.[34] Repeated participation in rituals of exorcism is often necessary for the maintenance of the balanced state.[35] The depth of the trance and the degree of dissociation vary considerably in different individuals; even in the same individual, the degree fluctuates from occasion to occasion. Besides, in modern possession-trance rituals, there is much play acting.[36] The cultural and even physical environment where the healing takes place are of crucial importance and deeply affect the patients, so much so that the same traditional healers who are successful in their home shrines do not attain similar results when invited into psychiatric wards.[37] A number of people must participate in the assembly in order for it to provide a setting conductive to successful healing and preservation of the sanity of the initiated. The communal nature of the healing procedure offers the patient social reinforcement, achieved in the process of ritual or symbolic manipulation.[38] This requires the development of some institutionalised organisation of the believers, headed by one or several cult leaders. Thus, persons with abnormal behavioural features, who have been treated by a certain ecstatic technique and obtained a state which is recognised in a given society as sanity, can maintain it only if they experience that same altered state of consciousness from time to time. These alterations of consciousness are often considered to be inspired by the same divinity or spirit who had inflicted the illness in the first place. The ceremony serves as an initiation to the cult of this divinity, and the victim is liberated from the illness as a result of an ecstatic rite.

These studies suggest a plausible model for understanding of the Corybantic rites. People cured by means of a Corybantic initiation needed to experience initiatory *mania* over and over, as means of maintaining both their mental health and the order of the ceremonies. They performed their rites in associations, which had to meet more or less regularly and were focused on a charismatic exorcist, who had probably been healed of insanity him- or herself. If, however, only former mad people participated in the Corybantic initiations, this phenomenon would not have been so widespread. The majority of the *korubantiôntes* must have been quite sane.

The cultural framework and social environment determine that certain kinds of alteration of consciousness and associated behaviour are encouraged as desirable; this socially accepted behaviour is controlled and never leads to pathological disability. On the contrary, it apparently has a wholesome effect on the sane majority who benefit from the resolution of personal stress and other salutary consequences of the ecstatic experience. And it reminds us of C.G. Jung (1875–1961), who spoke of *katharsis* and recommended submission to the state of being outside oneself, in order to regain wholeness. For he quoted 'the ancient motto of the Mysteries', namely: 'Let go of what you have, then you will receive.'[39]

'Talking cure'

Quite a different way of treatment appears to have been known since the fifth century BCE at the latest: this was the 'talking cure', re-invented more than two thousand years later by Sigmund Freud.[40] The method appears to have been developed by several Athenian intellectuals and experts in rhetoric, known as the sophists,[41] in particular by Gorgias and Antiphon.

Gorgias' practical interest in the subject which would be defined today as psychology and psychotherapy is attested to by the epigram inscribed on the monument erected by his great-nephew Eumolpus: 'No mortal has discovered a better art of training the soul for the contests in virtue, than Gorgias.'[42] He was famous as one of the greatest teachers of rhetoric, and his 'technique of personal coaching' was based on the art of persuasion.[43] Gorgias was aware of the power of words over the soul, and wrote: 'Speech is a great potentate, who by means of the tiniest and most invisible body achieves the most godlike results', for 'it is able to dispel fear (*phobos*), to assuage grief (*lupê*), to inculcate joy, and to evoke pity.'[44] Furthermore, in his opinion, persuasion added to speech could 'mould the mind as it wishes',[45] not only producing immediate effect, but influencing the character.

These are the powers of the rhetoric art. Gorgias could be quite serious about the force of witchcraft and magic, and of 'inspired incantations (*entheoi epôidai*) in words'.[46] He was convinced that these were effective only if combined with 'opinion of mind'[47]—a very enlightened understanding of the way suggestion and autosuggestion work. Accordingly, it is quite likely that when members of the audience believed in the capacity of charms to influence them—and even Socrates seems to have been convinced that incantations were effective—Gorgias' magic might work.[48] In fact, Gorgias explicitly draws a parallel between rhetoric and medicine:

> The power of speech has the same relationship to the order of soul as does the order of drugs to the nature of bodies. For just as different drugs draw different humors from body, and some put an end to sickness, some to life, so some speeches induce grief, some joy, some fear, some instil courage in the audience, and some drug and bewitch the soul with a kind of pernicious persuasion.[49]

Gorgias was indeed acquainted with the medical practice, and probably even used his art for medical purposes: Plato has the great rhetor remark that he used to accompany his brother Herodicus and other physicians on their visits to patients, and persuaded those unwilling to accept the pains of the prescribed treatment to consent to it.[50] In the *Encomium (Praise) of Helen*, Gorgias expresses his confidence in the power of the words to heal and manipulate the soul—anticipating as it seems Isocrates' designation of rhetoric as *psychagogia*, literally 'soul-leading'.[51]

Application of the art of speaking to the cure of disturbed minds attracted the attention of other Athenian intellectuals, as well. An author of a tract on the lives of orators, known as Pseudo-Plutarch, attributes to Antiphon authorship of a work entitled *Art of Avoiding Distress (Technê alupias)* and the establishment in Corinth of a clinic where patients tormented by grief and pain were treated by means of *logoi*:[52]

> While he [Antiphon] was still involved with poetry, he contrived an art of removing grief, like the treatment of doctors for the sick. He procured a workshop in Corinth beside the agora, and put out a notice that he was able to treat the grief-stricken through words. He assuaged the sick, inquiring into the causes. But thinking the art to be beneath him, he turned to rhetoric.[53]

Another version, attributed to Philostratus, a sophist of the Roman imperial period, is that Antiphon 'announced pain-removing lectures, in the belief that people would tell no grief so terrible that he could not remove it from their mind'.[54]

This testimony, regarded by most scholars as authentic, probably reflects Antiphon's real activities, namely the invention or elaboration of an oral technique of assuaging grief.[55] Antiphon's interest in cognition and perception is attested to by almost a dozen quotations from his book *On Truth*, while several passages in his treatise *On Concord* contain astute observations on psychology and human behavior.[56] Finally, Antiphon's engagement in the interpretation of dreams, testified by his authorship of the tract *On Dreams*, as well as by his biographical tradition, appears as an attempt to refute traditional interpretations as ensuing from a primitive superstition.[57] Antiphon's attention to dreams might also reflect his interest in the way the human mind works—another hint at the overlap between his approach and psychoanalysis.[58] Hence, the passage cited above probably reflects Antiphon's real activities, namely, invention or elaboration of an oral technique of assuaging grief, and perhaps even penning a tract on the subject.[59] Most significantly, such details as discovering the causes of psychological troubles by questioning the patient and cure by means of speech are reminiscent of the approach that is still used in modern psychotherapy.[60]

Sophists seem to have perfected and developed the attitude which existed from times immemorial and was intuitively used by many compassionate friends or relatives of sufferers. Aeschylus indeed believed that 'words are physicians (*iatroi*) for the sickness of wrath'.[61] To be sure, Aristophanes lists persuasion by words as the first among several methods of treatment of insanity.[62] In addition, the conviction of many fifth-century (and later) intellectuals, such as Plato,[63] that 'diseases of soul' could ensue from ignorance, invited their cure by means of persuasion. In this respect, Socrates' and Plato's ideas on philosophy as a cure for souls neatly corresponded to practices attributed to Gorgias and Antiphon who tried to treat troubled souls by wise words.

Athenian dramatists must have had keen understanding of the depth of the human soul, and were probably updated on the development of the 'talking cure' by contemporary sophists. It is not a coincidence that Antiphon is reported to have authored tragedies, and composed his manual on avoidance of grief, while still engaged in poetry:[64] dramatists, orators, and psychotherapists cannot but share a profound interest in psychology.

The first surviving example of sophisticated therapy by words is perhaps the end of Euripides' *Bacchae*, where in the scene of recognition, Cadmus gradually leads Agave from (euphoric) madness to (painful) sanity.[65] Agave, the unfortunate mother of Pentheus who dared not to recognise the power of Dionysus, was made by the ruthless god the murderer of her own son: together with other women of Thebes, she participated in ecstatic rites of Dionysus, and in her god-induced frenzy took her son for a lion and tore him into pieces. Agave's father Cadmus had to reveal to her the horrible truth:

A(gave):	What part of this causes you disgrace or pain?
C(admus):	First turn your eye to the heavens.
A:	There! What did you mean that I look at?
C:	Does it seem the same to you or altered?
A:	It is brighter than before and clearer.

C:	Does your mind still feel giddy?
A:	I don't know what you mean. But I am coming somehow to my senses and have abandoned my former state of mind.
C:	Will you hear me and answer truly?
A:	Yes: I have forgotten what we said before, father.
C:	To what household did you come at your marriage?
A:	You married me to Echion, one of the Sown Men, they say.
C:	Well, what son was born in that house to your husband?
A:	Pentheus, his father's son and mine.
C:	Whose head do you have in your hands then?
A:	The hunters told me it's a lion's.
C:	Look at it properly: the effort of doing so is slight. [. . .]
A:	No, in my misery I hold Pentheus' head! [. . .] Who killed him?
C:	You killed him, you and your sisters. [. . .]
A:	But how did we get there?
C:	You were out of your wits, and the whole city was possessed by Bacchus.[66]

The accuracy of Euripides' psychological observations and their compatibility to modern treatment methods have been discerned by E.R. Dodds (1893–1971).[67] On the basis of clinical data and psychiatric theory, Georges Devereux (1908–1985) convincingly demonstrated 'the clinical plausibility' of the scene.[68] In this dialogue, Cadmus first makes Agave concentrate on an external object and brings her to perceive her actual surroundings. After Agave's 'pre-therapy' has proven to be successful, Cadmus restores his daughter to sensibility by tenderly asking her questions about her life and recent actions, thus leading her to re-itineration of the past, re-insertion into the cultural environment she belongs to, and confrontation with the dreadful present.

In addition to this scene in the *Bacchae*, based as it seems on 'insight-and-recall oriented psychotherapy', Euripides reveals his interest in the ailments and treatment of *psuchê* in a fragment from an unknown play.[69] Theseus says there that he learnt from a wise man to contemplate human misfortunes in advance, in order to train his mind and in this way to mitigate the suffering when a catastrophe really happens.[70] This passage—and the advice—were apparently well known, and are cited by later authors, such as Plutarch and Cicero.[71] In any case, it is known today that systematic preparation for exposure to stress dramatically reduces the percentage of PTSD (post-traumatic stress disorder) and ASD (acute stress disorder).[72]

In Aristophanes' *Wasps*, Philocleon, an elderly Athenian who is addicted to jury-service, is treated by his son by 'working on madness from "within"':[73] a psycho-drama set by the son leads the father to a collapse, which breaks Philocleon's obsessive habit and brings him back to sanity.[74] Accepting the madman's conviction and playing his game indeed were recommended by Celsus in the first century CE,[75] but in the fifth century BCE, this scene remains an isolated example of the otherwise unattested approach. In the modern world, various kinds of treatment by theatrical techniques, such as re-enactment of the patient's story by actors in playback theatre, are used successfully.[76]

In the *Bacchants*, Cadmus applies psychotherapeutic (or simply rhetorical, as some would argue) techniques to treat Agave's short-term dissociation, whereas Philocleon's son deals with an abiding disorder. Euripides' and Aristophanes' scenes seem to indicate that, by the late fifth century BCE, techniques of 'therapy of words' were quite elaborate, and at least the leading intellectuals were familiar with them.[77] Although various aspects of modern counselling and psychotherapy differ from ancient approaches, methods of prevention and treatment of mental disorders by means of conversation and persuasion, which were probably developed in Greece in the fifth century, resemble the modern 'talking cure'.[78]

Conclusion

The treatment of abnormal behaviour advocated in Hippocratic medicine was focused on the body of the patient: mental afflictions were attributed mainly to humoral misbalance or trauma. Hippocratic therapy was still based on purgation of the body—procedures which ensued from time-honoured techniques of purification. In so doing, medical science applied a new theoretical foundation, the concept of humours, to the existing ritual practice of cleansing—a paradoxical situation, given the fact that in their writings, Hippocratic physicians did not spare their efforts to denigrate traditional healers.

Traditional cultic treatment of madness remained extremely popular and involved purifications, exorcism by means of ecstatic rites, and in some cases administration of herbal medicine. Some elements of this complex could be efficient, especially when enhanced by the placebo effect. In addition, Corybantic initiates who did not suffer from any mental problem enthusiastically participated in the cathartic ceremonies, enjoyed them immensely, and developed emotional connection bordering on addiction to the rites.

Actual innovation in practical terms came from an unexpected direction: experts in the use of words recognised their healing power and began to elaborate methods of 'speaking therapy'. These methods may have been rooted, to a certain extent, in the age-long appreciation of compassionate conversation and the power of persuasion, and even in the ancient belief in the magic power of the words. On the other hand, therapy by persuasion evolved in close interaction with the ideas of contemporary thinkers on illness of the soul as ignorance, to be treated by education and wise words.[79]

Notes

1 For studies of madness and its treatment in antiquity, see A.C.Vaughan, *Madness in Greek Thought and Custom*, Baltimore, MD: Furst, 1919; A. O'Brien-Moore, *Madness in Ancient Literature*, Weimar: Wagner, 1924; G. Rosen, *Madness in Society: Chapters in Historical Sociology of Mental Illness*, Chicago, IL: University of Chicago Press, 1968; B. Simon,

Mind and Madness in Ancient Greece: The Classical Roots of Modern Psychiatry, Ithaca, NY: Cornell University Press, 1978; J. Pigeaud, *Folie et cures de la folie chez les médicins de l'Antiquité gréco-romaine*, Paris: Les Belles Lettres, 1987; J. Pigeaud, *La maladie de l'âme: Etude sur la relation de l'âme et du corps dans la tradition médico-philosophique antique*, Paris: Les Belles Lettres, 1989; J. Pigeaud, *De la mélancolie: Fragments de poétique et d'histoire*, Paris: Dilecta, 2005; G. Guidorizzi, *Ai confini dell' anima: I Greci e la follia*, Milan: Cortina, 2010; W.V. Harris (ed.), *Mental Disorders in the Classical World*, Leiden: Brill, 2013.

2 Hippocrates, *Nature of Man*, 4 (tr. W.H.S. Jones, Cambridge, MA: Harvard University Press, 1967, pp. 11–13).

3 Pigeaud, *La maladie de l'âme*, p. 70.

4 Hippocratic texts almost entirely ignore enduring mental disorders, regarding acute frenzy the as the main expression of mental pathology: see O'Brien-Moore, *Madness in Ancient Literature*, p. 9; A.J.L. van Hooff, *From Autothnasia to Suicide: Self-killing in Classical Antiquity*, London: Routledge, 1990, p. 99; R. Garland, *The Eye of the Beholder: Deformity and Disability in the Graeco-Roman World*, Bristol: Bristol Classical Press, 2010, p. 137; C. Gill, 'Ancient Psychotherapy', *Journal of the History of Ideas* 46, 1985, 307–325 (p. 316).

5 O. Temkin, 'Beiträge zur archaischen Medizin', *Kyklos* 3, 1930, 90–135 (p. 101); R. Joly, *Le niveau de la science hippocratique: Contribution à la psychologie de l'histoire des sciences*, Paris: Les Belles Lettres, 1966; cf. P. Laín Entralgo, *The Therapy of the Word in Classical Antiquity*, New Haven, CT: Yale University Press, 1970, p. 201; Pigeaud, *Folie et cures de la folie*, p. 177.

6 G.C. McDonald, 'Concepts and Treatments of Phrenitis in Ancient Medicine', unpublished PhD dissertation, Newcastle University, 2009, pp. 67–75; and F. Steckerl, *The Fragments of Praxagoras of Cos and His School*, Leiden: Brill, 1958, pp. 9–16.

7 For instance, Aristophanes, *Wasps*, 118 (ed. and tr. J. Henderson, Cambridge, MA: Harvard University Press, 1998, p. 235).

8 *Aphorisms* 5.1; cf. *Aphorisms* 5.4; 1.2 (ed. and tr. W.H.S. Jones, Cambridge, MA: Harvard University Press, 1967, pp. 159 and 99); I.M. Lonie, 'The Cnidian Treatises of the Corpus Hippocraticum', *Classical Quarterly* 15, 1965, 1–30 (p. 4); and G. Majno, *The Healing Hand*, Cambridge, MA: Harvard University Press, 1975, p. 189. On hellebore, white and black, see J.-H. Kühn and U. Fleischer, *Index Hippocraticus*, Göttingen: Vandenhoeck & Ruprecht, 1986, p. 252; S. Amigues (ed.), *Théophraste, Recherches sur les plantes*, Paris: Budé, 1988–2006, vol. 5, p. 138.

9 Majno, *The Healing Hand*, p. 188; also in Pigeaud, *Folie et cures de la folie*, p. 209.

10 F. Hoessly, *Katharsis: Reinigung als Heilverfahren: Studien zum Ritual der archaischen und klassischen Zeit sowie zum Corpus Hippocraticum*, Göttingen: Vandenhoeck & Ruprecht, 2001, pp. 310–313.

11 For further discussion, see I.M. Linforth, 'The Corybantic Rites in Plato', *University of California Publications in Classical Philology* 13(5), 1946, 121–162; H. Jeanmaire, *Dionysos: Histoire du culte de Bacchus*, Paris: Payot, 1970, pp. 131–138; Y. Ustinova, 'Corybantism: The Nature and Role of an Ecstatic Cult in the Greek Polis', *Horos* 10–12, 1992–1998, 503–520; R. Anderson, 'Emotion and Experience in Classical Athenian Religion: Studies in Athenian Ritual and Belief', unpublished Ph.D. dissertation, University of Cambridge, 2004. I am grateful to R. Anderson for sharing with me his dissertation.

12 Euripides, *Hippolytus*, 141–144 (ed. and tr. D. Kovacs, Cambridge, MA: Harvard University Press, 1995, pp. 137–139); Aristophanes, *Wasps*, 8 (p. 223).

13 Aristophanes, *Wasps*, 119 (p. 235).

14 For a detailed analysis of clinical and therapeutic data, see Jeanmaire, *Dionysos*, pp. 105–108.

15 A dedication to *Kurbantes* was discovered in a bathroom in a fourth-century house in the town of Toumba in Macedonia: see E. Voutiras, 'Un culte domestique des Corybantes', *Kernos* 9, 1996, 243–256.

16 Plato, *Ion*, 536c (tr. H.W. Fowler and W.R.M. Lamb, Cambridge, MA: Harvard University Press, 1962, p. 429); *Crito* 54d (tr. W.R.M. Lamb, Cambridge, MA: Harvard University Press, 1971, p. 190).

17 Plato, *Euthydemus*, 277d–e (tr. W.R.M. Lamb, Cambridge, MA: Harvard University Press, 1962, p. 399–401).

18 Plato, *Laws*, 790d–791a (tr. R.G. Bury, Cambridge, MA: Harvard University Press, 1952, p. 23).
19 Plato, *Ion*, 534a (p. 421); *Symposium*, 215c–d (tr. W.R.M. Lamb, Cambridge, MA: Harvard University Press, 1961, p. 219); *Crito*, 54d (p. 190); Linforth, 'The Corybantic Rites', pp. 141–142.
20 Plato, *Laws* 790d (p. 23); *Euthydemus*, 277d–e (pp. 399–401).
21 Offering sacrifices was the duty of the priests of the Corybantes at Erythrae (F. Sokolowski, *Lois sacrées de l'Asie Mineure*, Paris: De Boccard, 1955, pp. 60–61), and it is improbable that the Attic Corybantes did not deal with them.
22 Voutiras, 'Un culte domestique des Corybantes'; and F. Graf, *Nordionische Kulte*, Rome: Schweizarisches Institut in Rom, 1985, pp. 320–321. Bathing is also mentioned in Sokolowski, *Lois sacrées de l'Asie Mineure*, pp. 60–61.
23 The invention of the tambourine was ascribed to the Corybantes (Strabo 10.3.13, in Strabo, *Geography*, tr. H.L. Jones, Cambridge, MA: Harvard University Press, 1928, p. 103) or Rhea (Euripides, *Bacchae*, 55–58, ed. and tr. D. Kovacs, Cambridge, MA: Harvard University Press, 2002, p. 17) with whom they were intimately associated in mythology and cult. See, for example, Aristophanes, *Wasps*, 119 (p. 235); cf. Guidorizzi, *Ai confini dell' anima*, pp. 191–192.
24 Plato, *Euthydemus*, 277d–e (pp. 399–401); Dio Chrysostom gives a very similar description (a rite during which 'the performers of initiation seat the initiates and dance round them in circles'), attributing *thrónosis* to mystery rites in general (*Oration*, 12.33, in Dio Chrysostom, *Discourses*, tr. J.W. Cohoon, Cambridge, MA: Harvard University Press, 1934, p. 35). Among Orphic poems there were *Korybantikon* and *Enthronements for the Mother* (F. Graf and S.I. Johnston, *Ritual Texts for the Afterlife: Orpheus and the Bacchic Gold Leaves*, London and New York: Routledge, 2007, p. 147; and M.L. West, *The Orphic Poems*, Oxford: Oxford University Press, 1983, p. 27). The cult of the Corybantes and of Rhea or Mother of Gods were closely linked, at least during the Hellenistic-Roman periods: see F. Graf, '"The blessings of madness": Dionysos, Madness, and Scholarship', *Archiv für Religionsgeschichte* 12, 2010, 167–180 (p. 174). There is no evidence of early Athenian association of the two cults, but it becomes obvious in the fourth century, as attested to by Menander's *Theophoroumene (The Girl Possessed)*; see M. Balme (ed.), *Menander: The Plays and Fragments*, Oxford: Oxford University Press, 2001, p. 243.
25 Jeanmaire, *Dionysos*, p. 138.
26 P. Herrmann, 'Eine "pierre errante" in Samos: Kultgesetz der Korybanten', *Chiron* 32, 2002, 157–171.
27 Aristotle, *Politics* 1342a10 (tr. H. Rackham, Cambridge, MA: Harvard University Press, 1944, p. 671).
28 E.R. Dodds, 'Maenadism in the Bacchae', *Harvard Theological Review* 40, 1940, 155–176 (pp. 158 and 160).
29 Jeanmaire, *Dionysos*, pp. 119–131. On *zar* and *bori*, see T. Modarressi, 'The Zar Cult in South Iran', in R. Prince (ed.), *Trance and Possession States*, Montreal: R. M. Bucke Society, 1968, pp. 149–156; L.W. Saunders, 'Variants in Zar Experience in an Egyptian Village', in V. Crapanzano and V. Garrison (eds), *Case Studies in Spirit Possession*, New York and London: Wiley, 1977, pp. 149–156; and on various possession cults including *zar*, see W. Sargant, *The Mind Possessed: A Physiology of Possession, Mysticism and Faith Healing*, London: Heinemann, 1973, pp. 110–193.
30 T. Gilovich and K. Savitsky, 'Like Goes With Like: The Role of Representativeness in Erroneous and Pseudo-scientific Beliefs', in T. Gilovich, D. Griffin and D. Kahneman (eds), *Heuristics and Biases. The Psychology of Intuitive Judgement*, Cambridge: Cambridge University Press, 2002, pp. 617–624 (pp. 618–620).
31 Sargant, *The Mind Possessed*; and E. Cohen, *The Mind Possessed: The Cognition of Spirit Possession in Afro-Brazilian Religious Tradition*, Oxford: Oxford University Press, 2007.
32 E. Cardeña and S. Krippner, 'The Cultural Context of Hypnosis', in S.J. Lynn, J.W. Rhue and I. Kirsch (eds), *Handbook of Clinical Hypnosis*, Washington, DC: American Psychological Association, 2010, pp. 743–771; and P. McNamara, *The Neuroscience of Religious Experience*, Cambridge: Cambridge University Press, 2009, p. 184.

33 J.M. Atkinson, 'Shamanisms Today', *Annual Review of Anthropology* 21, 1992, 307–330 (p. 309); cf. A. Kleinman, *Patients and Healers in the Context of Culture: An Exploration of the Borderline between Anthropology, Medicine, and Psychiatry*, Berkeley and Los Angeles, CA: University of California Press, 1980, pp. 212 and 232.

34 S. Atran, *In God We Trust: The Evolutionary Landscape of Religion*, Oxford: Oxford University Press, 2002, p. 166.

35 Crapanzano and Garrison, *Case Studies in Spirit Possession*, pp. xiii and 15–17.

36 E. Bourguignon, *Possession*, San Francisco, CA: Chandler & Sharp, 1976, pp. 40–41.

37 Kleinman, *Patients and Healers in the Context of Culture*, p. 222.

38 Cardeña and Krippner, 'The Cultural Context of Hypnosis', pp. 743–771. Kleinman emphasises the contrast between group or family treatment in traditional societies (Chinese folk healing in his research) and modern Western medicine based on one-to-one medical practitioner-patient transactions (*Patients and Healers in the Context of Culture*, pp. 205–206 and 239).

39 C.G. Jung, 'Problems of Modern Psychotherapy', in *The Practice of Psychotherapy* [*Collected Works*, vol. 16], tr. R.F.C. Hull, Princeton, NJ: Princeton University Press, 1966, vol. 16, §114–§174 (pp. 53–75), here §134 (p. 59.)

40 Cf. G. Devereux, 'The Psychotherapy Scene in Euripides' *Bacchae*', *Journal of Hellenic Studies* 90, 1970, 35–48; and Gill, 'Ancient Psychotherapy', pp. 324–325.

41 The standard introduction to the Sophists remains G. B. Kerferd, *The Sophistic Movement*, Cambridge: Cambridge University Press, 1981; for an excellent overview of the subject, see R.W. Wallace, 'The Sophists in Athens', in D. Boedeker and K.A. Raaflaub (eds), *Democracy, Empire, and the Arts in Fifth-Century Athens*, Cambridge, MA: Harvard University Press, 1998, pp. 203–222. The standard edition of the fragments of Presocratic philosophers is H. Diels and W. Krantz, *Die Fragmente der Vorsokratiker*, 6th edn, 3 vols, Berlin: Weidmann; a recent edition of the major texts with English translation is D.W. Graham (ed.), *The Texts of Early Greek Philosophy: The Complete Fragments and Selected Testimonies of the Major Presocratics*, 2 vols, Cambridge: Cambridge University Press, 2010.

42 Graham, *The Texts of Early Greek Philosophy*, p. 731.

43 T. Buchheim, *Gorgias von Leontinoi: Reden, Fragmente und Testimonien*, Hamburg: Meiner, 1989, p. xxvi. T.J. Saunders demonstrates that Gorgias' practical solution to the problem of the weakness of the soul is by its training, in 'Gorgias' Psychology in the History of the Free-will Problem', *Siculorum Gymnasium* 38, 1985, 209–228 (p. 214).

44 *Encomium of Helen*, 8 (in Graham, *The Texts of Early Greek Philosophy*, p. 759). For further discussion, see D.M. MacDowell (ed.), *Gorgias, Encomium of Helen*, Bristol: Bristol Classical Press, 1982, p. 36; S. Constantinidou, *Logos into Mythos: The Case of Gorgias' Encomium of Helen*, Athens: Institut du livre, 2008, p. 35; C. Calame, 'Émotions et performance poétique: la "katharsis" érotique dans la poésie mélique des cités grecques', in P. Borgeaud and A.-C. Rendu Loisel (eds), *Violentes émotions: Approches comparatistes*, Geneva: Droz, 2009, 29–55 (p. 41). For discussion of the 'psychological foundation' of Gorgias' rhetorical art, see C.P. Segal, 'Gorgias and the Psychology of the Logos', *Harvard Studies in Classical Philology* 66, 1962, 99–155.

45 *Encomium of Helen*, 13 (Graham, *The Texts of Early Greek Philosophy*, p. 759); cf. Segal, 'Gorgias and the Psychology of the Logos', p. 105.

46 *Encomium of Helen*, 8, cf. *Encomium of Helen* 14.

47 *Encomium of Helen*, 10; Segal, 'Gorgias and the Psychology of the Logos', pp. 111 and 114; Constantinidou, *Logos into Mythos*, p. 163; Laín Entralgo, *The Therapy of the Word*, pp. 88–97.

48 Cf. Plato, *Charmides*, 157a (tr. W.R.M. Lamb, Cambridge, MA: Harvard University Press, 1964, p. 21); Laín Entralgo, *The Therapy of the Word*, pp. 108–125.

49 *Encomium of Helen*, 14 (in Graham, *The Texts of Early Greek Philosophy*, p. 761); cf. Laín Entralgo, *The Therapy of the Word*, pp. 92–93; Constantinidou, *Logos into Mythos*, p. 182; R. Sorabji, *Emotion and Peace of Mind, from Stoic Agitation to Christian Temptation*, Oxford: Oxford University Press, 2000, p. 19.

50 Plato, *Gorgias*, 456b (tr. W.R.M. Lamb, Cambridge, MA: Harvard University Press, 1961, p. 291).

51 Isocrates 9.10 (tr. L. van Hook, Cambridge, MA: Harvard University Press, 1961, p. 11).

52 In antiquity, Antiphon the Sophist was identified with Antiphon of Rhamnus, an oligarch executed after the overthrow of the Four Hundred in 411, until Didymus of Alexandria suggested to distinguish between the two, because of the difference between their literary styles. The weakness of this argument has been demonstrated by various authors (J.S. Morrison, 'Antiphon', *Proceedings of the Cambridge Philological Society* 187 (NS 7), 1961, 49–58; Kerferd, *The Sophistic Movement*, p. 50; M. Gagarin, *Antiphon the Athenian: Oratory, Law, and Justice in the Age of the Sophists*, Austin, TX: University of Texas Press, 2002, pp. 37–38), and a trend at 're-unification of Antiphon' seems to prevail nowadays (A. Hourcade, *Antiphone d'Athènes: Une pensée d'individu*, Paris: Ousia 2001, p. 25). On the ongoing debate on the identity of Antiphon, see G.J. Pendrick (ed.), *Antiphon the Sophist: The Fragments*, Cambridge: Cambridge University Press, 2002, pp. 1–26.

53 Pseudo-Plutarch, *The Lives of the Ten Orators* 833c; in Pendrick, *Antiphon the Sophist*, p. 95.

54 Philostratus, *Lives of Sophists* 1.15; in Pendrick, *Antiphon the Sophist*, p. 97. The word 'pain-removers' is immediately reminiscent of Helen's grief-assuaging drug, mentioned in the *Odyssey*, book 4, ll. 220–224 (Homer, *The Odyssey*, tr. A.T. Murray, Cambridge, MA: Harvard University Press, 1995, p. 135).

55 G.J. Pendrick considers this clinic a comic invention (*Antiphon the Sophist*, p. 241), but J.S. Morrison believes that this invention 'is likely to contain a seed of truth' ('Antiphon', p. 57), and many scholars accept the tradition, see C. Diano, 'Euripide auteur de catharsis tragique', *Numen* 8, 1961, 117–141 (p. 119); M. Untersteiner, *The Sophists*, Oxford: Clarendon Press, 1954, p. 255; Laín Entralgo, *The Therapy of the Word*, pp. 98 and 102–106; W. Furley, 'Antiphon der Athener: Ein Sophist als Psychotherapeut?', *Rheinisches Museum* 135, 1992, 198–216; Wallace, 'The Sophists in Athens', p. 217; Hourcade, *Antiphone d'Athènes*, pp. 27, 67–72; and Sorabji, *Emotion and Peace of Mind*, p. 19.

56 *On Truth*, fragments 1–1,1 in Pendrick, *Antiphon the Sophist*, pp. 103–189; cf. Gagarin, *Antiphon the Athenian*, pp. 80–84; and *On Concord*, fragments 49–59, in Pendrick, *Antiphon the Sophist*, pp. 190–211.

57 Untersteiner, *The Sophists*, p. 256; Gagarin, *Antiphon the Athenian*, pp. 99–100; Pendrick, *Antiphon the Sophist*, pp. 52–53.

58 Hourcade, *Antiphone d'Athènes*, p. 28.

59 Some critics doubt that a written *Art of Avoiding Distress* existed, since no fragment of such work has been preserved, see Untersteiner, *The Sophists*, p. 270; and Pendrick, *Antiphon the Sophist*, p. 241.

60 Hourcade, *Antiphone d'Athènes*, p. 68; and Furley, 'Antiphon der Athener'.

61 Aeschylus, *Prometheus Bound*, 380 (tr. H.W. Smyth, Cambridge, MA: Harvard University Press, 1963, p. 249).

62 Aristophanes, *Wasps*, 111 (p. 235).

63 Pigeaud, *La maladie de l'âme*, p. 52; T.M. Robinson, *Plato's Psychology*, Toronto: University of Toronto Press, 1995, pp. 107–110; M. Ahonen, *Mental Disorders in Ancient Philosophy*, New York: Springer, 2014, pp. 46–51. In a word, Plato's dialogues are 'medicinal works', intended to cure or mitigate the disease of thoughtlessness and to serve as *therapeia psuchês*, 'tendance of soul'; see Rosen, *Madness in Society*, p. xv; C.H. Kahn, 'Did Plato Write Socratic Dialogues?', in H.H. Benson (ed.), *Essays on the Philosophy of Socrates*, Oxford: Oxford University Press, 1992, 35–52 (p. 46). Plato's definition of the conception of the health of the soul as a moral concept had most important consequences for both medicine and philosophy.

64 Pseudo-Plutarch, *The Lives of the Ten Orators*, 833c; in Pendrick, *Antiphon the Sophist*, p. 95.

65 Euripides, *Bacchae*, 1216–1300 (pp. 133–143). This exchange between a father and an offspring recovering from an attack of insanity is perhaps an elaboration of an earlier scene, in Euripides' *The Madness of Hercules*, 1089–1428 (tr. A.S. Way, Cambridge, MA: Harvard University Press, 1972, p. 216); see K. Riley, *The Reception and Performance of Euripides' Heracles*, Oxford: Oxford University Press, 2008, p, 39; D. Shalev, 'Diagnostics of Altered Mental States: From Euripides' Bacchae to Medieval Arabic Texts', *Scripta Classica Israelica* 31, 2012, 161–183 (p. 165).

66 Euripides, *Bacchae*, 1260–1295 (pp. 137–143).

67 E.R. Dodds (ed.), *Euripides: Bacchae*, Oxford: Clarendon Press, 1944, pp. 215–217 (commentary on lines 1264–1277). Cadmus' step-by-step technique was noticed by G.A. Auden, in 'The Madness of Ajax, as Conceived by Sophocles, Clinically Considered', *Journal of Mental Science*, 72, 1926, 1–10 (p. 9). For Euripides' keen interest in medicine, see E.M. Craik, 'Medical References in Euripides', *Bulletin of the Institute of Classical Studies* 45, 2001, 81–95.

68 Devereux, 'The Psychotherapy Scene in Euripides' *Bacchae*', pp. 35–48. This interpretation has been accepted by various critics, including J. Roux, *Euripide, Les Bacchantes, II: Commentaire*, Paris: Les Belles Lettres, 1972, p. 609, R. Seaford (ed.), *Euripides: Bacchae*, Warminster: Aris & Phillips, 1996, pp. 247–248; Riley, *The Reception and Performance*, pp. 39–40; and Shalev, 'Diagnostics of Altered Mental States'. C. Gill and V. Leiniekes regard the scene rather as a form of verbal cure, an example of the art of persuasion (see Gill, 'Ancient Psychotherapy', p. 315; V. Leiniekes, *The City of Dionysos: A Study of Euripides' Bakchai*, Stuttgart: Teubner, 1996, pp. 120–121).

69 G. Devereux proposes that, during his stay in Macedonia, Euripides observed real-life insight-and-recall psychotherapy, and compares it to anthropologically attested shamanic techniques of treatment, based on this principle. In fact, Socrates praised Thracian—but not Macedonian—healers for their therapeutic approach based on 'treatment of the soul' (*Charmides*, 156b; tr. W.R.M. Lamb, Cambridge, MA; Harvard University Press, 1967, p. 19; cf. Laín Entralgo, *The Therapy of the Word*, pp. 109–126). Yet even if this claim was based on an opinion current among the Greeks, Socrates explicitly spoke about cure of bodily ailments, rather than mental disorders. Therefore, borrowing this technique from barbarians remains undocumented.

70 R. Kannicht (ed.), *Tragicorum Graecorum Fragmenta*, vol. 5. 2, *Euripides*, Göttingen: Vandenhoeck & Ruprecht, 2004, fragment 964, pp. 963–964; Kerferd, *The Sophistic Movement*, p. 51; and Diano, 'Euripide auteur de catharsis tragique', p. 122.

71 Plutarch, *Moralia*, 112d (tr. F.C. Babbitt, Cambridge, MA: Harvard University Press, 1962, vol. 2, p. 161; Cicero, *Tusculan Disputations* 3.14 (in Cicero, *Tusculan Disputations*, tr. J.E. King, Cambridge, MA: Harvard University Press, 1965, p. 263).

72 T.F. Oltmanns and R.E. Emery, *Abnormal Psychology*, Boston, MA: Pearson, 2012, p. 185. On PTSD in the Greek world, see Y. Ustinova and E. Cardeña, 'Combat Stress Disorders and Their Treatment in Ancient Greece', *Psychological Trauma: Theory, Research, Practice, and Policy* 6.6, 2014, pp. 739–748.

73 Gill, 'Ancient Psychotherapy', pp. 315–316.

74 Aristophanes, *Wasps*, 799–1007 (pp. 323–351).

75 Celsus, *On Medicine*, 3.18 (Celsus, *On Medicine*, tr. W.G. Spencer, Cambridge, MA: Harvard University Press, 1935, p. 295); and Gill, 'Ancient Psychotherapy', p. 316.

76 K.V. Hartigan, *Performance and Cure: Drama and Healing in Ancient Greece and Contemporary America*, London: Bloomsbury, 2009.

77 For methods and approaches in Hellenistic and Roman 'therapy of the soul', especially those of the Stoics and Galen, see Sorabji, *Emotion and Peace of Mind*; and C. Gill, *Naturalistic Psychology in Galen and Stoicism*, Oxford: Oxford University Press, 2010.

78 C. Gill puts an emphasis on two points of divergence between therapeutic dialogues and modern psychotherapy: first, ancient dialogue was explicitly moral, while modern psychotherapy allows the patient a 'morally neutral' place; and second, 'ancient philosophy approaches the person as a conscious agent', while psychotherapy analyses the unconscious level and bases the treatment on its understanding (Gill, 'Ancient Psychotherapy', pp. 324–325).

79 This chapter is a result of research supported by the Israel Science Foundation (ISF 1077/12).

4

ANTIQUITY AND ANXIETY

Freud, Jung, and the impossibility of the archaic

Alan Cardew

Ὁδὸς ἄνω κάτω μία καὶ ὠυτή (The way up and down is one and the same)
(Heraclitus, fragment 60)

What can account for Freud's anxieties about visiting Rome and Athens, and Jung's physical inability to travel to Rome, 'the smoking and fiery hearth of ancient culture'? Was the greatness of the classical ideal held up by German classicists from Winckelmann to Nietzsche, simply too imposing, too monumental to be faced?

In her book of 1935, *The Tyranny of Greece over Germany*, E.M. Butler (1885–1959) famously traced the overwhelming influence of Greek art and culture over the German mind from the eighteenth to the twentieth century, Greece representing both an ideal and a goal.[1] Clearly, this influence was not confined to Germany but extended throughout the German-speaking world, including Switzerland and Austria. A white and gold statue of Athene towers in front of the Austrian Parliament on the Ringstraße in Vienna, a building whose portico is an exact copy of the Erectheion on the Acropolis.[2] Across Switzerland, there were less imposing but strong and intricate links with the classical revival; Johann Heinrich Füssli (1741–1825) knew Winckelmann (1717–1768) and Jacques-Louis David (1748–1825), Johann Heinrich Meyer (1760–1832) was an important figure in Weimar classicism,[3] and classicism ran through Swiss culture from Arnold Böcklin (1827–1901) to Carl Spitteler (1845–1924), whose *Prometheus und Epimetheus* is subject to a long exegesis in Jung's *Psychological Types* (1921).[4] E.M. Butler notes that none of the early German classical writers ever visited Greece, and that 'Winckelmann and Goethe actually refused to do so when the opportunity was given them':

> Had they seen with their own eyes its wild, titanic landscapes and experienced its sometimes menacing moods, they would perhaps have recognised

that tragic element in Greek poetry and thought which they resolutely ignored and eliminated from their concept of the golden age of Greece. They might have seen what Nietzsche was later to stress so strongly, and Spitteler to illuminate so unforgettably, the dark background from which the Apolline art they worshipped sprang.[5]

Freud used a passage from Virgil as an epigraph for *The Interpretation of Dreams*: '*Flectere si nequeo superos, Acheronta movebo*'—'If I cannot move the higher powers, I will move the infernal regions' (*Aeneid*, book 7, l. 312). Could the unconscious, with all its repressed desires, condensations, displacements, and defensive obscurity, serve as a shield against that terrible, high ideal? Wielded rather in the manner of the aegis of Athena; alive with roaring snakes and the severed head of the Gorgon with its rolling eyes.

Like Juno in Virgil's poem, should we not wish to overturn the rule of Olympus, and proclaim defiance to the tyranny of perfect, immoderate greatness? Otherwise, we are mere imitators and epigones. George Steiner said of classical texts that you do not read them, they read you—they ask: 'are you worthy?'—a terrible demand![6] There is no doubt that classicism constituted a neurosis for both Freud and Jung— perhaps, *the* neurosis.

For Carl Jung, truth was not to be found in the Olympian, airy, inflated heights, but in the primordial depths, in the archaic, the autochthonous, in the unconscious. Jung studied at the University of Basel, and he might be called one of the representatives of the Basel school of classicism, along with Nietzsche, Burkhardt, and Bachofen. God had been pronounced dead by Nietzsche, and the ineluctable truth of things could only be found in the earliest periods of Greece and Rome; philosophy had ended with Socrates, art with Aeschylus—Nietzsche had even pronounced Euripides' *Bacchae* as a falling away from the original purity and a diminution of the terrible truth of tragedy. Diels and Kranz (and their edition of the Presocratics) were far preferable to Plato, Dionysus far preferable to Apollo. The darkness of the past was preferable to the careless occultation of the present. One way to survive classicism was to treat its order and culture merely as a beautiful Apollonian mask, which served to hide the abyss which lay beneath it. Humankind could live in a comfortable dream and so be spared the horror of reality, but sometimes—the mask slipped. In *The Birth of Tragedy* (1872), Nietzsche tells how King Midas asked Silenus what was the best and most desirable of all things for man; his answer was:

> Oh wretched ephemeral race, children of chance and misery, why do you compel me to tell you what it would be most expedient of you not to hear? What is best of all is utterly beyond your reach: not to *be*, to be *nothing*. But the second best for you is—to die soon.[7]

We find an echo of this pitiless judgement in Jung and Freud. Both were members of a Schopenhauerian aristocracy of gloom, who affected to live without the consolation of philosophy, as in the case of Jung, and the consolation of religion, as in the case of Freud. Jung concludes in what was intended to be a popular work, entitled *Man and His Symbols*:

> The sad truth is that man's real life consists of a complex of inexorable opposites—day and night, birth and death, happiness and misery, good and evil. We are not even sure that one will prevail against the other, that good will overcome evil, or joy defeat pain. Life is a battle ground. It always has been, and always will be; and if it were not so, existence would come to an end.[8]

The same pessimism can be found in Freud's study, *Civilization and Its Discontents* (1930), where Freud laments:

> We are threatened with suffering from three directions: from our own body; which is doomed to decay and dissolution and which cannot even do without pain and anxiety as warning signals; from the external world, which may rage against us with overwhelming and merciless forces of destruction; and finally from our relations to other men.[9]

Religion is no balm; Freud wrote:

> The whole thing is so patently infantile, so foreign to reality, that to anyone with a friendly attitude to humanity it is painful to think that the great majority of mortals will never be able to rise above this view of life.[10]

In *Memories, Dreams, Reflections* (1961), Jung tells how in 1912 he was sailing from Genoa to Naples, and how, when he crossed the latitude of Rome, he stood at the railing. 'Out there lay Rome, the still smoking and fiery hearth from which ancient cultures had spread, enclosed in a tangled rootwork of the Christian and Occidental Middle Ages', he recalled, reflecting further:

> I always wonder about people who go to Rome as they might go, for example, to Paris or to London. Certainly, Rome as well as these other cities can be enjoyed aesthetically but if you are affected to the depths of your being at every step by the spirit that broods there, if a remnant of a wall here and a column there gaze upon you with a face instantly recognised, then it becomes another matter entirely.[11]

In his old age—in 1949—he wished 'to repair the omission', but was stricken when buying tickets: 'After that the plans for a trip to Rome were once and for all laid aside', he added.[12]

This sort of resistance finds a parallel in Freud's difficult trip to Athens, of which Freud gives an account in a long letter he sent to Romain Rolland (1866–1944), later published in 1936 as 'An Account of a Disturbance of Memory on the Acropolis'.[13] Freud, travelling in Italy at the relatively late age of 48, had a chance to visit Athens by boat. He had initially experienced a good deal of resistance to the plan: it was impossible! there were too many difficulties! Although feeling 'morose' and 'irresolute', the passage was booked with disconcerting ease, albeit in 'remarkably distressed spirits'. 'Such behaviour', Freud notes, 'was strange.'[14] Reaching the Acropolis at last, Freud was plunged into a state of 'derealization' which led him to reflect on the nucleus of all neuroses. 'When I stood on the Acropolis on the afternoon after our arrival, and my eye took in the landscape, the curious thought suddenly came to me: *So this all really does exist, just as we learned in school!*', he thought.[15] In his later reflection on the experience, Freud detected both false memories and a feeling of guilt or inferiority: 'I am not worthy of such good fortune'; it was an *impiety* for him to be there.[16] Freud only allowed himself to travel to Rome once he had finished *The Interpretation of Dreams* in 1901; Rome was 'a victory', which had been won after much agonising, for Rome threatened him with a fear of failure.[17] It could be said that—in a convoluted, displaced, and roundabout way—*The Interpretation of Dreams* was itself a way to Rome, but with nothing of the directness of an Appian Way. In Chapter 5 of that work, Freud analyses a series of his own dreams of Rome; in one, he sees the Tiber and the Ponte Sant'Angelo from a railway-carriage window, but the train is moving away; in others, Lübeck and Prague masquerade as the Eternal City, or a mist frustratingly shrouds a distant prospect of the place. In 1897, Freud had managed to get within fifty miles of Rome, turning back near Lake Trasimene, just the location where Freud's childhood hero, Hannibal, had turned away from the city, never to realise his dream of revenge and conquest. For Freud, reaching Rome represented the ultimate wish-fulfilment.[18]

Rome was always stern and forbidding, a mountain of history, religion, and culture, which could take a lifetime to master, as reflected in Theodor Mommsen's formidable *History of Rome* (1854–1885); one thinks of George Eliot's Dorothea buckling under 'the weight of unintelligible Rome'.[19] In addition to the inexorable demands of civic virtue and Roman law which required absolute duty and supreme sacrifice, there were the endless transgressions; rapes, assassinations, murders, martyrdoms, and fierce civil strife. Tacitus begins his *Histories* with a particularly bleak summation that would certainly support the darkest pessimism:

> The history on which I am entering is that of a period [i.e., 69–96 CE] rich in disasters, terrible with battles, torn by civil struggles, horrible even in peace [. . .] Rome was devastated by conflagrations, in which her most ancient shrines were consumed and the very Capitol fired by citizens' hands. Sacred rites were defiled; there were adulteries in high places. The sea was filled with exiles, its cliffs made foul with the bodies of the dead. In Rome there was more awful cruelty. High birth, wealth, the refusal or acceptance of office—all gave ground for accusations, and virtues caused the surest ruin [. . .] Slaves were corrupted against their masters, freedmen against their patrons; and those who had no enemy were crushed by their friends.[20]

For Freud, the successive archaeological layers of the history of Rome were an analogy for the layers of experience in the history of the psyche, an idea which he develops in *Civilization and Its Discontents* (1930):

> Historians tell us that the oldest Rome was the *Roma Quadrata*, a fenced settlement on the Palatine. Then followed the phase of the *Septimontium*, a federation of the settlements on the different hills; after that came the city bounded by the Servian wall; and later still, after all the transformations during the periods of the republic and the early Caesars, the city which the Emperor Aurelian surrounded with his walls. We will not follow the changes which the city went through any further, but we will ask ourselves how much a visitor, whom we will suppose to be equipped with the most complete historical and topographical knowledge, may still find left of these early stages in the Rome of to-day. Except for a few gaps, he will see the wall of Aurelian almost unchanged. In some places he will be able to find sections of the Servian wall where they have been excavated and brought to light. If he knows enough—more than present-day archaeology does—he may perhaps be able to trace out in the plan of the city the whole course of that wall and the outline of the *Roma Quadrata*.[21]

Whereas, in Rome, the past only survives in fragments, for the psyche 'nothing that has once come into existence will have passed away and all the earlier phases of development continue to exist alongside the latest one', for 'in mental life nothing which has once been formed can perish—that everything is somehow preserved and that in suitable circumstances (when, for instance, regression goes back far enough) it can once more be brought to light.'[22] The primordial drives had not been superceded. The archaeological and psychological were analogous but distinct, and yet was there not a deeper value in pursuing the similarity? After all, had not the German 'prophet of Darwinism', Ernst Haeckel (1834–1919), proclaimed that 'ontogony recapitulates phylogeny', arguing that, in its embryonic stages, a living being goes through the same transformations as its ancestors went through in their evolution?[23]

In the study of antiquity in the period roughly from 1850 to 1950, there was a desire to bring to light the earliest phases of development, the archaic, the original—for example, the positing of the primordial worship of the matriarchal in the form of the Magna Mater which predated the patriarchal beliefs of Rome and Athens. We find the 'uncovery' of such a cult in *Das Mutterrecht* (1861) by Johann Jakob Bachofen (1815–1887), or later in work of Jane Ellen Harrison (1850–1928) and Robert Graves (1895–1985), or in *Ursprungsgeschichte des Bewußtseins* (1949), translated as the *Origins and History of Consciousness* (1954), by Erich Neuman (1905–1960).

The quest was to uncover a prehistorical, philological, foundational level built from rude cyclopean blocks of myth, like the Gate of the Lion uncovered by Heinrich Schliemann (1822–1890) at Mycenae (the burden of the classical was becoming massively heavier . . .). Late classical civilisation, especially Hellenism, was weak and etiolated, its buildings over-decorated, its literature and philosophy derivative, so that, like bourgeois culture, it was superficial, groundless. Better the rude, vigorous, tremendous, powerful, and original. The tufa and the bedrock of the deep archaeology of the late nineteenth and early twentieth centuries corresponded to the unconscious and to an entire rhetoric of Western discourse, with its heavyweight metaphors of foundation, basis, and the grounding of down-to-earth arguments, rooted arguments. Rome and Athens may exhibit this characteristic, but not such other later sites as Alexandria, Pergamum, or Apamea. Even in Rome itself, the focus was not the Temple of Apollo on the heights of the Palatine, but the murky, ancient depths of the Forum, of the Lacus Curtius, the *lapis niger*, and the *cloaca maxima*. Where men once looked up, they must now look down.[24]

For his part, Jung was deeply affected by a childhood dream in which he had descended a stone staircase and entered a long subterranean chamber, at the end of which stood a wonderful, rich golden throne. On it was standing something he first thought to be a tree trunk, but it was fleshy with a single eye and had a nimbus of light above it. It was, in fact, an immense phallus, which Jung later concluded was a subterranean god, 'not to be named'.[25] This dream constituted 'an initiation into the realm of darkness', he wrote, adding 'My intellectual life had its unconscious beginning at this time'.[26] Much later, Jung began recording his dreams and experiences in a 'Brown Notebook' from 1913. He strongly felt that this demanded a loss of reason, a Tertullian-like *sacrificium intellectus*; at the time, he noted: 'Give away all that one possesses and one shall receive.'[27] It was a *katabasis*, as he later referred to it, or a *nekia*, a *descensus ad inferos*, not of a Christ, but in order to find Christ.

Jung was prey to fears that he was losing command of himself. It was during Advent of the year 1913, on 12 December, as he was sitting at his desk considering his fears when, as he put it, 'I let myself drop'.[28] What followed was a vision that incorporated a hero and a solar myth, a drama of death and renewal, and a rebirth symbolised by the Egyptian scarab. The direction of these visions was always down—down to the unconscious, down to the mythic land of the dead, down to the land of the ancestors. Unpopular, ambiguous, and dangerous, it is, and always was, a voyage of discovery to the other pole of the world—the land of the dead, where one hears the voices of the Unanswered, the Unresolved and Unredeemed; a searching into the deep thoughts of God.

Jung had little time for those who looked upwards. The development of Platonic thought over the millennia after the founding of the Academy must have appeared extremely uncongenial to him. His profound interest in Gnosticism, which has been called the unconscious of Platonism, proved more important for the development of alchemy. Even Hermeticism, a halfway-house, is not greatly in evidence. Jung would spend much time examining the fragments of Basilides or Zosimos, but not the *Enneads* or the *Platonic Theology*, not Philo, Plotinus, Porphyry, Iamblichus, Proclus, or Damascius.

In fact, Jung was always very careful to separate himself from Platonism. In an essay on the mother archetype, Jung emphasises the difference between the Platonic Idea 'supraordinate and pre-existent to all phenomena' and his concept of the archetype as a sort of 'unconscious idea', nothing but a possibility of form without concrete content.[29] According to Jung, the Platonic Idea is lodged in 'a "place beyond the skies"'—he puts this in inverted commas (which always consign assertions to the limbo of unsound notions).[30] The Idea is the prototype of all phenomena in any particular instance, in other words, it has content, whereas Jung's archetype is empty and purely formal. He likens the latter to 'the axial system of a crystal' inherent in the matrix of a crystalline solution, which becomes manifest when ions and molecules aggregate.[31] The archetype is 'nothing but a *facultas praeformandi*, a possibility of representation which is given *a priori*'.[32] The archetype manifests itself by forming local content; its concrete appearance depends on innumerable local factors. It is empirically verifiable, unlike Plato's Ideas which have been utterly superseded by the development of observational science.

'Anyone who continues to think as Plato did', Jung argued, 'must pay for his anachronism by seeing the "supercelestial," i.e., metaphysical, essence of the Idea relegated to the unverifiable realm of faith and superstition, or charitably left to the poet.'[33] As he continued, 'the hopelessness of this position is obvious', since 'Greek natural philosophy with its interest in matter, together with Aristotelian reasoning, has achieved a belated but overwhelming victory over Plato.'[34] Jung is particularly slighting when he is analysing Plato's *Timaeus* in his essay 'A Psychological Approach to the Dogma of the Trinity' (1942; 1948). The opening of the dialogue seemed to confess a shortcoming on Plato's part, a lack: 'One, two, three—but where, my dear Timaeus, is the fourth . . .?'[35] On Jung's account, Plato's cosmology lacked substance; the philosopher was incapable of dealing with the 'fourth dimension' of materiality and had to 'content himself with the harmony of airy thought-structures that lacked weight, and with a paper surface that lacked depth'.[36] In short, Jung concluded, there was 'something unexpected and alien to [Plato's] thought, something heavy, inert, and limited which no μὴ ὄν [not being] and no *privatio boni* can conjure away or diminish'; and, as a result, 'even God's fairest creation is corrupted by it, and idleness, stupidity and malice, discontent, sickness, old age and death fill the glorious body of the "blessed god"'.[37] Thus the reader is left with 'truly a grievous spectacle, this sick world-soul, and unfortunately not as Plato's inner eye envisaged it' when, in the *Timaeus* (34a), he wrote:

> All this, then, was the plan of the everlasting god for the god who was going to be. According to this place he made the body of the world smooth and uniform, everywhere equidistant from its centre, a body whole and complete, with complete bodies for its parts. And in the centre he set the soul and caused it to extend throughout the whole body, and he wrapped the body round with soul on the outside. So he established one world alone, round and revolving in a circle, solitary but able by reason of its excellence to bear itself company, needing no other acquaintance or friend but sufficient unto itself. On all these accounts the world which he brought into being was a blessed god.[38]

Jung is intent on establishing that 'three', the number of the Trinity is incomplete, and that the fourth, the 'quadrivium' represents entirety and wholeness. This will establish a ground for a critique of the theology of the holy Trinity in Christianity. The fourth is spurned by consciousness as being evil, formless, material, and feminine; it is consigned to unconscious drives. But, for completeness, the fourth must be faced and included in the cosmic picture. Jung does acknowledge that the *Timaeus* contains a number of quaternities, and that they form a symbol of completeness, a mandala, as can be seen in the completeness of the world—'a blessed god', as described by Timaeus in the passage above.[39] Thus, Plato is employed to establish the critique of the Trinity, and to provide a model for Jung's quadripartite solution.

Philosophers have their uses, but Jung will suffer no ancient rivals, and in one of his seminars on Nietzsche's *Zarathustra* he sweepingly condemned ancient philosophy as being linguistically inadequate. 'Ancient philosophy really started from a different reality than ours, from a very different psychology', he argued, noting that 'you can see what trouble Plato had to express certain ideas which to us are now definite conceptions; he had to use parables and all sorts of means in order to express his philosophical thought.'[40] For Jung, the parable of the cave belonged to 'the theory of cognition, [as] we say nowadays', but Plato had had to express it 'by that clumsy apparatus'. Consequently, in reading medieval philosophy, 'one has to struggle with an extraordinary clumsiness of language'. And he perceived exactly the same problem in reading 'the very elegant Latin of Stoic philosophy or the New Platonists', where 'language was just not differentiated enough to express subtleties'; in contrast, Greek was 'in a way much subtler, but in comparison with a modern language, that also was exceedingly archaic'.[41]

In Jung's eyes, Christianity too shares these shortcomings; and its symbols should be 'banished to a sphere of sacrosanct unintelligibility'.[42] And in St Paul we encounter 'the stammering of the spirit'—'the word is what is merely left of the spirit after the spirit has passed'—and 'so modern development led first descent of spirit into mind, and from mind into words, and then the spirit was utterly gone'; Jung concluded that 'we don't know what spirit is'.[43]

The Platonic Ideas, the identification of metaphysical realities with states of consciousness, the philosophical development of the individual, the Ideas, anamnesis, the awakening of the individual psyche, all find correspondences, sometimes uncomfortably close correspondences, with Jung's archetypes, and the individuation process. At other times, they represent a complete inversion of analytical psychology. Jung was a fierce defender of his position. In the case of the archetype, Jung was infuriated when Mircea Eliade stated that the archetypes were imitations in the unconscious of the process by which consciousness and transconsciousness seek to obtain completeness and conquer freedom.[44] This statement led to a vituperative exchange of letters of which only one is in Jung's collected letters.[45]

Eliade follows Plato in the ascent to an 'upper world', the upward journey of the awakened soul to the region of the intelligible. Plato is anagogic, up out of the illusory darkness of the Cave towards the essential Form of Goodness, and this may be achieved through love, or an experience of beauty, the study of music or mathematics, remembering, or anamnesis. There is no rejection of the world, and God may be perceived through the Cosmos. The soul's goal is essentially contemplative; and the highest goal for contemplation is the life of the gods.

Yet Jung was quite happy to dismiss the myth of the cave in Plato's *Republic*, arguing (as we have seen) that 'the famous parable of the cave belongs to the theory of cognition [. . .] but he had to express it by that clumsy apparatus'.[46] In Jung's psychic speleology, there seems no space for ascent to a higher level, through contemplation, love, the experience of beauty or music. For Platonism, the soul is, in leaving the cave, returning to its proper state, to the Intelligible realm. This may be seen as a complete reversal of Jung's psychic deixis. Instead of the Jungian model of the psyche, the chthonic depths building up to higher levels of consciousness and objectivity, we have a top-down cosmos with Ideas, gods, humans, and the world itself in a state of suspension from the higher reaches of the ineffable One.

Philo of Alexandria said that with its Acropolis the Greek Polis had its roots in the heavens—a very different orientation from the classical city as described above.[47] Philo used this analogy to interpret the creation in the Book of Genesis (see *De Opificio Mundi*, or 'On the Creation').[48] In Neoplatonism, the movement of the soul is from above to below and then it makes the return to the high. In its journey the soul mirrors the movement of creation:

> This, we may say, is the first act of generation: the One, perfect because it seeks nothing, and needs nothing, overflows, as it were, and its superabundance makes something other than itself. This, when it has come into being, turns back upon the One and is filled, and becomes Intellect [Nous][49] by looking towards it. Its halt and turning towards the One constitutes being, its gaze upon the One, Intellect.[50]

Plotinus calls this movement of emanation and return 'procession' (*prohodos*, πρoόδoς). The emanation is the overflowing of the One, into Nous (intelligence), and then from there to the Psyche; the original simplicity then becomes multiplicity, the world. Return is the Good's drawing everything to itself. Everything longs to return to the original One and to its supreme entirety.

What is important for the individual soul is the very turning point, the 'metastrophe', the point where the soul begins to awaken and leave the cave in Plato's *Republic*:

> The power to learn is present in everyone's soul and [. . .] the instrument with which each learns is like an eye that cannot be turned around from darkness to light without turning the whole body. The instrument cannot be turned around from that which is coming into being without turning the whole soul until it is able to study that which is and the brightest thing that is, namely, the one we call the Good.[51]

The universal pattern of procession is reflected in a cosmic diagram, or mandala (Figure 4.1), that Jung includes in his 1934 work, 'A Study in the Process of Individuation'.[52] It is the work of a patient, which shows the sun surrounded by a rainbow-coloured halo dividing into twelve parts, like the zodiac. To the left it represents the descending, to the right the ascending transformation process.

Jung notes the number symbolism in the design and draws analogies with alchemy and Gnosticism. The common Neoplatonic pattern is quite evident, although it is not something on which Jung commented. The picture has a strong analogy to the mandala used by the Sakta School of Indian Hinduism, which represents in an austere, diagrammatic form the patterns of universal generation and return (Figure 4.2).

It would be a fruitful task to attempt a Neoplatonic commentary on the drawing of Jung's patient; further analogies to this drawing are to be found in the cosmic patterns to be found in Proclus's *Platonic Theology*.[55] Such an exercise is beyond the scope of the present chapter, yet one might well ask: are all these analogies a matter

FIGURE 4.1 Jung, *Works*, vol. 9/i, p. 309, fig. 2.
'At the top, the sun, surrounded by a rainbow coloured halo divided into twelve parts, like the zodiac. To the left, the descending, to the right the ascending, transformation process.'[53]

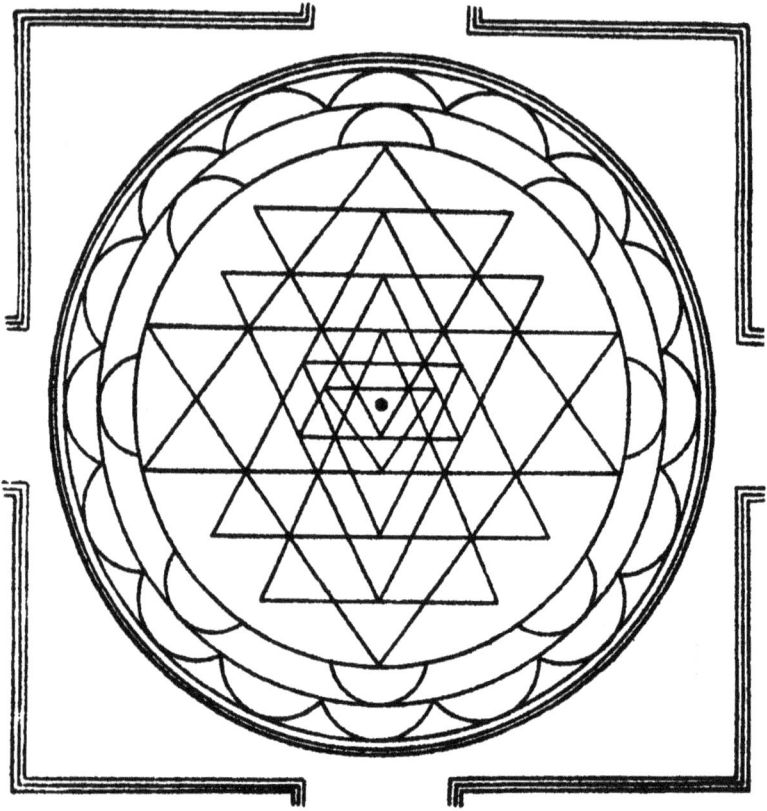

FIGURE 4.2 Giuseppe Tucci, *Theory and Practice of the Mandala.* Plate III.[54]

of archetypes or of the equally potent Platonic symbols, the *synthemata*? Indeed, are archetypes and *synthemata* the same?

For the Neoplatonic philosopher, what is important is the bringing around of the return in an individual's deepest being; this is the turn, the *epistrophe*. The philosopher is the saviour of himself. He must engage in *theōsis* (θέωσις, or assimilation to God) and follow the injunction of Plato in the *Theaetetus* that one should become as like to God as possible (see *Theaetetus*, 176b).[56] This process involves the philosophical practice of contemplation, or spiritual exercises, such as those employed by Plotinus to attain a merging with the One:

> Let us then, make a mental picture of our universe: each member shall remain what it is, distinctly apart; yet all is to form, as far as possible, a complete unity so that whatever comes into view, say the outer orb of the heavens, shall bring immediately with it the vision, on the one plane, of the

sun and of all the stars with earth and sea and all living things as if exhibited upon a transparent globe. Bring this vision actually before your sight, so that there shall be in your mind the gleaming representation of a sphere, a picture holding all the things of the universe moving or in repose, or (as in reality) some at rest, some in motion. Keep this sphere before you and from it imagine another, a sphere stripped of magnitude and spatial differences, cast out your inborn sense of Matter, taking care not merely to attenuate it: call on God, maker of the sphere whose image you now hold, and pray Him to enter. And may He come bringing his own Universe with all the gods that dwell in it—He who is the one God and all the gods, where each is all, blending into a unity, distinct in powers but all one god in virtue of that one divine power of many facets.[57]

Carefully employing images, symbols of completeness, using the cosmos to transcend the cosmos the seeker may be swept up in an ecstasy of rapture, beholding and becoming one with a marvellous beauty. Solitude, withdrawal, and contemplation are essential conditions for these spiritual exercises.

But all this is not for Jung. In his 'Introduction' to Evan Wentz's translation of *The Tibetan Book of the Great Liberation*, Jung argues that contemplation involves an extreme introversion which runs directly counter to the Western Mind which is extrovert, objective and depends on something external to it, and, although individual and differentiated, must rely on an external agency—be it Christ, power, or even money.[58] Self-transcendence is unintelligible, because undifferentiated. Jung was a strict Kantian and Jung's Lutheran—dare one say: Nicene?—theology is strictly against the Pelagian heresy that one can be saved entirely through one's own efforts. The transcendent Mind of Buddhism which has much in common with the Nous (Mind) of Platonism is a psychic projection. All 'metaphysical positions', be they called 'matter', 'energy', 'God', and even 'matter', all generalisations and hypostases must be treated strictly as mental phenomena, having no independent existence.

As a result, the possibility of divine union, transcendence, indeed of ecstasy, literally 'ecstasis' (ἔκστασις), i.e., standing outside oneself, becomes impossible. The human being must realise that he or she is 'shut up' inside his or her mind and 'cannot step beyond it, even in insanity', and that the experience of his or her world or gods very much depends on the individual's 'own mental condition'.[59] So far from being the culmination of human possibility, mystical experience is a reversion to a childish state. One cannot move outside one's psychic sphere; and it is impossible for the individual to have any intelligible understanding of such a state. The individual has to leave behind such a 'primitive' and 'child-like' condition and realise the limitations of consciousness; take up the challenge of scientific knowledge which is the 'last step out of humanity's childhood', and avoid at all costs the '*sacrificium intellectus*', of something so dearly won.

Freud shared this dismissal of transcendent experience. He, too, argued that such experience was a reversion to a primitive, infantile state. In a letter to Freud of December 1927, the poet Romain Rolland said that 'oceanic feeling' was the common denominator of all religious experience. He was writing in response to Freud's work on the origin of religion and its purpose, *The Future of an Illusion*, published earlier that year, in which Freud had asserted that the function of religion was to keep the destructive urges of the lazy, unintelligent, and indeed primitive masses that compose the bulk of humankind in check.[60] In *Civilization and Its Discontents* (1930), Freud responds to Rolland's intervention, arguing that religious experiences of unity and oneness, or 'oceanic feelings', have their source in the primitive-ego. The latter was the state when the infant has as yet no experience of selfhood, still being breast-fed, and not yet separated from its mother, hence being still one with the world. Any reaching back further in individual development than the stage of infantile helplessness, to reach an earlier, more primitive origin for religious feelings would appear to be hopelessly unclear. 'There may be something farther behind that, but for the present it is wrapped in obscurity', he warned.[61]

Freud sees any deliberate reaching for oceanic feelings through such exercises as yoga as being just 'coenaesthesia', and he dismisses such 'regressions to primordial states of mind' and 'obscure modifications of mental life' as 'trances and ecstasies'. Indeed, he is moved to exclaim in the words of Schiller's diver, 'Let him rejoice who breathes up here in the roseate light' (*Es freue sich, wer da atmet im rostigten Licht*).[62] There seem to be traces here of an aspiring Platonism, an innate yearning to escape from the cave of obscurity and to emerge into the light of consciousness. But the underlying, the primordial, the pre-historic, and indeed the obscure, have greater truth value than clarity, order, and consciousness. It would seem odd, absurd, and even heretical in this context to suggest that consciousness is stronger than the unconscious, and that it is the Mind that is the living and constant origin.

Jung's account of the development of the Self draws a good deal of its authority from parallels with Gnosticism; an attractively murky and contradictory movement, which emerged in late antiquity, a period which E.R. Dodds called the 'age of anxiety'.[63] Now Gnosticism particularly appealed to the cultural pessimism and nihilism of the late nineteenth and early twentieth centuries.[64] It is imbued with the most terrible apprehensions, forlornness, and dread. From the perspective of Gnosticism, humankind is trapped in a degraded world created by an imperfect god. We barely live, existing in a state of sleep, numbness, intoxication, 'poisoned by darkness'.[65] We cannot free ourselves from this bondage, the only hope for a Gnostic is to be rescued by an alien entity, a saviour, who will come, untainted, from a realm outside the spheres of existence, and lead humanity to a better, more perfect earth which is a closer reflection of the World of Intelligibles.

Gnosticism contains elements of Platonism, though reflected in a mirror of obsidian. Arthur Darby Nock (1902–1963) went so far as to call it 'Platonism run wild'.[66] Certainly, Platonists contemporary with the Gnostics, most notably Plotinus, thought this was the case. Plotinus launched a celebrated critique of Gnosticism in his *Enneads* (II. 9, 'Against the Gnostics'). He particularly dislikes the Gnostics' denigration of the cosmos. Could a better cosmos than this one be imagined? he asks:

> What reflection of that world could be conceived more beautiful than this of ours? What fire could be a nobler reflection of the fire there than the fire we know here? [. . .] And what globe more minutely perfect than this, or more admirably ordered in its course, could have been conceived in the image of the self-centred circling of the World of Intelligibles? And for a sun figuring the Divine sphere, if it is to be more splendid than the sun visible to us, what a sun it must be![67]

On this account, the world has not been abandoned but rather it is filled with an immanent power. It is a loss of vision which leads to the experience of alienation: 'The Soul's disaster falls upon it when it ceases to dwell in the perfect Beauty.'[68] Humankind's fall is just a misperception. However confused, however strong its sense of loss, the individual soul is still connected to the highest; for 'it stands, in part, always in the presence of the Divine Beings'.[69]

The development of the individual self is the struggle that leads the Soul to leave the cave of illusion and for it to confront the true reality, to gain wings. It is difficult to avoid Plotinus when examining Gnosticism, but somehow Jung manages it; a hermeneutics of suspicion would point at once to a significant lapse. The first glimpses of the self are found for Jung in the obscure, labyrinthine, and distinctly cheerless writings of Gnosticism.[70] It is curious that Jung begins his history of the development of the self with Gnostics and Patristic writing and does not include any of the considerable body of writing on the self in antiquity, from reflections on the injunction at Delphi ('Know Thyself'), via Plato's *Alcibiades I*, to Plotinus. The subject of the development of the self, its *paideia*, was a constant philosophical and religious concern in antiquity, a well-worn topic that is found Platonism, Stoicism, Epicurianism, Orphism, and the Mysteries.

One major obstacle is that the bulk of this literature, and chiefly that of Platonism, is not sufficiently archaic, for while it may trace its roots back to Orphism and Pythagoras, most of its major figures from Plato to Damascius cover an *historical* period from the fourth century CE and even beyond the closing of the Platonic Academy in Athens by Justinian in 529 CE. The Platonic tradition continues in Augustine and Dionysius the Areopagite up to Cusanus, Plethon, and the Renaissance, Ficino, and Pico, and it is important in the work of Hegel and Schelling. There would seem to be enough room for conjecture in a historical period with missing texts, sources, and fragments. Yet there is not the addictive mystery of an endless quest, the unappeasable yearning to go deeper, to find an earlier archaic grounding for the present.

The prelude to Thomas Mann's immense historical novel, *Joseph and His Brothers* (1935–1943), draws an analogy with an exploration of deep time with a 'Descent into Hell'. 'Deep is the well of the past. Should we not call it bottomless?', it asks, before going on to assert that, the deeper one delves into the underworld of the past, the more unfathomable the foundations of humankind's history and civilisation become. And those foundations become unfathomable because they constantly retreat 'into the bottomless depths', irrespective of the 'extravagant lengths' to which we 'unreel our temporal plumb line'.[71] Freud's psychic archaeology traces everything back to a primal anxiety caused by the destruction of ancient Crete.[72] In *Moses and Monotheism* (1939), Freud felt that he could have predicted the findings of Evans and Schliemann through psychological analysis, as there were still traces of the trauma to be found in the 'collective memory':

> With our present psychological insight, we could, long before Schliemann and Evans, have raised the question of where it was that the Greeks obtained all the legendary material which was worked over by Homer and the great Attic dramatists in their masterpieces. The answer would have had to be that this people had probably experienced in their prehistory a period of extreme brilliance and cultural efflorescence which had perished in a historical catastrophe and of which an obscure tradition survived in these traditions.[73]

All that is missing is a reversion to the myth of Atlantis; however, its sources, the *Timaeus* and the *Critias*, are regrettably Platonic.

In his last great work, *Mysterium coniunctionis: An Inquiry into the Separation and Synthesis of Psychic Opposites in Alchemy* (1955–1956) Jung returns to an enquiry into the opposition of elements in the psyche which he had first examined in 1921 in *Psychological Types*. In this earlier work, Jung developed the notion of introversion and extroversion, and he employs the Presocratic notion of 'enantiodromia' to account for the emergence of psychic opposites. Jung takes the conception of enantiodromia from Heraclitus, where the word means a 'running counter to':

> [It] is employed to designate the play of opposites in the course of events—the view that everything that still exists turns into its opposite. 'From the living comes death and from the dead life, from the young old age and from the old youth; from waking, sleep, and from sleep, waking; the stream of generation and decay never stands still.' 'Construction and destruction, destruction and construction. Just as the cosmos itself arose from the primal fire, so must it return once more into the same—a dual process running its measured course through vast periods of time, a drama eternally re-enacted.'[74]

In *Mysterium coniunctionis*, enantiodromia has primarily a compensatory function, but now there are symptoms of pessimism and a Gnostic anxiety:

> The more distinctly an idea emerges, the more consciousness gains in clarity, the more monarchic becomes its content, to which everything contradictory had to submit. This extreme state has to be reached, despite the fact that the climax always presages the end. Man's own nature, the unconscious, immediately tries to compensate, and this is distasteful to the extreme state,

which always considers itself ideal and is moreover in a position to prove its excellence with the most cogent arguments. We cannot but admit that it is ideal, but for all that it is imperfect because it expresses only one half of life. Life wants not only the clear but also the muddy, not only the bright but also the dark; it wants all days to be followed by nights [. . .].[75]

If we fully accept the nature of compensation, then might it not be time to balance the dark, the muddy, and the benighted with light and perfection? Should we not exchange dark conviction for bright assurance? It makes a sharp contrast with both Freud and Jung to believe, as Platonism does, that the cosmos reflects Mind, Beauty, and the Good, that it has its origin in knowing rather than primitive obscurity, and that Truth is found above rather than below. The Platonic represents a complete reversal of their psychic deixis.

With its aspiring lofty nature, Platonism was too great a contrast with the entire direction of psychic pre-history, which burrowed away into the depths, beneath both modernity and antiquity for some founding validation. In his account of Heraclitus, Jung steers dangerously towards a model of time based on the eternal return, but both Jung and Freud stuck to a Darwinian model of development through time, which was crossed with a Judaic, episodic model of Creation. For the psyche, the primitive earlier stages persist in the present either as collective memory, or displaced fragments, and its earliest stages still exist unchanged in non-modern tribal societies.[76]

In Plato's *Timaeus*, the temporal world is 'a moving image of eternity' (*Timaeus*, 37d), an eternity that is the principal subject of philosophical contemplation, *theoria*, which—in the words of Hans Jonas (1903–1993)—'beholds eternal objects in the forms of things, a transcendence of immutable being shining through the transparency of becoming'.[77] And, if it is true that all things have a timeless, transcendent origin[78] which is permanently present, then there is no development through time, and there can be no archaic.

Notes

1 E.M. Butler, *The Tyranny of Greece over Germany: A Study of the Influence Exercised by Greek Art and Poetry over the Great German Writers of the Eighteenth, Nineteenth, and Twentieth Centuries*, Cambridge: Cambridge University Press, 2005. Butler dedicated the book to Pallas Athene; it was placed on the Nazi Index shortly after publication.
2 Parliamentarians entering the building would pass through a vestibule with statues of Apollo, Athena, Zeus, Hera, Haephestus, Hermes, Demeter, Poseidon, Artemis, and Ares into a chamber decorated with a formidable statuary representing Roman worthies including Cincinnatus, Cato the Elder, Cicero, Augustus, Gracchus, and Seneca. To complete the classical model, the building was heated with a hypocaust. For his part, Freud amassed an extensive collection of largely classical figurines which were on his desk or otherwise disposed in his consulting room, his 'old and grubby gods'. Of them all, his favourite was a bronze figurine of Athena dating from the first or second century CE; he said that he 'felt proud and rich under the protection of Athena'; see Janine Burke, *The Sphinx on the Table: Sigmund Freud's Art Collection and the Development of Psychoanalysis*, New York: Walker, 2006, pp. 92–93.

3 Meyer was a contributor to a more abstract homage to the Acropolis: *Dropylaea* (*Die Propyläen*)—a journal, edited by Goethe, which proselytised the ideals of Weimar Classicism, and which was named after the monumental entrance to the Acropolis, the Propylaea. There is, of course, considerable evidence for the presence of Roman cultural influence on the German-speaking world which would make a pair with Butler's book.

4 Imposing, institutional, neo-classical buildings are to be found across Switzerland such as the vast Technological University in Zurich to the grand Federal Palace in Berlin.

5 Butler, *The Tyranny of Greece over Germany*, p. xi. Clearly, Butler is a firm member of the classical movement that was intent to overturn and upset the earlier classical movement of Romanticism and Idealism.

6 See George Steiner, *Errata: An Examined Life*, New Haven, CT: Yale University Press, 1997, p. 19. As a boy, Steiner too was seized by the terrible truth of life as demonstrated in *The Iliad*, for example in the scene in book 21 where the defeated Lycaon tearfully pleads that Achilles should spare his life:

> [. . .] Fool,
> don't talk to me of ransom. No more speeches.
> Before Patroclus met his day of destiny, true,
> It warmed my heart a bit to spare some Trojans:
> Droves I took alive and auctioned off as slaves.
> But now not a single Trojan flees his death,
> not one the gods hand over to me before your gates,
> none of all the Trojans, sons of Priam least of all!
> Come, friend, you too must die. Why moan about it so?
> Even Patroclus died, a far, far better man than you,
> And look, you see how handsome and powerful I am?
> The son of a great man, the mother who gave me life
> A deathless goddess. But even for me, I tell you,
> death and the strong force of fate are waiting.
> There will come a dawn or sunset or high noon
> when a man will take my life in battle too —
>
> (Steiner, *Errata*, p. 15)

7 F. Nietzsche, *The Birth of Tragedy* [1872], trans. W. Kaufmann, New York: Random House, 1967, §3.

8 C. G. Jung, *Man and His Symbols*, New York: Dell, 1968, p. 75.

9 S. Freud, 'Civilization and Its Discontents', in *The Standard Edition of the Complete Works*, ed. J. Strachey and A. Freud, 24 vols, London: Hogarth Press, 1963–1974, vol. 21, pp. 57–145 (pp. 69–70).

10 Freud, 'Civilization and Its Discontents', in *Standard Edition*, vol. 21, p. 70.

11 C. G. Jung, *Memories, Dreams, Reflections*, ed. A. Jaffé, tr. R. and C. Winston, London: Collins, 1963, p. 318.

12 Jung, *Memories, Dreams, Reflections*, p. 319.

13 S. Freud, 'A Disturbance of Memory on the Acropolis', in *Standard Edition*, vol. 22, pp. 239–249.

14 For a fuller account, see Burke, *The Sphinx on the Table*, pp. 198–199.

15 Freud, 'A Disturbance of Memory on the Acropolis', in *Standard Edition*, vol. 22, p. 241.

16 Freud, 'A Disturbance of Memory on the Acropolis', in *Standard Edition*, vol. 22, p. 247.

17 See Burke, *The Sphinx on the Table*, p. 182.

18 S. Freud, S. *The Interpretation of Dreams*, tr. J. Strachey, London: George Allen & Unwin, 1954, pp. 193–199; cf. Burke, *The Sphinx on the Table*, p. 175: 'Freud dreamed of Rome. In letters to Fleiss, he canvassed his desire to visit the city, admitting his longing was "deeply neurotic"' (see S. Freud, *The Complete Letters to Wilhelm Fliess, 1887–1904*, ed. M. Masson, Boston, MA: Harvard University Press, 1986, p. 285).

19 *Middlemarch*, chapter 20, in G. Eliot, *Middlemarch*, ed. B.G. Hornback, New York and London: Norton, 1977, p. 134.
20 Tacitus, *Histories*, book 1, chapter 2, in Tacitus, *The Histories; The Annals*, tr. C.H. Moore and J. Jackson, vol. 1, *The Histories: Books 1–3*, London: Heinemann; Cambridge, MA: Harvard University Press, 1962, pp. 5–7.
21 Freud, 'Civilization and Its Discontents', in *Standard Edition*, vol. 21, pp. 69–70. For an archaeological view of Freud's description of Rome, see A. Carandini, *Rome: Day One*, tr. S. Sartarelli, Princeton, NJ: Princeton University Press, 2001, pp. 1–10.
22 Freud, 'Civilization and Its Discontents', in *Standard Edition*, vol. 21, p. 70.
23 E. Haeckel, *Anthropogenie, oder Entwickungsgeschichte des Menschen*, Leipzig: Engelmann, 1874. For a discussion of Haeckel and his relationship to the history of psychiatry, see H.F. Ellenberger, *The Discovery of the Unconscious: The History and Evolution of Dynamic Psychiatry*, London: Allen Lane, 1970, pp. 233–234.
24 For an account of the now subterranean, earliest Forum area of Rome, see J. Rykwert, *The Idea of the Town: The Anthropology of Urban Form in Rome, Italy and the Ancient World*, Cambridge, MA: MIT Press, 1988. Much of the pressure to renounce the later classical world came from Sir Arthur Evans's excavations on Crete at Knossos. Primeval beliefs and buildings gave an impetus to an unsparing modernism. For further discussion, see C. Gere, *Knossos and the Prophets of Modernism*, Chicago, IL and London: University of Chicago Press 2009, especially the section on 'Freudian Archeology', pp. 153–160.
25 Jung, *Memories, Dreams, Reflections*, p. 28.
26 Jung, *Memories, Dreams, Reflections*, p. 30.
27 Jung, *Memories, Dreams, Reflections*, p. 211.
28 Jung, *Memories, Dreams, Reflections*, p. 203.
29 C.G. Jung, 'Psychological Aspects of the Mother Archetype' (1938; 1954), in *The Archetypes and the Collective Unconscious* [*Collected Works*, vol. 9/i], tr. R.F.C. Hull, Princeton, NJ: Princeton University Press, 1968, §148–§198 (§149).
30 Jung, 'Psychological Aspects of the Mother Archetype', §149.
31 Jung, 'Psychological Aspects of the Mother Archetype', §155.
32 Jung, 'Psychological Aspects of the Mother Archetype', §155.
33 Jung, 'Psychological Aspects of the Mother Archetype', §149.
34 Jung, 'Psychological Aspects of the Mother Archetype', §149.
35 C.G. Jung, 'A Psychological Approach to the Dogma of the Trinity', in *Psychology and Religion: East and West* [*Collected Works*, vol. 11], tr. R.F.C. Hull, London: Routledge and Kegan Paul, 1969, §169–§295 (§184); cf. *Timaeus*, 17a. The problem of the identity of the fourth guest was the subject of later Neoplatonic commentary on the dialogue. Ironically, Porphyry and Iamblichus give the very reverse argument to Jung; the missing person was someone too spiritual to endure the materialism of the *Timaeus*; cf. Proclus, *Commentary on the Timaeus* (*In Tim.*), I, 19–20. For a translation see Proclus, *Commentary on the 'Timæus' of Plato*, vol. 1 [*Thomas Taylor Series*, vol. 15], tr. T. Taylor [1820], Sturminster: Prometheus Trust, 2006, pp. 27–28. Counting Socrates in, then, there are four people involved in the discussion (the others being Timaeus, Critias, and Hermocrates). F.M. Cornford, on whom Jung relies for much of the analysis of *Timaeus*, declares that the problem of the identity of identifying the 'fourth' is a futile one; see F.M. Cornford, *Plato's Cosmology: The Timaeus of Plato*, London: Routledge, 1973, p. 3.
36 Jung, 'A Psychological Approach to the Dogma of the Trinity', §185.
37 Jung, 'A Psychological Approach to the Dogma of the Trinity', §185.
38 Jung, 'A Psychological Approach to the Dogma of the Trinity', §185; citing Cornford, *Plato's Cosmology*, p. 58 (translating *Timaeus*, 34a).
39 Cf. Jung, 'A Psychological Approach to the Dogma of the Trinity', §188–§192 (pp. 124–127). Plato's Atlantis is another mandala; the X in a circle which, according to Porphyry, represented the 'world soul' ('A Psychological Approach to the Dogma of the Trinity', §190; citing Proclus's commentary on the *Timaeus*, 261c; in Proclus, *Commentary on the 'Timæus' of Plato*, vol. 2

[Thomas Taylor Series, vol. 16], tr. T. Taylor [1820], Sturminster Newton: Prometheus Trust, 1998, p. 663).

40 C.G. Jung, *Nietzsche's 'Zarathustra': Notes of the Seminar Given in 1934–1939*, ed. J.L. Jarrett, 2 vols, London: Routledge, 1988, pp. 366–367.

41 Jung, *Nietzsche's 'Zarathustra'*, vol. 1, p. 367.

42 Jung, 'A Psychological Approach to the Dogma of the Trinity', §170.

43 Jung, *Nietzsche's 'Zarathustra'*, vol. 1, p. 367.

44 See Jung's letter to Mircea Eliade of 19 January 1955. In the first edition of *Le Yoga: Immortalité et liberté* (1954) Eliade had had the temerity to suggest that the unconscious 'apes' the conscious or the transconscious. This top-down view was too much for Jung— 'you seem to consider me so idiotic as never even to have thought about the nature of the unconscious'—and he argues strongly that the unconscious is conservative and not to be influenced (C.G. Jung, *Letters*, ed. G. Adler and A. Jaffé, 2 vols, Princeton, NJ: Princeton University Press, 1973–1975, vol. 2, pp. 210–212 [p. 212]). See editorial footnote 6 to this letter, which observes that 'on p. 230 of the French original, E[liade] uses the words "simiesque" (apish) and "singer" (to ape). In his reply to this letter [Eliade] expressed his regret about the misunderstanding, and he subsequently changed the words for the English edition of the book. The translation now reads: "The spontaneous rediscovery of the mandala by the unconscious raises an important problem. We may well ask if the 'unconscious' is not in this case trying to imitate processes by which 'consciousness' (or, in some cases, the 'transconscious') seeks to obtain completeness and conquer freedom" (p. 226), and on p. 227 there is the phrase "mimicking imitation"' (*Letters*, vol. 2, p. 210).

45 The 'missing' letters may be found in T. Velletri, 'Mircea Eliade and C. G. Jung: A Comparative Study', unpublished Ph.D. thesis, 2015, University of Essex.

46 Jung, *Nietzsche's 'Zarathustra'*, vol. 1, p. 367.

47 See L. Mumford, *The City in History*, New York: Harcourt Brace, 1961, which argues: 'The modest foundations of the village had been laid in the earth, but the city reversed the villager's values, and turned the peasant's universe upside down, by placing the foundations in the heavens. All eyes now turned skywards. Belief in the eternal and the infinite, the omniscient and the omnipotent succeeded over the millennia, in exalting the very possibilities of human existence. Those who made the most of the city were not chained by the animal limitations of human existence, they sought deliberately by a concentrated act of will, to transcend them' (p. 37). For a discussion of this passage and a wider expansion of its ideas, see S. Scully, *Homer and the Sacred City*, Ithaca, NY: Cornell University Press, 1990, chapter 2, 'The Sacred City'.

48 Philo, 'On the Creation' (*De Opificio Mundi*), especially §18, in *The Works of Philo*, tr. C.D. Yonge, Peabody, MA: Hendrickson, pp. 3–24 (p. 9).

49 'Intelligible' is the conventional and quite inadequate translation of *nous* (νοῦς). *Nous* is an immediate awareness without the mediation of discursive reason; It is pure intuitive apprehension. For Neoplatonism, *nous* is the nature of the intelligible realm which is just below the Divine.

50 Plotinus, *Enneads*, V.2, 'On the Origin and Order of the Beings which come after the First', §1, in Plotinus, *Ennead V*, tr. A.H. Armstrong, Cambridge, MA, and London: Harvard University Press, 1984, p. 59.

51 *Rep.*, 518c; Plato, *Republic*, tr. G.M.A. Grube, rev. C.D.C. Reve, in *Plato: Complete Works*, Indianapolis, IN: Hackett Publishing Company, 1977. For a full account of the pivotal theological importance of *metastrophe*, see A.D. Nock, *Conversion: The Old and the New in Religion from Alexander the Great to Augustine of Hippo*, Oxford: Oxford University Press, 1933.

52 C.G. Jung, 'A Study in the Process of Individuation', in *The Archetypes and the Collective Unconscious* [*Collected Works*, vol. 9/i], tr. R.F.C. Hull, Princeton, NJ: Princeton University Press, 1968, §525–§626 (pp. 290–354).

53 Jung, 'A Study in the Process of Individuation', in *The Archetypes of the Collective Unconscious*, p. 309, figure 2: 'Sketch of the picture from the year 1916'.

54 G. Tucci, *The Theory and Practice of the Mandala: With Special Reference to the Modern Psychology of the Subconscious*, tr. A.H. Broderick, London: Hutchinson, 1961, 'Appendix', pp. 137–141, which includes a long exegesis of this poem from the Tantrasāra of Abhinavagupta.

55 For a diagrammatic representation of these patterns in Proclus, see R. Chlup, *Proclus: An Introduction*, Cambridge: Cambridge University Press, 2012, figures 13 and 14.

56 Plato, *Theaetetus*, 176b: 'We should make all speed to take flight from this world to the other, and that means becoming like the divine so far as we can' (*Collected Dialogues*, ed. E. Hamilton and H. Cairns, Princeton, NJ: Princeton University Press, 1989, p. 881.

57 Plotinus, *Enneads*, V.8, 'On the Intellectual Beauty', §9, in Plotinus, *The Six Enneads*, tr. S. McKenna, abridged J. Dillon, Harmondsworth: Penguin, 1991, pp. 419–420.

58 C.G. Jung, 'Psychological Commentary on *The Tibetan Book of the Great Liberation*', in *Psychology and Religion: East and West* [*Collected Works*, vol. 11], tr. R.F.C. Hull, London: Routledge and Kegan Paul, 1969, §759–§830 (pp. 473–508).

59 Jung, 'Psychological Commentary on *The Tibetan Book of the Great Liberation*', in *Psychology and Religion: East and West* [*Collected Works*, vol. 11], §765.

60 In his Foreword of 1950 to the fourth (Swiss) edition of *Transformations and Symbols of the Libido* (1911–1912), published as *Symbols of Transformation*, Jung condemns the Freud of *The Future of an Illusion* as 'moving within the confines of the outmoded rationalism and scientific materialism of the late nineteenth century' (*Symbols of Transformation* [*Collected Works*, vol. 5], tr. R.F.C. Hull, Princeton, NJ: Princeton University Press, 1967, p. xxiii). It would be interesting to consider whether Jung deployed similar rationalist arguments in his response of 1954 to *The Tibetan Book of the Great Liberation*.

61 Freud, 'Civilization and Its Discontents', in *Standard Edition*, vol. 21, p. 69.

62 See Schiller, 'Der Taucher' (The Diver), in F. Schiller, *Sämtliche Gedichte und Balladen*, ed. G. Kurscheidt, Frankfurt am Main and Leipzig: Insel, 2004, pp. 59–63 (p. 61).

63 E.R. Dodds, *Pagan and Christian in an Age of Anxiety*, Cambridge: Cambridge University Press, 1965.

64 See H. Jonas, *The Gnostic Religion: The Message of the Alien God and the Beginnings of Christianity*, 2nd revised edn, Boston, MA: Beacon Press, 1962, 'Epilogue: Gnosticism, Existentialism, and Nihilism', pp. 320–340.

65 Jonas, *The Gnostic Religion*, p. 69.

66 A.D. Nock, 'Gnosticism', in *Essays on Religion and the Ancient World*, ed. Z. Stewart, 2 vols, Cambridge, MA: Harvard University Press, 1972, vol. 2, pp. 940–959 (p. 949). This issue is discussed further in J.H. Kennedy, 'The Platonism of the *Tripartite Tractate* (Nag Hammadi I, 5)' in *Neoplatonism and Gnosticism*, Albany, NY: State University of New York Press, 1992, pp. 187–206 (p. 187).

67 Plotinus, *Enneads*, II. 9, 'Against the Gnostics; or Against Those That Affirm the Creator of the Cosmos and the Cosmos itself to be Evil', §4, in Plotinus, *Enneads*, tr. McKenna, p. 113.

68 Plotinus, *Enneads*, II. 9, 'Against the Gnostics', §2; in Plotinus, *Enneads*, tr. McKenna, p. 111.

69 Plotinus, *Enneads*, II. 9, 'Against the Gnostics', §2; in Plotinus, *Enneads*, tr. McKenna, p. 111.

70 See the chapter entitled 'The Structure and Dynamics of the Self', in *Aion: Researches into the Phenomenology of the Self* [*Collected Works*, vol. 9/ii], tr. R.F.C. Hull, Princeton, NJ: Princeton University Press, 1968, §347–§421 (pp. 222–265). For an account of the vast ancient literature on the self, see M. Foucault, *The Hermeneutics of the Subject: Lectures at the Collège de France 1981–1982*, ed. F. Gros, tr. G. Burchell, New York: Palgrave Macmillan, 2005.

71 T. Mann, *Joseph and His Brothers* [1933–1943], tr. J.E. Woods, New York: Knopf, 2005, p. 3.

72 Compare with Freud's essay, 'Constructions in Analysis' (1937): 'Just as the archaeologist builds up the walls of the building from the foundations that have remained standing, determines the number and position of the columns from depressions in the floor and reconstructs the mural decorations and paintings from the remains found in the débris, so does the analyst proceed' (Freud, *Standard Edition*, vol. 23, pp. 256–269 [p. 259]); discussed in Gere, *Knossos and the Prophets of Modernism*, p. 157.

73 S. Freud, 'Moses and Monotheism', in *Standard Edition*, vol. 23, pp. 1–139 (pp. 70–71). See the discussion of this passage in Gere, *Knossos and the Prophets of Modernism*, p. 157.

74 C.G. Jung, *Psychological Types* [*Collected Works*, vol. 6], tr. R.F.C. Hull, Princeton, NJ: Princeton University Press, 1971, §708.

75 C.G. Jung, *Mysterium coniunctionis: An Inquiry into the Separation and Synthesis of Psychic Opposites in Alchemy* [*Collected Works*, vol. 14], tr. R.F.C. Hull, Princeton, NJ: Princeton University Press, 1970, §471.

76 For an account of Jung's encounter with the primitive, see B.W. Burleson, *Jung in Africa*, New York: Continuum, 2005.

77 Jonas, *The Gnostic Religion*, p. 338.

78 Many different models of time and existence were argued for and about in the ancient world, and there were many refutations that the world was created or emerged through a series of Theogonies, and arguments for a timeless continuum. For further discussion, see D. Sedley, *Creationism and Its Critics in Antiquity*, Berkeley and Los Angeles, CA, and London: University of California Press, 2007; and R. Sorabji, *Time, Creation, and the Continuum: Theories in Antiquity and the Early Middle Ages*, London: Duckworth, 1983.

PART II

Ecstatic-archaic history

5

I MUST GET OUT (OF MYSELF) MORE OFTEN?

Jung, Klages, and the ecstatic-archaic

Paul Bishop

This chapter explores the experience of the ecstatic-archaic in two key thinkers in the vitalist tradition, C.G. Jung (1875–1961) and Ludwig Klages (1872–1956), and in particular their readings of works by two major German writers, one—Friedrich Nietzsche (1844–1900)—usually associated with vitalism, the other—Friedrich Schiller (1759–1805)—hardly ever.[1] Using the intellectual frameworks offered by Jung and Klages as prisms through which to read these texts by Nietzsche and Schiller, this chapter seeks to make a contribution to uncovering the ecstatic dimension of the archaic. So first, Nietzsche.

In the fourth (and final) part of *Thus Spoke Zarathustra* (1883–1885, pub. 1883–1891), we come across a curious chapter (in this most curious of books), entitled 'At Midday'.[2] Occupying a central position in Part 4, it relates how Zarathustra falls asleep beneath an old tree embraced by a grape-vine and has a dream, or a vision, or an ecstatic experience of some sort, described as a 'strange drunkenness'. (In this respect, the chapter acts as an anticipation of the 'drunken song', or the night-wanderer's song, sung by Zarathustra in the penultimate chapter.) Our attention is drawn to this passage by C.G. Jung (1875–1961) in his paper on the archetype of rebirth.[3]

First given as an Eranos lecture in 1939, Jung's paper considers five different kinds of rebirth, i.e., metempsychosis, reincarnation, resurrection, rebirth (renovatio), and participation in the process of transformation' (§199–§205). This paper is an unusual one, inasmuch as it considers an archetype that is not a figure, but a *process*, yet Jung insists on its archetypal dimension: 'Rebirth is an affirmation that must be counted among the primordial affirmations of humankind', he argued, and 'these primordial affirmations are based on what I call archetypes' (§206). As an example of this fifth (and, it seems, for Jung, the most interesting) kind of rebirth, Jung mentions the ceremony of the Mass, but also the Eleusinian Mysteries.[4] He cites, for instance, the Homeric Hymn to Demeter, 'Happy is he among men upon earth who has seen these mysteries; but he who is uninitiate and has no part in them, never has lot of like good things once he is dead, down in the darkness and gloom',[5] and he refers to a text he identifies as one of the Eleusinian epitaphs: 'Truly the blessed gods have proclaimed a most beautiful secret: / Death comes not as a curse, but as a blessing to men' (§205, n. 2).[6]

In this way, Jung tries to resolve the problem of whether or how we can actually discuss the ancient Mysteries. For Jung, there is a basic proposition: 'There must be psychic events underlying these affirmations which it is the business of psychology to discuss—without entering into all the metaphysical and philosophical assumptions regarding their significance' (§207). In presenting what he thus conceives as a *phenomenology* of the archetypal experience of rebirth, Jung distinguishes between two kinds of archetypal rebirth experience: one of the transcendence of life in general (subdivided into ritual-induced and immediate experiences), the other of one's own subjective transformation (divided into a further eight sub-categories). For Jung, the noontide vision experienced by Zarathustra in 'At Midday' belongs in the former category of the transcendence of life, and constitutes a classic example of the spontaneous, ecstatic, or visionary experience. Indeed, Jung considered its details to be so accurate that he wrote 'it is just as if Nietzsche had been present' at a performance of the mysteries of Eleusis (§210).[7] 'Nietzsche, as we know', Jung argues, 'substitutes for the Christian mystery the myth of Dionysus-Zagreus, who was dismembered and came to life again. His experience has the character of a Dionysian nature myth: the Deity appears in the garb of Nature, as classical antiquity saw it'—Jung refers to the passage about 'an old, bent and gnarled tree, hung with grapes'—'and the moment of eternity is the noonday, sacred to Pan' (§210): 'Hath time flown away? Do I not fall? Have I not fallen—hark!—into the well of eternity?' In the image of the 'golden ring', the 'ring of return', Jung believes (and he draws on the Nietzschean interpretation of Ernst Horneffer for support)[8] that Nietzsche saw 'a promise of resurrection and life' (§211). According to Jung, this kind of 'spontaneous, ecstatic, or visionary experience' can offer 'all that the mystery drama represents and brings about in the spectator' (§210), and on the basis of his reading of 'At Midday', Jung confidently concludes that 'it is just as if Nietzsche had been at a performance of the mysteries' (§210).

In a sense, Jung is entirely correct to associate Nietzsche with the great Mysteries, inasmuch as Socrates remarks in the *Phaedo*, 'many bear the emblems, but the devotees are few', and 'these devotees are simply those who have lived the philosophical life in the right way'.[9] For other remarks elsewhere by Nietzsche bear out Jung's interpretation, and perhaps none so more powerfully than his gnomic observation in *Ecce Homo*: 'The fortunateness of my existence, its uniqueness perhaps, lies in its fatality: to express it in the form of a riddle, as my father I have already died, as my mother I still live and grow old.'[10]

This enigmatic statement has been interpreted variously by such commentators as Jacques Derrida, Rudolph Gasché, Pierre Klossowski, Sarah Kofman,

Thomas Steinbuch, and Michel Onfray; yet surely it cries out to be read in a Jungian sense. On such a reading, in *Ecce Homo* Nietzsche casts off his masculine, patriarchal side, and embarks on (or acknowledges) the discovery of the feminine, intuitive side of the self.[11] Part and parcel of this discovery is Nietzsche's realisation, his acceptance, his insight into the inevitability, even the utility, of death. After all, 'mother', 'maternal', and 'matrix' (= womb) (*mater*) appear to be etymologically related to 'matter' (*materia*) of which we are made and to which we return. Famously, Nietzsche designated himself as 'the *last* disciple of the philosopher Dionysos',[12] and as such as 'the *first* to take seriously that wonderful phenomenon which bears the name Dionysus as a means to understanding the older Hellenic instinct'.[13] In the *Twilight of the Idols*, Nietzsche does not mince his words—the Dionysian is tied up with 'the orgy'. Out of these quintessentially physiological, psychological, and above all *ecstatic* experiences evolved, he claims, the Dionysian mysteries:

> The *fundamental fact* of the Hellenic instinct—its 'will to life'—expresses itself only in the Dionysian mysteries, in the psychology of the Dionysian state. *What* did the Hellenes guarantee for themselves with these mysteries? *Eternal* life, the eternal recurrence of life; the future promised and consecrated in the past; the triumphant Yes to life beyond death and change; *true* life as collective continuation of life through procreation, through the mysteries of sexuality.[14]

Yet this is not a comfortable vision by any means: 'In the teachings of the mysteries', Nietzsche emphasises, '*pain* is sanctified.'[15]

Now for the German vitalist thinker Ludwig Klages, this ecstatic aspect of Nietzsche's thinking can be found in all kinds of unexpected ways in his work. For instance, at one point Klages cites the conclusion of §337 in *The Gay Science*:

> We present-day humans are just beginning to form the chain of a very powerful future feeling, link by link—we hardly know what we are doing [. . .] This is actually the colour of this new feeling: Anyone who manages to experience the history of humanity as *his own history* will feel in an enormously generalized way [. . .] a happiness that humanity has not known so far: the happiness of a god full of power and love, full of tears and laughter, a happiness that, like the sun in the evening, continually bestows its inexhaustible riches, pouring them into the sea, feeling richest, as the sun does, only when even the poorest fisherman is still rowing with golden oars![16]

For Klages, this passage in Nietzsche is 'extremely important', and for an appreciation of its significance he draws on the work of Alfred Schuler (1865–1923), a fellow member of the so-called *Kosmiker-Kreis* (or 'Cosmic Circle').[17] Klages can help us to understand the ecstatic dimension of the archaic in Nietzsche as it is identified by Jung. For the category of the ecstatic receives from Klages an extensive analysis in the work where he cites this passage from Nietzsche's *Gay Science*—a work that excited the interest of Walter Benjamin (1892–1940) and that Jung himself likely knew (after all, in 'On Rebirth' Jung cites the same Eleusinian epitaphs in the same order as Klages does). The work in question is a short but dense monograph published in 1921 and reprinted in an extended second edition in 1926, entitled *Of Cosmogonic Eros*.[18]

The ecstatic is a category investigated by Klages at various points in his extensive writings, including the writings of his early years, edited and published by Klages himself in 1944 as *Rhythmen und Runen*; in a major essay of 1914, 'Of Dream Consciousness' ('Vom Traumbewußtsein'); and in his *magnum opus*, translated in three volumes (1929–1932), *The Spirit as Adversary of the Soul* (*Der Geist als Widersacher der Seele*).[19] By far his most extensive discussion, however, is in *Of Cosmogonic Eros*, where Klages devotes two chapters to the 'condition' (*Zustand*) and then to the 'essence' or 'nature' (*Wesen*) of ecstasy.[20] His discussion takes place against the background of the distinction, which is fundamental to his philosophical system, between 'spirit' (*Geist*) and 'soul' (*Seele*) (*SW* 3, 390–391; *KE*, 63–65). Elsewhere, Klages argues that human ego-consciousness is based on the participation in spirit (*Geist*) (*SW* 3, 391; *KE*, 66),[21] yet in Klages's system, it transpires that spirit or *Geist* is something highly suspicious, even sinister. For it is, in the words of his great multi-volume treatise, the 'enemy' or the 'opponent' (*Widersacher*) of the soul.

Like Jung, Klages likes to present evidence for his claims on the basis of language, i.e., etymology (*SW* 3, 392, cf. 393; *KE*, 66, cf. 67–68). For Klages, ecstasy is not just the decoupling of soul from spirit, it is the decoupling of the soul from the self (*das Selbst*). Correspondingly, 'ecstasy'—from the Greek *ekstasis*, deriving from *existanai*, 'to put out of place'—does not simply mean to be 'carried away' (*Weggerücktsein*), but to be 'outside oneself' (*Außersein = außer dem Ich sein*). So someone who is drunk or otherwise intoxicated is no longer 'himself' but is 'off his head' or 'out of his mind', can 'forget himself' and later 'come round to himself' again.[22]

Klages makes a distinction between the effect of a drive (*der Trieb*) and ecstasy. 'In the drive', he writes, 'the excess of individual life weakens the spirit [*den Geist*]; in ecstasy [the spirit] is weakened, even if mediated through it [i.e., individual life], by the vital force of the world' (*SW* 3, 392; *KE*, 66–67). On the basis of lines taken from the *Ghazals* of the thirteenth-century Persian poet, Rūmī (1207–73), as translated by Friedrich Rückert (1788–1866)—

> For when the flames of love arise,
> Then Self, the gloomy despot, dies.
> [*Denn, wo die Lieb' erwachet, stirbt*
> *Das Ich, der dunkele Despot.*][23]

—Klages insists that ecstasy is not 'the decoupling of the body from the soul', but rather 'its decoupling from the self and hence its decoupling from the spirit [*Entgeistung*]' (*SW* 3, 393; *KE*, 68). Carefully, forensically, and—above all—phenomenologically, Klages works out what is happening in the ecstatic experience.

On Klages's account, every ecstatic experience has two phases: first, a preparatory phase (*der vorbereitende Teil*) when the ego perishes, and second, a realisatory phase (*der erfüllende Teil*) when life arises in its stead (*SW* 3, 393; *KE*, 68–69). In support of his view, he cites the view of Synesius (in turn, quoting Aristotle) that 'those who are being initiated into the mysteries are to be expected not to learn anything but to suffer some change, to be put into a certain condition, i.e., to be fitted for some purpose',[24] i.e., the point of the Mysteries was not *mathein*, but *pathein*.[25] According to Pierre Boyancé, what the initiate saw most likely involved the contemplation of divine symbols or divinities,[26] and as we shall see, Klages's view is similar.

Klages's reading is confirmed by other ancient sources, for instance: 'I came out of the mystery hall feeling like a stranger to myself' (Sopatros, *Rhetores Græci*, VIII: 114–115); Aelius Aristides, a Greek orator and an author of the Second Sophistic, described Eleusis as 'the most frightening and the most resplendent of all that is divine for humankind' ('Eleusinios', *Orations*, 19.2); according to Plutarch (*Moralia*, 47a), in the Mysteries terror, anxiety, and bewilderment turned to wonder and clarification, and darkness turned to light; while elsewhere (frag. 168 Sandbach = Stobaeus *Anthologium* 4.52.49) Plutarch drew on the Mysteries to describe experience of the soul at the moment of death:

> The soul suffers an experience similar to those who celebrate great initiations [. . .] Wandering astray in the beginning, tiresome walkings in circles, some frightening paths in darkness that lead nowhere; then immediately before the end all the terrible things, panic and shivering and sweat, and amazement. And then some wonderful light comes to meet you, pure regions and meadows are there to greet you, with sounds and dances and solemn, sacred words and holy views; and there the initiate, perfect by now, set free and loose from all bondage, walks about crowned with a wreath, celebrating the festival together with the other sacred and pure people, and he looks down on the uninitiated, unpurified crowd in this world in mud and fog beneath his feet.[27]

From the evidence *he* cites, Klages draws the conclusion that 'the path to life goes through the death of the ego' (*SW* 3, 393; *KE*, 69).

At the same time, Klages goes to distinguish many different sorts of ecstasy—for instance, when interpreting Goethe's famous poem, 'Sacred Yearning' (*Selige Sehnsucht*), he distinguishes between the ecstasy of an inner explosion and the ecstasy of an inner melting away (*SW* 3, 394; *KE*, 71)—and there are distinctly Dionysian aspects to his discussion (*SW* 3, 397–398; *KE*, 74–76). Overall, however, Klages distinguishes between three core varieties (*Grundformen*) of ecstasy—between its 'heroic', 'erotic', and 'magic' forms

(*SW* 3, 398; *KE*, 76). The 'heroic-tragic' form of ecstasy involves the death of the ego through the death-in-combat of the body; its 'magic' form consists in a dual relation to the distant firmament of the night sky and to the realm of the dead; but what about its 'erotic' form?

This turns out to have very little to do with the erotic as one would usually understand the term, but instead is bound up with what (in an earlier chapter) Klages had called 'elementary Eros' or Eros Kosmogonos (*SW* 3, 386–387; *KE*, 56–57).[28] In this respect, erotic ecstasy consists of a union that takes place *internal to the individual*, or as Klages puts it, 'the *gamos* of erotic ecstasy is an inner *gamos* or self-copulation of a being extended into the world, thus generating *and* receiving and hence *pregnant*' (*SW* 3, 399; *KE*, 77). In the language of myth, such a *gamos* consists of the fertilized egg *and* the god that hatches from it: embrace, pregnancy, and birth (*SW* 3, 399; *KE*, 78).[29] In the language of pathology, it involves not just *idiopathic*, but *sympathetic* aspects (*SW* 3, 399–402; *KE*, 78–83).[30] (This distinction was introduced in the second edition of *Of Cosmogonic Eros*, as Klages's note to the 1926 edition explains.)

At this point in his argument, Klages sees himself confronted by a huge question:

> How can [erotic arousal] remain sympathetic, when it becomes true ecstasy merely out of feeling? If someone in an ecstatic state has left not only his ego, but even the limitations of his individuality, and has himself become a trinity in which the poles of the world have become internalized, then where in his intoxication would there be still be room for the joint intoxication of another being? This *seems* to be impossible and, if it nevertheless happens, then it is the soul's deepest and ultimate secret. We shall not lift the veil, but merely lead to the threshold [. . .].
>
> (*SW* 3, 409; *KE*, 94–95)

We shall return to this image of the veil in a moment, but let us note here Klages's emphasis on the curiously non-sexual sense in which he understands the erotic: 'Sexual union has *not* led the lovers to the "crown of life" [cf. Revelation 2:10], it has *not* transferred them out from the transitoriness of individual existence into the "eternal life", it has *not* given them the mystical initiation!', he declares (*SW* 3, 410; *KE*, 96). In relation to these experiences, the copulative drive is really an adiaphoron (cf. the Stoic concept of *adiaphora* or 'indifferent things') and the ecstasy of gratification is an illusion, albeit one that brings pleasure:

> By contrast, even in the shudder of highest fulfillment Eros remains an *Eros of distance* and the intoxicated individual is to his intoxicated partner something secondary, never to be mixed with, of unfathomable depth, an eye of the universe looking at him from a crimson night! To surrender oneself to this does not mean to desire it; to embrace it, does not mean to become one with it; and to perish in it means: to awake!
>
> (*SW* 3, 410; *KE*, 96)

It is at this juncture that Klages makes his boldest move yet, proposing 'the solution to the so-called riddle of the world'—hence a riddle associated with Nietzsche, as well as with the vitalist biologist, Ernst Haeckel (1834–1919).[31]

According to Klages, this solution to the world-riddle is 'the ecstatic internalization of the mystery of the world' (*die Lösung des sogenannten Rätsels der Welt ist die ekstatische Innerung des Mysteriums der Welt*) (*SW* 3, 410; *KE*, 96). In turn, this statement this leads him to pose another series of questions: why are the questions of the sphinx fatal for human beings? Why does the gorgon's gaze turn people into stone? And why does it bring ruin to lift the veil of Isis? For Klages, the answer to these questions is bound up with 'the archaic question of fate' which itself provided 'the knowledge providing emblem', namely that 'only something *eternally distant* is granted with enrapturing bliss' (*SW* 3, 410; *KE*, 96).

Arising out of a correspondence with Gertrude Hunziker, one of Klages's followers based in Munich,[32] Klages wrote as a kind of appendix included in *Of Cosmogonic Eros* an excursus, also published in various forms as separate articles, entitled 'Why does it Bring Ruin to Lift the Veil of Isis?'.[33] Now the motif of the veil worn by the statue of the Egyptian goddess, Isis, in her temple at Sais in Egypt has been the subject of various analyses by scholars in recent times, including Ernst Gombrich (1909–2001),[34] Jan Assmann's *Das verschleierte Bild zu Sais* (1999),[35] and Pierre Hadot's *Le Voile d'Isis* (2004).[36] (One might also mention the work done on this topic by Rudolf Steiner.)[37] In the nineteenth and twentieth centuries, the motif was treated by the visual arts in various ways, e.g., the statue of a veiled Isis in the Luisium Park in Dessau, the depiction of Isis as veiled goddess with an inscription in French on the pedestal at the Herbert Hoover National Historic Site, or the statue, *Nature Unveiling Herself Before Science* (*La Nature se dévoilant à la Science*), an allegorical work on display in the Musée d'Orsay made in Art Nouveau style in 1899 by Louis-Ernest Barrias (1841–1905). So to return to the question: Why *shouldn't* one lift the veil on the statue of the goddess Isis at Sais?

In answering this question, Klages takes as his starting-point, not the account given by Plutarch of an inscription at the shrine of Neith-Isis-Minerva at Sais in Egypt, 'I am all that hath been, and is, and shall be; and my veil no mortal has hitherto raised',[38] nor even Madame Blavatsky's famous occult work, *Isis Unveiled: A Master-Key to the Mysteries of Ancient and Modern Science and Theology* (1877), but rather a ballad written by Friedrich Schiller in 1795 (and published that year in *Die Horen*), 'The Veiled Image at Sais'.[39] For Klages, this text by Schiller acquires a significance that transcends its literary context—on the one hand, the account of the initiation into the mysteries of Isis in the conclusion of the *Metamorphoses* (or *The Golden Ass*) of Apuleius of Madauros; and, on the other, the famous verses expressing the *Liebstod* from Richard Wagner's *Tristan and Isolde*—and turns it into a moment of genuine insight into the problem of why one should never lift the veil of Isis.

(Although Klages does not mention it, that literary context includes Friedrich von Hardenberg, known as Novalis (1772–1801), who provides the epigram to

Of Cosmogonic Eros, cf. the following aphorism taken from Novalis's *Miscellaneous Sketches*: 'the exterior is an interior elevated into a *mysterious state*';[40] cf. the alternative ending to *The Apprentices of Sais*: 'One was successful—he lifted the veil of the goddess at Sais. / But what did he see? He saw—marvel of marvels—himself.'[41] It is intriguing that Klages chooses as his reference-point not Novalis, the German Romantic poet and thinker, but instead Schiller, a writer associated with the exact opposite of Romanticism—i.e., with classicism.)

According to Schiller's ballad, whoever lifts the veil of the statue of the goddess *sees* the secret of the world. So either the goddess herself is this secret or she possesses the power to make it *visible*. This fact raises another question: to what extent is it *seeing* the mystery that is so ruinous to human beings? To answer this question in the terms that is posed by this Schillerian ballad, Klages turns back to the literature of antiquity. First, he reminds us that the voices of antiquity are unanimous in declaring that the sight of the gods is dangerous for a human being. In the *Argonautica Orphica*, it is said of Artemis-Hecate (another form of Isis) that she is 'terrible for men to see, and terrible to hear, unless one approaches the sacred rites and purification'.[42] And Klages cites from the so-called 'Leidener Weltschöpfung', the text of a Greco-Egyptian initiation ceremony, in which one reads: 'When the god enters, do not look directly at him, but look at your feet.'[43] (Klages associates this with the ban on looking at Yahweh directly in the Hebrew Scriptures.)

Second, as the account found in Apuleius's *Metamorphoses* suggests, the final inititation rite in the (Eleusinian) Mysteries involved the *epopteia* or 'vision' (*Schauung*). As the figure of Lucius in Apuleius's novel puts it, 'I came to the boundary of death and [. . .] I came face to face with the gods below and the gods above and paid reverence to them from close at hand.'[44] From this example, one may conclude that the sight or vision vouchsafed by the Mysteries is not dangerous for everyone, but only for the uninitiated! In turn, this prompts the question: in what did initiation consist?

As Schiller's ballad suggests, no mortal can lift the veil until the goddess herself raises it. In other words, the initiation is something that the individual receives or is given, not something that he or she takes, and it is the goddess herself who grants the initiation. In secret ceremonies across the world, this act of reception is imagined as a 'gamos' or union with the deity, in which the soul of the initiate plays the role of the feminine component. As Klages explains in *Of Cosmogonic Eros* and in his correspondence with Hunziker (known as his 'Mythological Letters'), the sacred marriage signifies a mystical transformation: the visionary takes the god into himself (usually under the form of a ritual meal), becomes the god, and from henceforth the secret is no longer external to him (*SW* 3, 478; *KE*, 213). As the theurgist says in the Egyptian magic papyri, cited by Klages: 'I am Osiris, called the water, I am Isis, called the dew.'[45]

Accordingly, Klages argues, the vision of the secret takes place only because of the becoming-one with the deity, which—in contrast to profane copulation—does not annul the duality of the two poles (*SW* 3, 478; *KE*, 213). The human being can, however, only participate in this vision (and in this union) in a state of extreme *Pathik*, which seemingly involves the extinction of the ego and hence as death. But why, in Schiller's ballad, does the young man *want* to lift the veil? The answer can surely only be: out of the desire to discover or, put simply, out of curiosity. For Klages, both motives derive from a unsettling of the understanding, and the understanding is unsettled by everything that it does not yet *possess*.

On this account, the drive to know is the same as the drive to possess, if only in an intellectual sense. Whoever wishes to investigate the secret of the world has to gain power over the world, as opposed to the initiate, who gives himself up to the world and who is overpowered by it. Thus the intellectual will to gain power is *sacrilege against life*, and this is why the revengeful response of life strikes down the one who commits this sacrilege. In other words, Klages is taking a stand against the rationalistic disenchantment of life.

Having answered the first question (why does it bring ruin to lift the veil?), Klages turns to the second question, namely: what did the youth actually see? Although Schiller shrinks back from depicting what the youth saw, for Klages there can only be one answer to this question: that what the youth saw was, in one go, the truth which presents itself to the inquisitive understanding as the ultimate truth (*SW* 3, 479; *KE*, 214). But what kind of a truth is this? Here we arrive at the heart of Klages's critique of modernity in general and science in particular.

Pursuing scientific inquiry right to the end, into such questions as: what is matter? what is energy? what is the material world? what is the soul?, etc., one realises (or so Klages would have us believe) that all these directions of scientific inquiry end up in nothing, that is, in the projection of the nullity of the intellect itself. For the question for knowledge, Klages argues, can only lead to universal doubt. Hence the will to comprehensible truth is really the will to make the world itself unreal. And so the youth, who with one leap attains his goal—that is, the only goal which the curiosity of the understanding can attain—sees eternal death, the nothingness that consumes all space and time (*den ewigen Tod, das welt- und raumverschlingende Nichts*) (*SW* 3, 479; *KE*, 215)!

Yet how else could the deity of life show itself to him? For, however strange the thought might seem, only the deity can *show* (*zeigen*) itself to a human being. For Klages, the intellect or thinking mind always stands *outside* life, and so for the intellect, nothingness is itself a position and hence identical with everything. Only when it is thrown back from life does this nothingness reveal itself for what it is—as purposelessness, meaninglessness, sterility, destruction, and eternal nullity in every respect. From this perspective, even life itself appears in the guise of a self-destruction that knows neither beginning nor end (*SW* 3, 480; *KE*, 215). In the philosophy of Klages, this perspective is linked to the agent identified as mind, intellect, or *Geist*, as opposed to life itself.

Thus the truth of which Schiller's ballad speaks is the 'the truth of the self-perfecting, i.e., despairing, understanding' (*die Wahrheit des sich vollendenden, das heißt aber des verzweifelnden Verstandes*) (*SW* 3, 480; *KE*, 216), a truth associated by

Klages with the Buddha as well as with Schopenhauer, Lord Byron, or Giacomo Leopardi. It is *this* truth which 'a sacrilegiously infringed life shows to the youth of Sais in the form of a *terrible symbol*', for he sees 'eternal death, eternal meaningless-ness, eternal vanity [*Umsonst*]'—and this is what, in Klages's view, everyone will find who, 'instead of sacrificing it to the deity, chooses as its guide the inquisitive-ness [*Fürzwitz = Vorwitz*] of self-legitimating understanding' (*SW* 3,481; *KE*, 216). (In this respect, there is a good deal of overlap between Klages's analysis and the position of the Frankfurt School with its critique of instrumental reason.)[46]

Now what would such a symbol look like? Klages offers some cultural refer-ence points for his readers, referring to the series of woodcuts by Hans Holbein (1497–1543) called the *Dance of Death* (1538) and to the crucifixion scene in the Isenheimer Altar painted by Matthias Grünewald (*c.* 1470–1528). But the context is ultimately not just cultural but also political and historical: accord-ing to Klages, the millions of lives lost in the First World War might make it easier to understand Grünewald's horrific depiction of the Crucifixion. These works—and these events—can help us to understand why, in the words of Schiller's ballad, 'deep-rooted sorrow / Hurried him fast to an untimely grave' (*Ihn riß ein tiefer Gram zum frühen Grabe*). As Klages summarises the central message of this ballad, 'for anyone who confronts it and tries to understand it intellectually [*geistig erfassend*] reality is not so much tragic as of unthinkable horror—the Gorgon Medusa!' (*SW* 3, 481; *KE*, 217).[47]

Finally, Klages elaborates on 'the particular twist given to the interpretation of the sacrilegiously treated statue of Isis' in *Of Cosmogonic Eros* as follows. What does, he asks, the understanding *do* to everything that it really tries to make its own? The answer, he says, is that it 'counts, weighs, and measures'. And what happens as a consequence to life? It becomes, Klages concludes, 'disenchanted' (*SW* 3, 481; *KE*, 217). Here Klages sounds a major theme of twentieth-century thought, one that resonates in the theme of disenchantment in Max Weber's 'Science as a Vocation' (*Wissenschaft als Beruf*) (1917) and the first chapter of Georg Simmel's *The Philosophy of Money* (*Philosophie des Geldes*) (1907). For Klages, this disenchant-ment has, so to speak, a negative and a positive aspect.

Negatively, it involves a loss of—well, enchantment: 'In myth and for "primi-tive people"', Klages writes, 'in a storm a horde of daimons rides the clouds; for the understanding, it is floating moisture, soullessly and mechanically following the calculable mechanism of the air flows' (*SW* 3, 481; *KE*, 217). (One is tempted to think here of the change in the world-view depicted in another great poem by Schiller, 'The Gods of Greece' (*Die Götter Griechenlands*) (1787, pub. 1788).)[48] Positively, by 'disenchantment', Klages means 'reification' (*verdinglichen*)—and when this happens, the entire world becomes susceptible to strategies of calcula-tion and management: 'Whatever is reified [*verdinglicht*] can be brought into the proximity of the clearest possible vision', and hence 'to grasp' (*begreifen*) and 'to seize' (*erfassen*) are used to express the function of the understanding, while the 'touching' (*Antasten*) of sacred images was used in earlier times to describe an act of sacrilege towards sacred images (*SW* 3, 481; *KE*, 217).

So 'the disenchantment of the world consists in the erasure of *what it contains that is distant*': in the categories of Klagesian thinking, 'human drives are Eros inasmuch as they participate in cosmic Eros', but 'cosmic Eros is *the Eros of distance*' (*SW* 3, 481–482; *KE*, 217).[49] To the extent that the drive to possess negates distance, it kills 'Eros', and 'the nimbus of the world',[50] and ultimately '*reality itself*' (*SW* 3, 482; *KE*, 217). Thus is revealed 'the secret and the bliss-endowing knowledge of the initiate': it is 'to view the sacred image in its distance, even if he merges with it', and Klages recalls the conclusion to Apuleius's *Metamorphoses*: 'in the middle of the night I saw the sun flashing with bright light'.[51]

****

In conclusion, one might feel entitled to ask: what kind of reality is it that Jung and Klages are talking about in their respective conceptions of the archaic and the 'ecstatic'? It is surely significant that, in the case of both thinkers alike, they choose to draw on ancient sources *and* on more recent literary ones (on Nietzsche's *Thus Spoke Zarathustra*, in the case of Jung; on Schiller's ballad, in the case of Klages). What ultimately happened in the Mysteries of Eleusis, in the cult of Isis, or in any of the other ancient mystery cults lies beyond the scope of our discussion here. Yet we might wonder whether, in the case of Jung and Klages alike, we are dealing with the ritual-interpretative equivalent of what Sonu Shamdasani has called a 'biography in books'—is the 'collective unconscious' a kind of 'library within'?[52] Is cosmogonic Eros ultimately product of a kind of textual self-creation?

If it is the case that 'Jung's self-experimentation was largely undertaken while seated in his library', so that while 'Jung's self-investigations marked a turn away from scholarship, his fantasies and his reflections upon them palpably remained those of a scholar', is Klages's conception of the archaic–ecstatic equally a precipitate of his scholarly reading? Or should we turn the proposition around: does Jung—and, by extension, does Klages—show us 'a new understanding of how to read'?[53] Maybe it is no coincidence that when, in §1 of *The Birth of Tragedy*, Nietzsche mentions 'the cry of the Eleusinian mysteries', he refers, not to the Homeric Hymn to Demeter, but to Schiller's 'Ode to Joy': 'Do you prostrate yourselves, millions? Do you sense your Maker, world?'[54] Nietzsche was, of course, not so patently anachronistic as to have believed that, in the celebration of the Mysteries of Eleusis, the initiates recited Schiller; even if one of Schiller's (early) poems is called 'The Eleusinian Festival' (*Das Eleusische Fest*) (1798, pub. 1799).[55] Rather, the fact that Nietzsche quotes from Schiller points to the role played by classical and Romantic literature in providing a form of continuity in our engagement with the great traditions of the past: and to this extent its contribution to ensuring the availability, especially in our modern, postmodern or even post-postmodern times, of a sense of the archaic and the ecstatic.

Finally, one might note the importance for both Jung and Klages of another canonical, 'classical' text—Goethe's *Faust*. There are numerous allusions in *Of Cosmogonic Eros* to *Faust*, and the work closes with a quotation from the Sirens' song that leads to the climactic conclusion at the end of the scene, 'Rocky Inlets of the Aegean Sea', in *Faust*, Part II, Act 2:

> What lights us the billows, what fiery wonder
> Sets blazing their clashes and sparkling asunder?
> It lightens and wavers and brightens the height:
> The bodies, they glow on the courses of night,
> And ringed is the whole by the luminous wall;
> May Eros then reign who engendered it all!
> [*So herrsche denn Eros, der alles begonnen!*][56]

In his commentary on this passage, Cyrus Hamlin observes that, in 'their response to the mystery of Homunculus's self-sacrifice' offered 'in exalted, hymnic tones', the Sirens perceive and describe 'the blending and fusion of opposites'—that is, 'of fire and water, of spirit and substance, of the masculine and feminine'—'through which life is created in the sea'.[57] And, rightly, Hamlin emphasises that *this* Eros is not the daimon celebrated in Plato's dialogue, the *Symposium*, and certainly not the cute, playful Cupid of later mythological tradition, but rather 'a much more ancient, even primal, concept, the original creative force that produces life and light out of chaos'.[58] It is, in other words, a far more Hesiodic, and thus a far more Klagesian, Eros.

Equally, one might recall Jung's comment from his paper on rebirth—made in the context of his extensive discussion of the figure of al-Khidr (i.e., the verdant one) in the *Qu'ran*, Sura 18, 'The Cave'—to the effect that the early scenes with Mephistopheles in *Faust*, Part I, offer us 'a key to our understanding of the highly enigmatic German soul' (§254). And elsewhere, in his writings on the Second World War, Jung repeatedly invokes the figure of Faust.[59] So what will happen today, now that the culture of the ancient Greeks and the Romans is no longer taught, and the mediation of this ancient worldview through the texts of classical and Romantic literature no longer takes place, since their texts, too, are no longer taught? Are the gods, daimons, and other primordial forces that inform and haunt great works of literature dead, or will they find other forms and ways in which to manifest themselves? To paraphrase Nietzsche and Jung, *are the gods dead? Or are they more alive than ever before?*[60]

Taken together, Jung and Klages stand as exponents of the importance of cultivating and nurturing a *cultural memory* (Assmann), and both warn us that, if we do not cultivate this cultural memory, what is not so much repressed as forgotten or excluded can and maybe will return in dangerous forms. For the archaic in general and in its ecstatic form in particular is a striking case of something that is, in the parlance so dear to postmodernism, 'always already' there, and it is something that we, quite literally, ignore at our peril.

Notes

1 For an assessment of and an introduction to the life and thought of Ludwig Klages, see P. Bishop, *Ludwig Klages and the Philosophy of Life: A Vitalist Toolkit*, London and New York: Routledge, 2017.

2 F. Nietzsche, *Thus Spoke Zarathustra*, tr. G. Parkes, Oxford: Oxford University Press, 2005, pp. 240–242.

3 C.G. Jung, 'On Rebirth', in *The Archetypes and the Collective Unconscious [Collected Works*, vol. 9/i], trans. R.F.C. Hull, 2nd edn, Princeton, NJ: Princeton University Press, 1968, §199–§258.

4 Those and other Mysteries formed a reference point for Plotinus in his Ennead, 'The Good or the One' (see *The Essential Plotinus: Representative Treatises from the Enneads*, ed. and tr. Elmer O'Brien, Indianapolis, IN: Hackett, 1964, pp. 72–89): 'Therefore it is so very difficult to describe this vision, for how can we represent as different from us what seemed, while we were contemplating it, not other than ourselves but perfect at-oneness with us? This, doubtless, is what is back of the injunction of the mystery religions which prohibit revelation to the uninitiated. The divine is not expressible, so the initiate is forbidden to speak of it to anyone who has not been fortunate enough to have beheld it himself' (p. 87).

5 Hesiod, *The Homeric Hymns and Homerica*, trans. H.G. Evelyn-White, London: Heinemann; Cambridge, MA: Harvard University Press, 1982, p. 323.

6 I have been unable to identify the source of this epitaph, but Jung also refers to it in his early work, *Transformations and Symbols of the Libido* (1911–1912) (see CW 5 §532), cf. *Psychology of the Unconscious*, tr. B.M. Hinkle, New York: Moffatt, Yard, 1917, p. 378) and on several other occasions; also cited by Ludwig Klages in *Vom kosmogonischen Eros*, end of chapter 6.

7 Jung, 'On Rebirth' (CW 9/i §210). For further discussion of the significance of the Eleusinian Mysteries from a Jungian perspective, see C.G. Jung and C. Kerényi, *Essays on a Science of Mythology: The Myth of the Divine Child and the Mysteries of Eleusis*, tr. R.F.C. Hull, Princeton, NJ: Princeton University Press, 1969. For more recent discussion, see C. Sourvino-Inwood, 'Festival and Mysteries: Aspects of the Eleusinian Cult', in M.B. Cosmopoulos, *Greek Mysteries: The Archaeology and Ritual of Ancient Greek Secret Cults*, London and New York: Routledge, 2003, pp. 25–49; J. Larson, *Ancient Greek Cults: A Guide*, New York and London: Routledge, 2007, chapter 6, 'Mistresses of Grain and Souls: Demeter and Kore/Persephone', pp. 69–85; and H. Bowden, *Mystery Cults in the Ancient World*, London: Thames & Hudson, 2010, pp. 26–48, as well as the synthetic overview in H.P. Foley, 'Background: The Eleusinian Mysteries and Women's Rites for Demeter', in Foley (ed.), *The Homeric 'Hymn to Demeter': Translation, Commentary, and Interpretive Essays*, Princeton, NJ: Princeton University Press, 1994, pp. 65–75.

8 E. Horneffer, *Nietzsches Lehre von der ewigen Wiederkunft und deren bisherige Veröffentlichung*, Leipzig: Naumann, 1900.

9 *Phaedo*, 69d; Plato, *The Collected Dialogues*, ed. E. Hamilton and H. Cairns, Princeton, NJ: Princeton University Press, 1989, p. 52.

10 F. Nietzsche, *Ecce Homo*, 'Why I Am So Wise', §1, in *Ecce Homo: How One Becomes What One Is*, tr. R.J. Hollingdale, Harmondsworth: Penguin, 1979, p. 38.

11 For a thoroughgoing interpretation from a Jungian standpoint of Nietzsche's entire life, which reads this statement as 'the riddle that enclosed the enigma of his own fatality' and as 'evidenc[ing] the orphic paradox of being trapped between the dead and the living', see G. Ostfeld de Bendayan, *Ecce Mulier: Nietzsche and the Eternal Feminine: An Analytical Psychological Perspective*, Wilmette, IL: Chiron, 2007, p. 138.

12 F. Nietzsche, 'What I Owe to the Ancients', §4; in *Twilight of the Idols; The Anti-Christ*, tr. R.J. Hollingdale, Harmondsworth: Penguin, 1968, pp. 110–111; my emphasis. For further discussion, see R. Pfeffer, *Nietzsche: Disciple of Dionysus*, Lewisburg, PA: Bucknell University Press, 1972.

13 F. Nietzsche, *Twilight of the Idols*, 'What I Owe to the Ancients', §4, in *Twilight of the Idols*, p. 108; my emphasis.

14 'What I Owe to the Ancients', §4, in Nietzsche, *Twilight of the Idols*, p. 109; and F. Nietzsche, *The Anti-Christ, Ecce Homo, Twilight of the Idols and Other Writings*, ed. A. Ridley and J. Norman, tr. J. Norman, Cambridge: Cambridge University Press, 2005, pp. 227–228.

15 'What I Owe to the Ancients', §4, in Nietzsche, *Twilight of the Idols*, p. 110.

16 F. Nietzsche, *The Gay Science*, §337, 'The "humaneness" of the future', in *The Gay Science: With a Prelude in German Rhymes and an Appendix of Songs*, ed. B Williams, tr. J. Nauckhoff and A. del Caro, Cambridge: Cambridge University Press, 2001, pp. 190–191; *The Gay Science: With a Prelude in Rhymes and an Appendix of Songs*, ed. and tr. W. Kaufmann, New York: Vintage, 1974, pp. 268–269.

17 For an overview of the Cosmic Circle, see P. Bishop, 'Stefan George and the Munich Cosmologists', in J. Rieckmann (ed.), *A Companion to the Work of Stefan George*, Rochester, NY, and Woodbridge: Camden House, 2005, pp. 161–187.

18 L. Klages, *Vom kosmogonischen Eros*, 2nd edn, Jena: Diederichs, 1926 (henceforth referred to as *KE*). Also cited here from the following edition: L. Klages, *Sämtliche Werke*, ed. E. Frauchinger et al., 9 vols, Bonn: Bouvier, 1964–1992, vol. 3, *Philosophische Schriften*, pp. 353–497 (henceforth referred to as *SW*).

19 L. Klages, *Rhythmen und Runen: Nachlaß herausgegeben von ihm selbst*, Leipzig: Barth, 1944; *SW* 3, 155–238; and *SW*, vols 1 and 2.

20 For further discussion, see R. J. Kozljanič, 'Die Formen der Ekstase bei Klages und in der Antike', *Hestia: Jahrbuch der Klages-Gesellschaft* 21, 2002/2003, 67–84.

21 For further discussion, see the section entitled 'The Carrier of Consciousness' in *On the Nature of Consciousness* (1921), in *SW* 3, 267–274.

22 In his writings Jung repeatedly refers to the idea of *Ergriffenheit*, i.e., being 'seized', 'gripped', or 'caught', sometimes but not always in a political context, as in his essay on 'Wotan' (1936). Here Jung wrote that what was happening in Germany in the 1930s could be summed up as *Ergriffenheit*, a term which postulates 'not only an *Ergriffener* (one who is seized) but also an *Ergreifer* (one who seizes)', and he identified Wotan as 'an *Ergreifer* of men' (Jung, 'Wotan', in *Civilization in Transition* [*Collected Works*, vol. 10], tr. R. F. C. Hull, Princeton, NJ: Princeton University Press, 1968, §371–§399 [§386]). For further discussion, see P. Bishop, *The Dionysian Self: C. G. Jung's Reception of Friedrich Nietzsche*, Berlin and New York: de Gruyter, 1995, chapter 12, 'Jung's Reception of Nietzsche in his Writings 1935–1945: Wotan—The Shadow of Dionysos', pp. 298–322; and, more recently (and more critically), C. B. Dohe, *Jung's Wandering Archetype: Race and Religion in Analytical Psychology*, London and New York: Routledge, 2016, chapter 6, 'Wotan and "the Archetypal *Ergriffenheit*"', pp. 159–191. For his part, Klages uses the notion in a social or cultic-cum-ritual, rather than a political, context when in *Of Cosmogonic Eros* he writes: 'In an orgiastically aroused crowd a psychological contagion is without doubt spread around which can penetrate and eventually threatens to overpower even the coolest observer. Anyone who is gripped in this way [*der solcherart Ergriffene*] stands with each of the others who have been gripped [*jedem der übrigen Ergriffenen*] in the same medium; even if *what* turns him upside down, crushes him, transports him into ecstasies, is not something he shares at all with the others' experience of being crushed!' (*SW* 3, 400; *KE*, 79–80).

23 This passage is also quoted by Freud in one of his great case-studies, his analysis of Schreber; see 'Psychoanalytic Notes on an Autobiographical Account of a Case of Paranoia (Dementia paranoides)' [1911], in *Case Histories II*, tr. James Strachey, ed. Angela Richards, Harmondsworth: Penguin, 1979, pp. 131–223 (p. 203).

24 See Synesius, *Dio*, 10.48a, citing Aristotle: 'As Aristotle claims that those who are being initiated into the mysteries are to be expected not to learn anything but to suffer some change, to be put into a certain condition, i.e., to be fitted for some purpose' (*The Works of Aristotle*, ed. D. Ross, vol. 12, *Select Fragments*, Oxford: Clarendon Press, 1952, 'Fragments on Philosophy', no. 15, p. 87; cf. Synesius of Cyrene, *The Essays and Hymns*, tr. A. Fitzgerald, 2 vols, Oxford: Oxford University Press; London: Humphrey Milford, 1930, vol. 1, p. 163). For further discussion, see W. Burkert, *Greek Religion: Archaic and*

Classical [*Griechische Religion der archaischen und klassischen Epoche*] [1977], tr. J. Raffan, Oxford: Basil Blackwell, 1985, p. 286: 'Aristotle states, however, that the important thing was not to learn anything but to suffer or experience (*pathein*) and to be brought into the appropriate state of mind through the proceedings.'

25 For further discussion, see J. Larson, *Understanding Greek Religion: A Cognitive Approach*, London and New York: Routledge, 2016, pp. 269–273.

26 P. Boyancé, 'Sur les mystères d'Eleusis', *Revue des Études grecques* 75, 1962, 460–482.

27 For all these sources, see Foley, 'Background: The Eleusinian Mysteries and Women's Rites for Demeter', in *The Homeric 'Hymn to Demeter'*, pp. 69–70.

28 In a text from 1902 that formed part of his unpublished correspondence with Franziska zu Reventlow, Klages emphasised that Eros is 'not beautiful, blind, animal lust', which 'merely nourishes him'; rather, Eros is 'lust which at the same time can *see*' (*die Wollust, die zugleich sehend ist*). 'Whoever is overcome by Eros-Dionysos is a daimon, even while yet remaining a human being. He sees through the shadow body of things into the flaming night of the images. He himself is destiny, is Gorgonian dread. The streams of the earth, the storms of the heavens, the paths of the stars are *in* him and his power reaches beyond Saturn's orbit' (*Rhythmen und Runen*, p. 523).

29 There are notable parallels between Klages's description of the *gamos* and the experiences transcribed by Jung in his *Red Book*, especially the chapters 'The Conception of the God' and 'Mysterium Encounter' in *Liber primus*, and 'The Opening of the Egg' in *Liber secundus*; see C.G. Jung, *The Red Book: Liber novus*, ed. S. Shamdasani, tr. M. Kyburz, J. Peck, and S. Shamdasani, New York and London: Norton, 2009, pp. 242–245, 245–248 and 286–288.

30 Derived from the Greek words *idios* = 'one's own' and *pathos* = 'suffering', an idiopathy is literally 'a disease of its own kind', i.e., a disease of apparently spontaneous origin or whose pathogenesis is at any rate unknown. Here it would seem that the force of Klages's distinction is between an ecstasy that arises spontaneously within an individual and an ecstasy that arises in relation to another being.

31 On several occasions Nietzsche refers to the 'riddle of the world' (*Welträtsel*), and in 1899 Ernst Haeckel published *Die Welträthsel: Gemeinverständliche Studien über Monistische Philosophie*, Bonn: Emil Strauß, 1899; translated into English as *The Riddle of the Universe*, 1901.

32 H.E. Schröder, *Ludwig Klages 1872–1956: Centenar-Ausstellung 1972*, Bonn: Grundmann, 1982, pp. 71–72. See also H.E. Schröder, *Ludwig Klages: Die Geschichte seines Lebens*, vol. 2/1, *Das Werk (1905–1920)*, Bonn: Bouvier, 1996, pp. 860, 870, and 901.

33 See 'Der Schleier der Isis', in *Der neue Merkur* 6, 1924, 42–50; 'Das verschleierte Isisbild', in *Magische Blätter: Mitteilungen über praktische Geheimwissenschaften* 8, 1924, 240–248; and 'Warum bringt es Verderben, den Schleier des Isisbildes zu heben?', in *Didaskalia: Beilage der Frankurter Nachrichten*, 30 November 1924.

34 E.H. Gombrich, 'The Symbol of the Veil: Psychological Reflections on Schiller's Poetry', in P. Horden (ed.), *Freud and the Humanities*, London: Duckworth, 1985, pp. 75–109.

35 J. Assmann, *Das verschleierte Bild zu Sais: Schillers Ballade und ihre griechischen und ägyptischen Hintergründe*, Stuttgart and Leipzig: Teubner, 1999.

36 P. Hadot, *Le Voile d'Isis: Essai sur l'histoire de l'idée de Nature*, Paris: Gallimard, 2004; *The Veil of Isis: An Essay on the History of the Idea of Nature*, tr. M. Chase, Cambridge, MA, and London: Belknap Press of Harvard University Press, 2006.

37 See Rudolf Steiner, *Aus der Akasha-Forschung: Das Fünfte Evangelium* [1913–1914] [= *Gesamtausgabe*, vol. 148], Dornach/Schweiz: Rudolf Steiner Verlag, 1992, pp. 165–169; and *Innere Entwicklungsimpulse der Menschheit: Goethe und die Krisis des neunzehnten Jahrhunderts* [1916] [= *Gesamtausgabe*, vol. 171], Dornach/Schweiz: Rudolf Steiner Verlag, 1984, pp. 166–167 and 192–193.

38 See Plutarch, 'Isis and Osiris', §9, 354c: 'In Saïs the statue of Athena, whom they believe to be Isis, bore the inscription: "I am all that has been, and is, and shall be, and my robe no mortal has yet uncovered"' (Plutarch, *Moralia*, vol. 5, tr. F.C. Babbitt, Cambridge, MA, and

London: Harvard University Press, 1936, p. 24). Schiller also refers to this passage in his essay 'Of the Sublime' (1793), where he writes: 'All that is wrapped up and full of mystery contributes to fright, and therefore is susceptible to sublimity. Of this kind is the inscription that could be read at Sais in Egypt, on the temple of Isis: "I am all that has been, that is, and all that shall be; no mortal has yet raised my veil"' (Schiller, *Werke: Nationalausgabe*, ed. J. Petersen and G. Fricke, N. Oellers and S. Seidel, im Auftrage des Goethe- und Schiller-Archivs, des Schiller-Nationalmuseums und der Deutschen Akademie, 43 vols, Weimar: Hermann Böhlaus Nachfolger, 1943ff., vol. 20, pp. 171–195 (p. 191), translated in Hadot, *The Veil of Isis*, p. 278).

39 See 'Das verschleierte Bild zu Sais', in F. Schiller, *Sämtliche Gedichte und Balladen*, ed. G. Kurscheidt, Frankfurt am Main and Leipzig: Insel, 2004 pp. 187–189. For translations, see 'The Veiled Image at Sais', *The Poems and Ballads of Schiller*, tr. E.B. Lytton, 2 vols, Edinburgh and London: Blackwood, 1844, vol. 1, pp. 66–69; and *The Minor Poems of Schiller of the Second and Third Periods*, tr. J.H. Merivale, London: Pickering, 1844, pp. 128–131.

40 Novalis, 'Das allgemeine Brouillon', §295; in *Werke, Tagebücher und Briefe*, Bd. 2, *Das philosophisch-theoretische Werk*, ed. H.-J. Mähl, Munich: Hanser, 1978, p. 527.

41 Translated in R. Cardinal, *German Romantics in Context*, London: Studio Vista, 1975, p. 35; see Novalis, *Werke und Briefe in einem Band*, ed. A. Kelletat, Munich: Winkler, 1968, p. 139.

42 *Argonautica Orphica*, trans. Jason Colavito. Available online from: www.argonauts-book. com/orphic-argonautica.html. Accessed 30 December 2015.

43 *Abrasax: Ausgewählte Papyri religiösen und magischen Inhalts*, vol. 5, *Traumtexte*, ed. R. Merkelbach, Wiesbaden: Springer, 2001, p. 26; cf. *Abrasax: Ausgewählte Papyri religiösen und magischen Inhalts*, vol. 3, *Zwei griechisch-ägyptische Weihezeremonien (die Leidener Weltschöpfung; die Pschaei-Aion-Liturgie* [*Papyrologica Coloniensa*, 18.3], Opladen: Westdeutscher Verlag, 1992.

44 Apuleius, *Metamorphoses*, book 11, p. 341; *in Metamorphoses: Books VII–XI*, ed. and tr. J. Arthur Hanson, Cambridge, MA, and London: Harvard University Press, 1989, p. 341.

45 C. Leemans (ed.), *Papyri Graeci Musei Antiquarii Publici Lugdini-Batavi*, vol. 2, Leiden: Lugduni Batavorum; Brill, 1843, pp. 26–27. For further discussion, see S. Feist, 'Die religionsgeschichtliche Bedeutung des ältesten Runeninschriften', *Journal of English and Germanic Philology* 21 (4), October 1922, 601–611 (p. 610).

46 For further discussion of the parallels between Klagesian thought and critical theory, see G. Stauth, 'Critical Theory and Pre-Fascist Social Thought', *History of European Ideas* 18 (5), 1994, 711–727; G. Stauth and B.S. Turner, 'Ludwig Klages (1872–1956) and the Origins of Critical Theory', *Theory, Culture and Society* 9 (3), August 1992, 45–63; A. Honneth, '"L'esprit et son objet": Parentés anthropologiques entre la "Dialectique de la raison" et la critique de la civilisation dans la philosophie de la vie', in G. Raulet (ed.), *Weimar ou l'explosion de la modernité: Actes du colloque 'Weimar ou la modernité'*, Paris: Anthropos, 1984, pp. 97–111; and M. Großheim, '"Die namenlose Dummheit, die das Resultat des Fortschritts ist": Lebensphilosophische und dialektitische Kritik der Moderne', *Logos: Zeitschrift für systematische Philosophie* 3 (2), 1996, 97–133.

47 See Freud's essay 'Medusa's Head' (1922), published posthumously (S. Freud, *Writings on Art and Literature*, Stanford, CA: Stanford University Press, 1997, pp. 264–265). The original manuscript dated 14 May 1922 appears to be a preliminary sketch for a much larger work. In this short paper, Freud links the gaze of the Medusa with the fear aroused in the young boy on seeing the female genitalia and thus developing the castration complex.

48 Schiller, *Sämtliche Gedichte*, pp. 220–225 and 124–127; *Minor Poems*, pp. 16–21. For the most recent discussion of this poem, see S. Lyons, 'The Disenchantment/Re-enchantment of the World: Aesthetics, Secularization, and the Gods of Greece from Friedrich Schiller to Walter Pater', *Modern Language Review* 109 (4), October 2014, 873–895.

49 In *Of Cosmognic Eros*, Eros is 'cosmic' or 'elementary', inasmuch as 'the individual being gripped by it experiences itself as pulsating and throbbing as if with an electric current

which, similar in nature to magnetism, allows the most distant souls irrespective of their limitations to feel each other in a connecting pull, itself the means of everything that happens to separate bodies, transforms time and space into the omnipresent element of an embracing ocean washing around and joins together the *poles of the world* in such a way as to leave untouched their irreducible difference' (*SW* 3, 387; *KE*, 58). And it is 'cosmogonic' inasmuch as it is 'a state of plenitude that pours forth from itself, in such a way that what is internal—immediately giving birth to itself—in a trice becomes something external, world, and phenomenal reality' (*SW* 3, 387–388; *KE*, 58). As Klages explained in *Of Cosmogonic Eros*, the view that Eros could be *cosmogonic* (literally, 'world-creating') can be traced back in part to Hesiod and in part to the Orphic cult. Its doctrines taught how, 'out of the aether and the unfathomable void', Chronos fashioned 'the silver world-egg', from which there emerged 'the shining god Phanes-Eros-Dionysos', hermaphroditic in aspect and bearing within him the seeds of all other deities (*SW* 3, 376; *KE*, 36; cf. L. Klages, *Cosmogonic Reflections: Selected Aphorisms from Ludwig Klages*, tr. J.D. Pryce, London: Arktos, 2015, p. 70). Compare with the passage from Klages's correspondence with Franziska zu Reventlow (*Rhythmen und Runen*, p. 523), cited above, as well as with the early aphorisms 'Sexual drive and Eros' (*Rhythmen und Runen*, pp. 348–349)—'Eros lives in the world of images; he snatches everything his fire melts away from temporality; he makes it eternal and deifies it. Sexuality lives in the world of things and, if aroused by Eros, it deifies objects' (p. 349)—and the second appendix added to *Of Cosmogonic Eros*'s second edition in 1926, 'On Sexus and Eros' (*SW* 3, 483–490; *KE*, 218–227): 'We can compare sexuality to the harsh light of a shining electric wire, but Eros to the opalescence of the frosted glass that surrounds it, and erotic vitality to an elegant lamp that casts its light as an equally dispersed illumination' (*SW* 3, 490; *KE*, 226) (cf. *Cosmogonic Reflections*, pp. 16 and 79). Evidently, then, Eros is about much more than sex … In 1929, the physician and sexologist Felix A. Theilhaber (1884–1956) published a major study of Goethe in relation to these two categories, see *Goethe: Sexus und Eros*, Berlin-Grunewald: Horen-Verlag, 1929.

50 For the Klagesian notion of the nimbus, see *The Spirit as Enemy of the Soul* (*SW* 2, 844). For a discussion of the notion of 'nimbus' in the work of Klages, see G. Moretti, 'Nimbus: Nota sulla questione dell' "aura" in Ludwig Klages', *Rivista di Estetica* 53 (1), 2013, 149–159.

51 Apuleius, *Metamorphoses*, book 11, §23; in *Metamorphoses: Books VII–XI*, p. 341.

52 S. Shamdasani, *C.G. Jung: A Biography in Books*, New York and London: Norton, 2012, p. 49.

53 Shamdasani, *C.G. Jung: A Biography in Books*, pp. 90 and 83.

54 F. Nietzsche, *Basic Writings*, ed. and tr. W. Kaufmann, New York: Modern Library, 1968, p. 38.

55 Thanks to Wilhelm von Humboldt (1767–1835), we know that 'The Eleusinian Festival' picks up one of Schiller's favourite ideas, namely, 'the formation of the crude, natural individual by means of culture and art': 'Even on the beginnings of civilization itself, the transition from nomadic life to agriculture, on—as he so beautifully expressed it—the trustingly undertaken alliance with the devout, maternal earth, is where his fantasy would by preference linger. What mythology had to offer in relation to this, he keenly fixed on: remaining true to the traces of the fable, he represented Demeter, the main figure in this context, by allowing human feelings to divine ones in her breast, as a correspondingly wondrous phenomenon that moves one deeply' (Wilhelm von Humboldt, 'On Schiller and the Path of His Intellectual Development' [1830], in *Werke in fünf Bänden*, ed. Andreas Flitner and Klaus Giel, vol. 2, Stuttgart: Wissenschaftliche Buchgesellschaft, 1961, pp. 357–394 [pp. 372–373]).

56 *Faust II*, ll. 8474–8479; in J.W. von Goethe, *Faust: A Tragedy*, ed. C. Hamlin, tr. W. Arndt, 2nd edn, New York and London: Norton, 2001, pp. 239–240.

57 Goethe, *Faust*, ed. Hamlin, p. 239, note 7.

58 Goethe, *Faust*, ed. Hamlin, p. 239, note 8.

59 See Bishop, *The Dionysian Self*, pp. 315–322, for discussion of the context to such remarks by Jung as the following: 'Faust never attains the character of reality: he is not a real human being and cannot become one (at least not in this world). He remains the German idea of a human being, and therefore an image—somewhat overdone and distorted—of the average German' ('After the Catastrophe'; CW 10 §423). Intriguingly, in this essay Jung also invokes Klages when he writes that the Faustian condition arises from an 'inner contradiction and dichotomy' from which arises 'his longing of "hungering for the infinite" [...], that "Eros of distance" [*"Eros der Ferne"*], that eschatological expectation of great fulfilment' (CW 10 §423).

60 See Nietzsche, *The Gay Science*, §125: 'God is dead. God remains dead. And we have killed him' (*The Gay Science*, ed. and tr. W. Kaufmann, New York: Random House, 1974), p. 181; and Jung, *The Red Book*, 'Scrutinies': 'God is not dead. He is as alive as ever' (Jung, *Red Book*, p. 348).

6

ECSTATIC ATOMS

The question of Oresteian individuation

Ben Pestell

The archaic mind may be broadly described as one which is at home to the sorts of dualities which confuse the modern mind. This is intimated by the paradoxical qualities of 'primal words', and the porous boundaries between personal and external agency.[1] Such dualities, oppositions, or contradictions find form in myth, tragedy, and analysis.[2] Combining these forms, the mythic drama of Aeschylus's Oresteian tragedy anticipates much that appears in Jung's work, notably the theory of individuation. This coincidence of tragedy and individuation suggests a new opposition, namely that between the selfhood of the individuated subject and the loss of self in drama's communal *ekstasis*. Can this be reconciled? To address this, I consider the roles of actor, character and audience, and the interaction between them. Naturally, this question of ecstatic individuation invokes the spirit of Nietzsche's Dionysian and Apollonian, but I proceed without recourse to Nietzsche's work (which is viewed sceptically by classicists), to focus instead on mediation between Jung and classical scholarship, and the role of individual in society.

Tragedy explores themes which are at once specific and universal. This assertion has been a mainstay of criticism since Aristotle, who held that poetry gave consideration to general statements as expressed through individual characters.[3] Witness Oedipus, whose private pollution despoils his land, and who was an exemplary individual figure for Aristotle in a dramatic medium which evokes collective catharsis. Twenty-three centuries later, Oedipus re-emerged as the mythical figure whose personal misfortune stood, for Freud, for universal male sexual anxiety. Tragic drama is a pre-eminent artistic form for performing and revealing the practical connections between individual and society, and between psychic and material life.

The *Oresteia* is the only surviving complete trilogy of Greek tragedy, comprising the plays *Agamemnon*, *Choephoroi* (or *Libation Bearers*), and *Eumenides*. It relates the events following the victorious return of Agamemnon the king to Argos from the decade-long war at Troy. The drama is filled with murder. The focus is the House of Atreus, and its attendant curse, which stemmed from the grievous rancour between brothers Thyestes and Atreus. Thyestes slept with Aërope, Atreus's wife, and, in revenge, Atreus arranged for his brother a feast of Thyestes' own children. When the truth of the meal is revealed, Thyestes, vomiting, declaims a fast-clinging curse on the family line. The bloodshed continues. We hear that Atreus's son, Agamemnon, before he set out to Troy, sacrificed his daughter, Iphigeneia, to the goddess Artemis for the winds to permit his fleet to sail to Troy, and release them from their harbour-bound decline. This becomes the principal (though not exclusive) motivation for Agamemnon's own death at the hands of his wife, Clytemnestra, upon his return home. Clytemnestra, in turn, is killed by their son, Orestes. The end to the cycle of vengeance is brought about by a court case presided over by Athena, in which Apollo stands as advocate for Orestes against the archaic goddesses the Erinyes (Furies). The *Oresteia* ends with Orestes' absolution, and with the salvation of Athens from the Erinyes' destructive threats. The drama initially presented these two outcomes as mutually exclusive, but the opposed outcomes are achieved by Athena's persuasive technique which prefigures the talking cure of analysis, and establishes both individual (Orestes) and community (Athens) on a path analogous to individuation.

I suggest that Orestes is the crucial figure in Greek tragedy for the healthy mind in general, and for individuation in particular. I approach his trilogy from three related perspectives. First I assess the extent to which we can discuss tragic protagonists as individual characters, with reference to the long-established distinction of the operation of character (*ēthos*) and divinity (*daimon*) as motivating the protagonists' actions. I argue that this is consistent with Jung's view of archaic thought, and that Orestes represents the possibility of overcoming the undue influence of unconscious or divine impressions. This leads to the second part of the chapter, which considers prior symbolic interpretations of *Eumenides* and its resolution of opposed forces, particularly with regard to Jungian individuation. The character of Orestes fades from the play, and the focus shifts to the city of Athens, so, in the third part, building on an example from a recent production of the *Oresteia*, I evaluate the scope for tragedy as bridging divisions between individual and society, thus extending personal individuation to the collective sphere. I conclude with an affirmation of the activity of archaic thought in the present, and of the transformational power of the artwork.

Tragic protagonists: character and divinity

Tragedy is an art form of excess. Its protagonists are amplified, flawed heroes. In terms of psychology, we can allegorise their plots as 'complexes'.[4] But what of the psychology of tragic characters themselves? Are they pure expressions of force and affect? Or are they conceived as individuals with realistic inner lives? In the *Oresteia*'s three murderers (Agamemnon, Clytemnestra, and Orestes), we have strong examples of how motivation is driven by both one's character and also by something impersonal—the gods.

Despite the attention paid in the *Poetics* to the position of tragic protagonists, Aristotle was not concerned with the psychological subject. Instead, his view is that tragedy is 'a *mimēsis* not of people but of their actions and life', and consequently the depiction of character (*ēthos*) and intellect (*dianoia*) over action (*praxis*) would not result in as successful a tragic drama.[5] The emphasis on *praxis* supports the view of tragedy as the instrumentalisation of symbols, forces, and emotions in the body of the characters. Contrary to this, however, much recent criticism in classical studies has charged Aristotle with neglecting the chorus and the collective nature of tragedy, and thereby over-emphasising the individual. Summarising the criticisms, Miriam Leonard observes, 'The problem with Aristotle is not just that he reduces the significance of the choral voice within the tragedies themselves but that, through the concept of *catharsis*, he posits the individual psyche as the natural receptacle of tragic angst.'[6] Aristotle's critics thus see in the *Poetics* a problematic neglect of the social sphere, both off the stage and on. The famous complaint that the text omits any explanation of *katharsis* does not help his cause. As such, we risk perceiving tragedy as the action of atomised individuals performed in the presence of an audience of atomised individuals who experience *katharsis* as a personal, private, and non-social purgation.

This is not, however, the inevitable consequence of reading Aristotle, and Leonard credits his individualist focus with enabling the existential tragic interpretations of German idealism. As Leonard observes, both Schelling and Hegel locate 'the *real* "performance" of tragedy not in the action on the stage but in the abstract interaction of metaphysical forces'.[7] This reading abstracts the *praxis* yet further from the body of the protagonist: where Aristotle focuses on the general sweep of the hero's action rather than the nuances betrayed in speech, the idealist view regards—in the combination of *praxis*, *dianoia*, and *ethos*—the swelling and surging of cosmic ideas and powers. Hegel states this distinctly:

> The chief conflict treated most beautifully by Sophocles, with Aeschylus as his predecessor, is that between the state, i.e. ethical life in its spiritual universality, and the family, i.e. natural ethical life. These are the clearest powers that are presented in tragedy, because the full reality of ethical existence consists in harmony between these two spheres and in absence of discord between what an agent has actually to do in one and what he has to do in the other.[8]

Here we may agree with Leonard's rebuttal of the criticisms of Aristotle, seeing, with Hegel, that rather than inspiring asocial introspection, the individualised response to tragedy promotes deep reflection on ethical life and on the conflicting demands of social existence. Furthermore, Hegel underscores the essential dualistic *agōn* of the tragic structure. Schelling sees a similar symbolic abstraction in the focus on the tragic hero:

Necessity and freedom, inasmuch as they are universal concepts, must in art necessarily appear symbolically. Since only human nature is subjected to necessity on the one hand, yet capable of freedom on the other, both concepts must be symbolized in and through that human nature, which itself must be represented by individuals who—as just such natures in which freedom and necessity are bound to one another—are called persons.[9]

Schelling appears to say to Aristotle's twenty-first-century critics that to see only individuals on the stage is to ignore the immense symbolic weight of mythology. Of course, one may further argue that Aristotle himself, in his fourth-century logocentric way, was rather blind to mythic symbolism. Schelling, however, was deeply sympathetic to the tautegoric truth of the mythological artwork.[10] Joshua Billings notes that Schelling, in common with Hegel and Hölderlin, maintained an interest in myth as 'negotiating a relationship with the divine [. . .]. Mythology's representation of divinity in corporeal form achieves an interpenetration of universal and particular, and so forms the bridge between the absolute and the world of sense'.[11] Following Schelling, one may regard tragic protagonists as personifications of forces—comparable to the action of divinity. The extreme action of tragic characters can be seen to justify this. Antigone and Creon, in Hegel's example, give full vent to the irreconcilable extremity of their respective positions, summarised—albeit reductively—as family against the state (although divinity lends authority to both sides as a complicating factor). The clash, or *agōn*, has the same sublime affect as crunching continental plates. Individuals they may appear to be, but they act on a colossal scale.

For Hegel, harmony between conflicting spheres is a precondition of ethical existence. The *Oresteia*, over the course of its three plays, dramatises the symbolic conflict, played out by monstrously amplified characters, until its harmonisation. In the *Oresteia*, Agamemnon's monstrousness is epitomised by his sacrifice of his daughter; Clytemnestra's by her erotic exulting in Agamemnon's spurting blood (*Ag.* 1388–1392). As such, it is tempting to regard them less as portrayals of humans in all their emotional and psychological complexity, and more as monumental embodiments of force and feeling.

Nevertheless, depth psychological responses to the *Oresteia* have fruitfully examined individual characters and the psychology of the play itself as a prescient dramatisation of psychic life. George Devereux holds that the dreams in Greek tragedy are 'authentically dream-like', and suggests that Menelaus' dream (*Ag.* 410–426) 'is practically an epitome of Freud's great study *Mourning and Melancholia* [. . .]. There are few passages in the world's treasury of poetry which confirm so well Freud's repeated assertion that the poets had *intuitively* anticipated much of his work.'[12] Thus, despite the seeming monstrousness of the *Oresteia*'s characters, they lend themselves to psychological study, to the extent that Melanie Klein was able to provide coherent judgements of their behaviour. She deduces that Agamemnon's 'successes not only satisfied his *hubris*; they increased it and led to a hardening and *deterioration of his character* [. . .] Agamemnon reporting his triumphs and the destruction of Troy seems neither lovable nor able to love.'[13] Similarly, she describes Clytemnestra's deterioration as follows: 'early hate and grievances, stirred up by external situations, reawaken destructive impulses; they come to predominate over loving ones, and this involves a change in the states of fusion between life and death instincts.'[14] Klein coherently, if somewhat abstractly, accounts for Clytemnestra's seeming neglect of her other children, Orestes and Electra. In Klein's view, Aeschylus' dramatisation of this mythical plot is true to human psychic life. Moreover, the process of the trilogy represents, for Klein, the establishment of internal peace, with Athena characterised as the 'mature super-ego'. The goddess's casting vote integrates a divided self. Klein affirms, 'In Aeschylus this state of mind is shown by the songs of joy with which the Trilogy ends.'[15] For Klein, then, the *Oresteia* is not only psychologically coherent, it also accurately parallels a successful process of analysis.

If, following this necessarily brief survey, we accept that the conclusions of Hegel and Schelling, and those of Klein and Devereux are not mutually exclusive, we must accept that the well-drawn tragic protagonist therefore embodies a balance between a believable psychological life and the transgressive, sublime force of nightmarish amplifications of reality. The tragic hero is never just an individual, but is also the representation of a network of symbols. The distinction between the transcendent power recognised by German idealists and the inner life uncovered by depth psychology is best translated into Greek terms as a balance between *daimon* and *ēthos*. Jean-Pierre Vernant expresses the balance: 'All that the hero feels, says and does springs from his character, his *ēthos* [. . .]. But at the same time these feelings, pronouncements, and actions also appear as the expression of a religious power, a *daimōn* operating through them.'[16] In the world of tragedy, the hero never acts solely by intellect.

An appreciation of these depersonalising forces is essential to understanding the actions of the tragic figures. Witness Agamemnon's state of mind at the moment of his sacrifice of Iphigeneia, as described by the Argive elders: the Greek word is *parakopē*, commonly translated as 'madness' (Thomson), 'derangement' (Collard), or 'frenzy' (Fagles), but literally, 'struck aside'.[17] The action implies a striker and a victim, and thus presumes the agency of a god who commits the strike.[18] As we speak of those who are 'touched' with madness, the idea of losing one's wits as a condition inflicted from preternatural forces retains popular currency. Vernant acknowledges the similarity of *parakopē* to *atē*, 'the religious power sent by the gods to mislead men and bring them to their doom'.[19] This is the ruin which the Agamemnon of the *Iliad* invokes to explain his quarrel with Achilles. In the *Iliad*, Agamemnon blames Zeus, Moira (Fate), and the Erinyes for sending the *atē* which in turn caused him to provoke Achilles' rage (XIX.86–95). E.R. Dodds notes:

> Had he acted of his own volition, he could not so easily admit himself in the wrong; as it is, he will pay for his acts. Juridically, his position would be the same in either case; for early Greek justice cared nothing for intent—it was the act that mattered.[20]

Dodds's assessment echoes Aristotle's emphasis on tragic *praxis* over *dianoia*. This is not to say that protagonists cannot be held accountable for their actions—indeed, the operation of inherited guilt means that they are often also held accountable for others' actions—but that there is a constant sense of the ineffable divine directing the most lamentable course through life.

Conversely, John J. Peradotto contends that Agamemnon's assent to sacrifice his daughter depends

> less upon Zeus or Artemis than upon the kind of man he is, his ethos [. . .] Agamemnon has inherited his father's predatory and teknophonous ethos, an ethos incidentally which is quite consistent with the portrayal of Agamemnon in the literary tradition.[21]

Agamemnon lets the sacrificial frenzy in: he effectively invites the strike. Like the party-goer who never refuses a refill, Agamemnon welcomes intoxication. As Bernard Williams says of this scene,

> we might see the rage as something that was necessary to Agamemnon if he was to do this thing at all. This is not a text that invites us very far into psychological interpretation, but still less does it beckon us towards blame.[22]

He is at once responsible for, and the victim of, his madness: acting as he is acted upon. And yet it could not be otherwise.

A confusion of divine and mortal agency is suggested by the last reported speech from Agamemnon in the Chorus's account. The imagery partakes wholly of the wind. The Chorus tells us that before he is 'struck aside' and commits the sacrifice, he says, εὖ γὰρ εἴη: 'May all be well.'[23] It is a short sentence, a curt, hopeful, but grimly ironic prayer, consisting mainly of vowels but for a velar—the gamma, a soft consonant voiced at the back of the throat—and the trilling rho. So Agamemnon's last reported words before the sacrifice are breathy, like the *tuchē* (fortune) he blows with (συμπνέων, *Ag.* 187), and the winds he intends to change. In the next strophe the Chorus tells us of the *parakopē* and Agamemnon's impure, unholy 'mental wind' (φρενὸς πνέων, *Ag.* 219). He is struck aside, but one could believe that he wills it. His *ēthos* enables the *daimon*, his personal action embodies a divine will. He stands in the wind and blows with it.

Agamemnon's state of mind is echoed by C.G. Jung's comments on thought in archaic people: 'the primitive does not think *consciously*, but [. . .] thoughts *appear*. The primitive cannot assert that he thinks; it is rather that "something thinks in him."' Moreover, 'he is incapable of any conscious effort of will; he must put himself beforehand into the "mood of willing," or let himself be put'.[24] Jung distinguishes the 'primitive' from the 'civilised' in this way: in the extent of the role of conscious thoughts. Tragedy's portrayal of *ēthos* and *daimon*, and Agamemnon's blowing with fate's wind amply evoke this archaic 'mood of willing' in which the conscious mind is powerfully influenced by something non-conscious, whether external or unconscious. The non-conscious influence is experienced as the contradictory power of divine contact, as pithily expressed by the chorus of Argive elders in the *Agamemnon* in their 'Hymn to Zeus':

δαιμόνων δέ που χάρις βίαιος

σέλμα σεμνὸν ἡμένων

From the awesome throne of the divine, grace comes with violence.[25]

The Chorus knows well that divine intervention truly is a violent grace: *charis biaios*. When the *daimon* irrupts into the world, a mortal can be touched with a benediction, or derangement, or both simultaneously. *Charis*—grace—is a gift or a transaction, but often a traumatically disruptive one. As a recipient of Olympian *charis*, Agamemnon bends his *ēthos* with it, embracing the monstrosity.

The action of the subsequent killers, Clytemnestra and Orestes, underscores the role played by personal *ēthos* in that both are driven by *daimon*, but their *ēthos* points them in different ways. *Daimon* of a different sort works on Clytemnestra. She has a double motivation for Agamemnon's murder: one is human (Iphigeneia), the other divine (primordial curse).[26] Clytemnestra reveals the true locus of the divine impulse to murder when she is momentarily possessed by the numinous *alastōr*, as vividly rendered by Robert Fagles:

> You claim the work is mine, call me
> Agamemnon's wife – you are so wrong.
> Fleshed in the wife of this dead man,
> the spirit lives within me,
> our savage ancient spirit of revenge [ἀλάστωρ].
> In return for Atreus' brutal feast
> he kills his perfect son.[27]

Clytemnestra speaks as the instrument of the *alastōr* which—like the Erinyes—symbolises the curse on the House of Atreus. Clytemnestra is clearly here more than the avenging mother: she is the physical manifestation of vengeance itself. She is at once human and transcendent force.

The *Oresteia*'s three murderers, Agamemnon, Clytemnestra, and Orestes, are not equally touched with monstrousness: Orestes is unique among them in being the only one to question his actions seriously beforehand, and to bewail them instantly. Orestes is continually conscious of the two sides of his situation: he was divinely commanded by Apollo, but his matricide is abhorrent, and the revenge perpetuates his family's pollution. Having killed his mother, rather than rejoicing, Orestes tells the Chorus,

> for I am beaten, my rebellious senses [φρένες]
> bolt with me headlong and the fear [Φόβος] against my heart
> is ready for the singing and dance of wrath [Κότῳ].[28]

Although his *ēthos* is healthier and less destructive than his parents', he is still subject to the operation of *daimon*. He has already acted in accordance with the wishes
of the Olympian Apollo, and here he is afflicted by a more amorphous presence.
Two forces are personified as divinities: Phobos (fear) at his heart, choreographed
by Kotos (Wrath). The tragic hero is always bound to greater, external forces. The
mental activity of these forces may be explicable on a psychological level—for
Klein, Orestes has to some extent experienced stable internalisation of the good
object[29]—but they also operate on the symbolic, mythic level to maintain the
interplay between individual and society. For Agamemnon, his Troy-sacking coa-
lition of Argive warriors can only sail if he kills his daughter, turning the violence
on his own house. For Clytemnestra, her personal motivation is subsumed by the
spirit of the house. As for Orestes, his private vision of singing and dancing Phobos
foreshadows the sinister song and choreography of the chorus of Erinyes, soon to
appear on the stage in a terrifying personification of primordial awe which jeop-
ardises the city of Athens. But Orestes offers the symbolic hope of overcoming the
daimonic and unconscious influences over his selfhood.

Oresteian individuation

Although Freud famously described the revelations in *Oedipus Tyrannus* as a process akin to psychoanalysis,[30] arguably it is Aeschylus' *Oresteia* which most plainly
dramatises a talking cure. Athena carefully deploys persuasive language to guide the
vengeful Erinyes towards reconciling their primordial instincts with the cultured
legalities of Athenian society. A comprehensive Jungian reading of the *Oresteia* has
been produced by Richard Trousdell, who asserts, 'By using the power of language
to evoke emotional response, Athena models a "talking cure," the uniquely human
capacity to use verbal symbols to represent inner experience in order to know and
to be known.'[31]

In the final play, *Eumenides*, the Erinyes constitute the chorus: they are present, active participants of the dramatic action, and so too are the gods Athena
and Apollo. Athena presides over a court case on the Athenian Acropolis, with
the Erinyes prosecuting Orestes for his matricide, and Apollo standing as Orestes'
advocate. The jury of Athenian citizens is equally divided on the case, but Athena's
casting vote acquits Orestes, who may return home, free and purified. The Erinyes
are outraged at this, feeling dishonoured, and threatening Athens with all manner
of ruin and barrenness. Athena's resolution is momentous in its language and transformational power. She enshrines the principle of wondrous terror (τὸ δεινὸν, *Eum.*
698) at the heart of the *polis*, and the Erinyes are placated and exalted. Athena's
use of persuasion dissolves the implacable opposition of Orestes and Erinyes: she
acknowledges the irrational element of the awesome chthonic goddesses, and
brings them into civic life. Thereby Athena integrates the political with the magical, the individual with the social, and the historical with the mythical.

There is a long-standing tradition of reading *Eumenides* as an allegory of the
transition from matrilineal social relations to a patriarchal system.[32] A key argument

in this reading is that the Erinyes, who defended Clytemnestra (the mother killed by her son, voiceless after death with no redress sought by her family) are forced by the motherless, warlike Athena to give up their fury and their protection of the maternal line, and are literally repressed by being housed under the Acropolis. The case is rarely stated with more force than by Hélène Cixous, here identifying with the Erinyes: 'Justice does not satisfy us. It forces us to convert our grief. Its secret ambition, that of Athena, is to make us stifle our rages so that peace can reign.' Thus, for Cixous, 'the blow of repression' subjugates maternal passion.[33] The text hardly requires a loose interpretation to support this: the sexist ideology which dictates Athena's vote is stated explicitly.[34]

It is indeed unarguable that the system exalted by Athena is resolutely patriarchal—Aeschylus was, after all, reflecting his contemporary political reality—but the text does permit a more positive interpretation of the Erinyes' fate. Rather than being repressed by the city, these primordial goddesses are brought into consciousness. In the first two plays of the trilogy, the Erinyes, the daughters of Mother Night (*Eum.* 321–322, 416, 745, 1033), were invisible to all but the mantic Cassandra (*Ag.* 1190) and the guilt-maddened Orestes (*Cho.* 1061–1062), but now they are visible, participating interlocutors on the stage. They also state that—in their fearsomeness—they are guardians of the *phrenes* (the mind or soul, *Eum.* 517–519): they are already psychologically internalised.[35] Their condition is succinctly stated by Helen Bacon: 'In the course of the trilogy the Furies advance from being outcasts, inhabitants of outer darkness, working unseen by gods and mortals, to being legitimised members of the cosmic community, part of the *consciousness* of mortals and gods.'[36] Thus, as opposed to dramatising a literal repression of guilt through the incorporation of the Erinyes, Aeschylus shows the archaic spirits being addressed, conversed with, respected, brought into the open, made conscious, and accommodated before being allotted an exalted, ritual space.[37]

Athena herself has been interpreted as representing patriarchal subjugation of the maternal. She was born from the head of Zeus after he swallowed the Oceanid, Metis,[38] but Aeschylus elides this fact: 'No mother gave me birth', Athena states in *Eumenides*.[39] Trousdell, however, finds in Athena a creative balance:

> Apollo argues that Athena is only her father's child, a purely patriarchal representation of the feminine (lines 665–677). But by the spell of her voice and its transforming power, Aeschylus implies that Athena is also Zeus's inner feminine counterpart, his new voice of persuasion. In this sense, Athena restores the lost voice of her own mother, Metis, whom Zeus had swallowed. As the scene progresses, this inner voice of maternal compassion emerges in Athena as a creative counterbalance to temper the punitive force of fury and thunderbolts.[40]

The normative binary which equates the feminine with compassion, persuasion and 'the spell of her voice' and the masculine with force and punishment is part of the network of confused and conflicting oppositions which drive the *Oresteia* (male–female, human–animal, light–dark, and so on). Yet Trousdell here states that the opposites are balanced in the single figure of Athena. The goddess's persuasive language is no mere sop to the diminished feminine, but the accomplishment of balanced oppositions. As Richard Buxton explains, the context of her speech to the Erinyes 'is political, yet the vocabulary (*meiligma, thelkterion*) used to qualify the persuasion at work in that context is erotic'.[41] In her crossing of boundaries and mingling of registers, Athena embodies the harmonious balance that she envisages for her city if the Erinyes accept the position she offers them.

Trousdell claims the Oresteia 'offers a full and clear example of the psychological process that Jung termed individuation'.[42] He finds that *Choephoroi* conducts much of 'the hard, repetitive, and even boring work of individuation', with Orestes and Electra 'in a dangerous liminal space between helplessness and power, the seen and the unseen, old gods and new ones'.[43] The time spent in the liminal state allows the trilogy to perceive discriminatingly the ways to divide and balance the dangerous confusion of forces. The success of the *Oresteia*'s process is confirmed by the 'aim of individuation' as explained by Jung in 'The Relations Between the Ego and the Unconscious'. Jung says the aim 'is nothing less than to divest the self of the false wrappings of the persona on the one hand, and of the suggestive power of primordial images on the other'.[44] Of these two aims, Athena undoubtedly does the latter by bringing primordial goddesses into full civic employment. As for the former, the persona is the mask or barricade which 'feigns individuality',[45] and she allows Orestes to return to Argos literally undisguised (unlike his clandestine return to kill Clytemnestra), and free from the compulsion to enact the curse on the collective psyche of his family.

We may identify in Orestes' role certain aspects of Jung's unifying child archetype—most appositely, the child may be a 'young *hero*', who has experienced 'abandonment'.[46] Jung explains:

> the 'child' paves the way for a future change of personality. In the individuation process, it anticipates the figure that comes from the synthesis of the conscious and unconscious elements in the personality. It is therefore a symbol which unites the opposites.[47]

The child archetype described by Jung cannot be mapped on to the *Oresteia* without some imaginative leaps of interpretation. What applies least to Orestes is the 'miraculous birth' of the archetypal child hero and the activity of the archetype as the unconscious, irrational mediator between opposites.[48] In Jung's words, 'The hero's main feat is to overcome the monster of darkness: it is the long-hoped-for and expected triumph of the conscious over the unconscious.'[49] Orestes' personal individuation is synchronous with the moment of overcoming conflict, and Athena is the agent who enables the redefinition of Orestes' personal status, and that of the Erinyes within the *polis*. Orestes is the conflict's focus, not its resolution, and he disappears almost entirely from the play's attention the moment he is released.

But he is symbolic of the end to an agonistic curse as the Night-born Erinyes are brought into consciousness.

Where individuation is said to involve a union of opposites, it is better to regard union (*Vereinigung*) not in terms of merging, but of the *hieros gamos* (as Jung put it throughout his work). In this way, Jung can be read sympathetically with Richard Seaford's study of Aeschylean opposites, in which he argues that, in the *Oresteia*, a Heraclitean unity is overcome by a Pythagorean discrimination. Heraclitus is famed for his aphoristic contradictions—at his most confounding is the Blakean assertion, 'Cold warms up, warm cools off, moist parches, dry dampens'.[50] In general, we may regard his work as expressing a world of perpetual metamorphosis. This Heraclitean world, Seaford argues, pervades the 'cosmos of *Agamemnon* and *Choephoroi*', but *Eumenides* introduces 'a stable cosmology pervaded by the prevalence of one opposite over the other. This is the kind of cosmology propounded by early Pythagoreanism.'[51] For Seaford, the value of Pythagoras is in his mediating opposites through a third term.[52] Thus rather than achieving a resolution through a unity of opposites, the *Oresteia*, Seaford writes

> projects onto the cosmos (as the Olympian and chthonian deities) a controlled interaction of opposites. At first it represents opposites—as do Anaximander and Herakleitos—as a unity, identical with or giving rise to each other; but finally it represents them—as does Pythagoreanism—as asymmetrically reconciled.[53]

Here, the opposites are neither confused nor separate, but 'interconnected' while yet differentiated, with one side attaining prevalence over its opposite:[54] 'conflict (victory–defeat), gender (male–female), reciprocity (positive–negative), ritual utterance (paian–lament), cosmology (Olympian–chthonic)'.[55]

The political structure of Athena's state may be lamentably patriarchal and bellicose towards those outside its political alliances, but it also promises fecundity after sterile chaos. The dangerous, chaotic confusion of victory and defeat in the corpse of Troy-conquering Agamemnon, or the destructive meshing of human and divine agency in the three intra-familial killers has been replaced by a decisive double victory (for Orestes and the Erinyes) and the establishment of a human court of justice under an Olympic charter succeeding chthonic vengeance. Orestes' acquittal is the final element of a personal purification ritual. It signifies his release from divine compulsion and finds him safely on the path of individuation. It is mirrored on a collective scale by the constructive balancing of Olympian and chthonic, or conscious and unconscious, or civil and archaic spirits in Athens. But Orestes does not stay on stage to witness the city's salvation: the last quarter of the play goes on without him. Assuredly, the healthy mind is dramatically uninteresting to tragedy; but more significantly, his role is symbolically subsumed by the good relationship between Athens and his city of Argos. This implies a meaningful interplay between individual and society in the concluding moments of the tragedy.

Ecstatic or atomised performance

Thus far we have seen how the action and characterisation on the tragic stage resonates with twentieth-century psychology. The theatre, of course, functions on two planes of experience (if not more): the world of the drama, and the world of the spectator—the symbolic and the material. Does the individuation process on stage lend itself to a similarly enlightening experience for the audience? Naturally, this is in the hands of the performing company. Of the three distinct productions of the *Oresteia* in the UK in 2015, the version adapted and directed by Robert Icke at the Almeida in London was the most celebrated.[56] Icke's version included three decisions which underscore the psychological potency of the tragedy: he dramatised the events surrounding Iphigeneia's sacrifice; he explicitly named Orestes' 'trauma', and he deviated from reading for psychological unity in favour of fragmentation in his conclusion. This third decision in particular runs contrary to claims of individuation in the tragedy. Crucially, we note that where, in Aeschylus, Orestes is absent from the conclusion, for Icke, Orestes ends the play.

There is an ancient precedent for dramatising the story of Iphigeneia's sacrifice, namely Euripides' *Iphigeneia at Aulis*, which was produced about fifty years after the *Oresteia*. Here Euripides presents the pre-transgressive, human side to Agamemnon and Clytemnestra, arguably complicating the psychological portrait of the protagonists. Aeschylus gives only brief insight into Agamemnon's pre-sacrificial agonies (*Ag.* 202–204), but Euripides opens his tragedy with Agamemnon's wracked countermanding of his own duplicitous summoning of his daughter. More affectingly, we follow Clytemnestra as she moves from anticipating the marriage of her daughter to Achilles, to her realisation of Agamemnon's true intentions. Her hopeless situation is expressed in her compassionate entreaty to Achilles:

> She is my child. She comes first. I must fight for her [. . .] It was for you that I garlanded her and led her here to marry you. But as it is I have brought her to be slaughtered [. . .] I have no altar to take refuge at except your knees, and there is no friend nearby. You hear of the cruelty of Agamemnon who will stop at nothing. As you see, I have arrived here, a woman in a camp full of unruly sailors who are bold when it comes to evil deeds.[57]

This is a marked contrast to the outrageously amplified Clytemnestra of the *Oresteia*. Although *Iphigeneia at Aulis* is set in a period of extreme tension and anxiety, in focusing on the situation before the trauma of child-murder, Euripides has available to him the portrayal of a more compassionate scene.

In recent times, Euripides' play has occasionally been appended to Aeschylus', the effect of which is to shift the dramatic focus to the violence done to Iphigeneia and the sorrow of Clytemnestra.[58] This innovation appears to have unconsciously influenced Icke's version, although he has denied an overt connection, stating he added the sacrifice to present the whole story to the audience.[59] Nevertheless, it is hardly unknown for a plot to begin in the aftermath of a trauma: the structure of a play is an artistic decision. The overall effect of Icke's addition, beyond informing a contemporary audience of the key narrative events, is to present a more complete view of the interactions of the family. Although reconfigured as a Blairite ruler, Icke's Agamemnon is given a plausible family life, with scenes set at the dinner table with Clytemnestra, Orestes, Electra, and Iphigeneia.[60] The naturalistic tone offsets to powerful emotional effect the horror of Iphigeneia's quiet, clinical death from a modern pharmaceutical compound administered by Agamemnon. Although Agamemnon's conflicting obligations to family and state are fully realised in Icke's production, the wider machinations of state and warfare are extremely abstract (the enemy, for example, is dramatically remote, and never named). As such, the emotive drive of Icke's play is personal and individual: the family unit rather than the social sphere.

The action of Icke's *Oresteia* is complemented by a simultaneous commentary between Orestes and a figure named 'Doctor' in the text, though to the audience (to whom character names are not provided), the analyst-patient relationship may also be seen as one of lawyer-defendant. The distinctions between the process of analysis and that of justice are blurred in performance, but towards the close, the doctor openly names the trauma,[61] as the play is revealed as an obsessive re-enactment crossed with a criminal reconstruction. Despite these manifest overtures to analytical procedure, Icke's production does not resolve Orestes' case along the lines of Klein's reading nor Jungian individuation. Instead, the play leaves Orestes, and the audience, in a desolately indeterminate denouement. Icke's Orestes is left isolated on an alienated, deserted stage without support or direction, hopelessly repeating 'What do I do?'.[62] It serves to highlight the human, individual, psychological side of the tragedy: despite his juridical acquittal and the verdict of 'innocent', Orestes is left with his trauma. He laments, 'But I still killed her [. . .] Perhaps I always *feel* guilty.'[63] Orestes here is an utterly atomised, twenty-first-century subject; thus Icke's play spoke deeply to the concerns of London's theatre-goers.

The conclusion of Icke's *Oresteia* is an inversion of Aeschylus: for Aeschylus, Orestes is absent from the stage, and the *polis* is foregrounded; for Icke, the *polis* is abstracted and Orestes is the sole presence in the final moments. It is a marked contrast to the experience of Marxist classicist George Thomson whose own view of the conclusion is as inclusive as Icke's is withdrawn. In Thomson's *Aeschylus and Athens*, he concludes his reading of the *Oresteia* by recounting his memories of a production of extracts from the trilogy which accompanied a lecture of his in Athens in 1961:

> By his introduction of the Panathenaic procession, the poet has brought the
> story out of the darkness of antiquity into the brilliant light of the Athens of
> his day. It began in the remote and barbarous past, it ends here and now. It is
> as though at the close of the trilogy he invited his audience to rise from their
> seats and carry on the drama from the point where he has left it.
>   [. . .] The tumultuous applause that greeted the finale, and the light that
> shone in so many tear-stained faces, showed that the Athenians respond to
> the contemporary appeal of their greatest poet as deeply today as they did
> twenty-four centuries ago.[64]

Aeschylus set the *Eumenides* on the Athenian Areopagus: the outcrop of rock that
still stands today, a few minutes' walk from the Theatre of Dionysus where the play
was first performed. The dramatic location merges with that of the performance
space. In 1961, Thomson personally experienced the affect of the expansion of
time and space from mythical stage to material society that is central to Aeschylus's
text. This spatial connection augments the emotional resonance of the play with
the audience. Therefore, the new charter pronounced by Athena inspires *praxis* in
the social sphere.

How may we conceive of the transaction between actor, protagonist, and
audience? The Attic stage was highly stylised (utilising all-male casts, masks,
music, dancing, and so on), but modern audiences would surely recognise a
familiar commitment to emotional verisimilitude. In fourth-century Athenian
comedy, the actors' convincing inhabiting of psychological roles was seen as
vital to a production's success. In Aristophanes' *Thesmophoriazusae*, the actor-
poet must inhabit the character. As Ismene Lada-Richards notes, '*mīmēsis*
cannot leave the imitator's own identity intact'.[65] Similarly, in *Ecclesiazusae*,
female actors will impersonate men and must banish 'personal thoughts and
feelings'.[66] Such comic moments of method acting suggest a keen appreciation of the psychological complexities of impersonation in the century after
Aeschylus, at least.

Yet the actors of Attic tragedy had to impersonate multiple characters in a single
play. Lada-Richards is succinct in explaining the difference between ancient and
modern approaches to acting:

> while we have a tendency to reconstruct a play's action mentally around
> notions of psychological consistency and unity of character, what holds an
> ancient Greek play together on the stage is the continuity provided by the
> actor's own body, that marvellously pliant instrument which lends a presence
> and a voice to both the matricide son and the murdered mother in Sophocles'
> *Electra*, or to both the scheming Odysseus and the deified Heracles in the
> prologue and the closing scene of Sophocles' *Philoctetes*.[67]

This is not to deny the characters' psychological consistency, but to enforce
the remarkable fact that ancient actors would often be called upon to inhabit

the personae of radically opposed protagonists. Therefore the audience must appreciate in a single moment the distinct planes of narrative consistency and acting skill.

The theatre, then, has always been the site of some form of transcendence of reality. The dissolution of boundaries between material and symbolic realities, it has been argued, lies at the origin of the dramatic act. Commenting on a paean on Theseus by Bacchylides, Bruno Snell says:

> at the end of the poem the chorus is in the same situation as the mythical beings with whom the song concerns itself. The song of the mythical chorus becomes the song of the performing chorus. Here is the germ of drama, the source of impersonation.[68]

The paean's formalised stimulation of identification with the myth is also a controlled instance of *ekstasis* (standing outside one's self). *Ekstasis* is defined by Charles Segal as a condition in which the participant of the drama, or of a Bacchic ecstasy, 'temporarily relinquishes the safe limits of personal identity in order to extend himself sympathetically to other dimensions of experience'.[69] Echoing Segal's words, Lada-Richards imagines a similarly magical scene to Snell's in which Dionysian *ekstasis* results in 'both the actor's "stepping out" of himself and the spectator's sympathetic fusion with the acting stage figure'.[70] In drama, the planes of reality are dissolved: that which was separated is commingled. At the risk of summoning the spectre of Nietzsche again, we may ask, can the expansion of *ekstasis* co-exist with the differentiation of individuation?

The ancient theatre provided the space for performing, processing, and resolving the paradoxes that afflict the psychic life of the community. Tragedy thus offers the potential to expand the affective power of individuation beyond the solitary individual. The *ekstatikos* component of individuation is evocatively expressed by Trousdell, who claims that, while 'the individuation process is uniquely personal [. . .] this process is also part of a shared effort to expand consciousness and meaning'.[71] He elaborates:

> something beyond words persuades, a dynamic the theater chooses as its primary medium: the living presence of mind, body, and spirit. In the Greek theater space, gathered around a circular *orchestra*, the audience acted as part of an attentive field of focused looking and listening that created a containing space, a *temenos*, in which cathartic action could take place. Without the audience's focused emotional engagement, the performance would fall flat, just as a therapist's affective participation creates the attentive field in which psychological transformation may happen.[72]

The abstract sacred or psychic language of '*temenos*' (sacred precinct) and 'attentive field' may fail to persuade sceptics, but it accurately describes the affect of the dramatic work (the identification of actor, character, and spectator), and the conditions for *ekstasis*. Here, the audience becomes part of the artistic creation in which the actors' identity temporarily departs, or merges with the mythical figure's. The artwork holds the potential to transform reality.

Conclusion

If individuation defines the self from the mass, is it the opposite of *ekstasis*? And if not, is ecstatic individuation a regression? This chapter has argued that the tragic theatre, in particular, the *Oresteia*, provides the conditions for beginning or continuing a process of individuation that is shared beyond the solitary agent. By way of illustration, I conclude with complementary thoughts from Freud and Jung on the relationship of the imaginary with reality. Freud contends:

> Only in art does it still happen that a man who is consumed by desires performs something resembling the accomplishment of those desires and that what he does in play produces emotional effects—thanks to artistic illusion— just as though it were something real.[73]

The power that Freud locates in art influences material reality on an emotional level. For Jung, the divisions between worlds are yet more porous, and he describes the spirit world as

> the experience, the conscious acceptance of a reality in no way inferior to that of the material world. I doubt whether primitives exist anywhere who are not acquainted with magical influence or a magical substance. ('Magical' is simply another word for 'psychic.')[74]

Jung collapses the hierarchy of the material over the spiritual, and eliminates semantic questions of the distinction between mental life and magic. In so doing— and read together with Freud's comments on art—we may see how art enacts the spirit world. In particular, the *Oresteia* performs an individual and a social integration as Athena's language influences material circumstance. The opposites at play are not perfectly resolved or removed: the Erinyes retain their powers for blessing and for destruction, but the latter injurious power is subordinated. Through Athena's divine authority as judge, analyst, or super-ego, we are shown a living myth which holds the potential to transmit its emotional and social power today. In tragic action, Athena transforms reality, and transforms the collective experience of the audience as we each recognise the archaic, irrational forces which persist in civic life.[75] Myth, tragedy, and psychology are thus seen to have a united purpose in performing the harmonisation of contradictory forces in both individual and society.

Notes

1 On primal words, see S. Freud, 'The Antithetical Sense of Primal Words' [1910], in *On Creativity and the Unconscious*, tr. M.N. Searl, New York: Harper & Row, 1958, pp. 55–62. On agency, see the ensuing discussion of this chapter.
2 The seminal work on the role of opposition in myth is C. Lévi-Strauss, *Anthropologie Structurale*, Paris: Plon, 1958, translated as *Structural Anthropology*, tr. C. Jacobson and B. Grundfest Schoepf, New York: Basic Books, 1963. On tragedy and analysis, see comments on Hegel and Jung, respectively, below.
3 Aristotle, *Poetics*, tr. M.E. Hubbard, in *Classical Literary Criticism* [1972], ed. D.A. Russell and M. Winterbottom, Oxford: Oxford University Press, 1989, pp. 51–90 (p. 62, 1451b).
4 The Oresteian myth inspired Jung's 'Electra Complex'; see C.G. Jung, 'The Theory of Psycho-Analysis [1913], in *Freud and Psychoanalysis* [*Collected Works*, vol. 4], tr. R.F.C. Hull, London: Routledge & Kegan Paul, 1961, §203–§522 (§347–§349). This claim for gender equivalence was completely rejected by Freud; see S. Freud, 'Female Sexuality' [1931] in *The Future of an Illusion, Civilization and Its Discontents and Other Works* [*Standard Edition of the Complete Psychological Works of Sigmund Freud*, vol. 21 (1927–1931)], ed. and tr. J. Strachey et al., London: Hogarth Press, 1964, pp. 221–243 (pp. 228–229).
5 Aristotle, *Poetics*, tr. Hubbard, p. 59, 1450a.
6 M. Leonard, *Tragic Modernities*, Cambridge, MA: Harvard University Press, 2015, p. 133. Leonard focuses on the criticisms by Simon Goldhill (*Sophocles and the Language of Tragedy*, Oxford: Oxford University Press, 2012) and Page duBois ('The Death of the Character', *International Journal of the Classical Tradition* 21 (3), October 2014, 301–308).
7 Leonard, *Tragic Modernities*, p. 143.
8 G.W.F. Hegel, *Aesthetics: Lectures on Fine Art*, tr. T.M. Knox, Oxford: Oxford University Press, 1975, vol. 2, p. 1213.
9 F.W.J. Schelling, *The Philosophy of Art* [1859], tr. D.W. Stott, Minneapolis, MN: University of Minnesota Press, 1989, p. 249.
10 For Schelling's discussion of tautegory (i.e., saying what is impossible to say any other way), see F.W.J. von Schelling, *Historical-Critical Introduction to the Philosophy of Mythology* [1842], tr. M. Richey and M. Zisselsberger, Albany, NY: State University of New York Press, 2007, Lecture 8. See also J.-P. Vernant, 'The Reason of Myth' [1974] in *Myth and Society in Ancient Greece* [1980], tr. J. Lloyd, New York: Zone, 1988, pp. 203–260: on Aristotle's rejection of mythology in *Metaphysics* 1000a (pp. 210–211), and tautegory in Schelling (pp. 223–224).
11 J. Billings, *Genealogy of the Tragic: Greek Tragedy and German Philosophy*, Princeton, NJ: Princeton University Press, 2014, p. 124.
12 G. Devereux, *Dreams in Greek Tragedy: An Ethno-Psycho-Analytical Study*, Oxford: Blackwell, 1976, pp. ix, 59.
13 M. Klein, 'Some Reflections on "The Oresteia"' [1963], in *Envy and Gratitude and other works 1946–1963* [1975], London: Virago, 1988, pp. 275–299 (pp. 282–283); my emphasis.
14 Klein, 'Some Reflections on "The Oresteia"', pp. 296–297.
15 Klein, 'Some Reflections on "The Oresteia"', p. 298.
16 J.-P. Vernant, 'Tensions and Ambiguities in Greek Tragedy' [1969], in J.-P. Vernant and P. Vidal-Naquet, *Myth and Tragedy in Ancient Greece*, tr. J. Lloyd, New York: Zone, 1990, pp. 29–28 (p. 37).
17 All references to the Greek text are to this edition: Aeschylus, *Oresteia: Agamemnon, Libation-Bearers, Eumenides*, ed. and tr. A.H. Sommerstein, Cambridge, MA: Harvard University Press, 2008, '*parakopē*': *Agamemnon* l. 223. Translations from Aeschylus, *The Oresteia: Agamemnon, Choephoroe, Eumenides* [1938], tr. G. Thomson, New York: Everyman, 2004, *Agamemnon* l. 234 (p. 9); Aeschylus, *Oresteia*, tr. C. Collard, Oxford: Oxford

University Press, 2002, *Agamemnon* l. 222 (p. 8); Aeschylus, *The Oresteia: Agamemnon, The Libation Bearers, The Eumenides*, tr. R. Fagles, Harmondsworth: Penguin, 1977, *Agamemnon* l. 220 (p. 110).

18 There are comparable examples of *parakopos* in Euripides' *Bacchae* where it is used to describe Bacchic madness (ll. 33, 1000).

19 J.-P. Vernant, 'Intimations of the Will in Greek Tragedy' [1972] in Vernant and Vidal-Naquet, *Myth and Tragedy in Ancient Greece*, tr. M. Lloyd, pp. 49–84 (p. 76).

20 E.R. Dodds, *The Greeks and the Irrational*, Berkeley, CA: University of California Press, 1951, p. 3.

21 J.J. Peradotto, 'The Omen of the Eagles and the *Ethos* of Agamemnon' [1969], in *Oxford Readings in Classical Studies: Aeschylus*, ed. M. Lloyd, Oxford: Oxford University Press, 2007, pp. 211–244 (pp. 235–236).

22 B. Williams, *Shame and Necessity*, Berkeley, CA: University of California Press, 1993, p. 134.

23 Aeschylus, *Oresteia*, tr. Sommerstein, *Agamemnon* l. 217.

24 C.G. Jung, 'The Psychology of the Child Archetype' in C.G. Jung and C. Kerényi, *The Science of Mythology* [1941], tr. R.F.C. Hull [1951], Abingdon: Routledge, 2002, pp. 83–118 (p. 86).

25 Aeschylus, *Agamemnon* ll. 182–183; my translation.

26 An influential discussion of Clytemnestra's motivation is in R.P. Winnington-Ingram, *Studies in Aeschylus*, Cambridge: Cambridge University Press, 1983, p. 80.

27 Aeschylus, *The Oresteia*, tr. Fagles, *Agamemnon* ll. 1526–1532 (p. 165) = Greek ll. 1497–1504.

28 Aeschylus, *Oresteia: Agamemnon, The Libation Bearers, The Eumenides*, tr. R. Lattimore, Chicago, IL: University of Chicago Press, 1953, *Libation Bearers*, ll. 1023–1025 (pp. 129–130).

29 Klein, 'Some Reflections on "The Oresteia"', p. 286.

30 Sigmund Freud, *The Interpretation of Dreams* [1900], ed. A. Richards, tr. J. Strachey [1953], Harmondsworth: Penguin, 1991, p. 363.

31 R. Trousdell, 'Tragedy and Transformation: The *Oresteia* of Aeschylus', *Jung Journal: Culture & Psyche* 2 (3), Summer 2008, 5–38 (p. 31). Jung himself did not produce a sustained reading of the *Oresteia*. His comments on *Eumenides* are consistent with the standard psychological view that it dramatises repression: he argues that the Erinyes are renamed Eumenides (*sic*.: in the surviving manuscript they are called 'Semnai [Theai]'—'Awesome Goddesses'—not 'Eumenides') as an apotropaic euphemism to make the complex 'unreal' (C.G. Jung, 'A Review of the Complex Theory' [1948], in *The Structure and Dynamics of the Psyche [Collected Works*, vol. 8], tr. R.F.C. Hull, London: Routledge & Kegan Paul, 1960, §194–§219 (§206).

32 This reading stems from J.J. Bachofen, *Das Mutterrecht: Eine Untersuchung über die Gynaikokratie der alten Welt nach ihrer religiösen und rechtlichen Natur* (1861), the essential passage translated as 'Athens', in *Myth, Religion, and Mother Right*, tr. R. Manheim, London: Routledge & Kegan Paul, 1967, pp. 157–172; see also Freud, *Moses and Monotheism* (1939).

33 Hélène Cixous, 'The Coup' [1985], tr. S. Lhomme and H. Carr, *Women: A Cultural Review*, vol. 5, no. 2, Autumn 1994, 113–119 (p. 116). The theme of psychological repression in *Eumenides* has found strong support in a recent study by E. Zakin, 'Marrying the City: Intimate Strangers and the Fury of Democracy', in *Bound by the City: Greek Tragedy, Sexual Difference, and the Formation of the Polis*, ed. D. E. McCoskey and E. Zakin, Albany, NY: State University of New York Press, 2009, pp. 177–196.

34 For one example among many, Athena states, 'I shall not set a higher value on the death of a woman, when she had killed her husband, the guardian of the house' (Aeschylus, *Eumenides*, ll. 739–740, tr. Sommerstein, p. 449).

35 The *phrenes* were also associated with the midriff, as opposed to the modern tendency to equate the mind with the brain. The ancient belief accurately represents the fact that

emotions are often felt in the gut. Whatever the precise location, the *phrenes* are clearly internal.

36 H.H. Bacon, 'The Furies' Homecoming', *Classical Philology* 96 (1), January 2001, 48–59 (p. 57).

37 I have discussed the role of the Erinyes at greater length elsewhere; see B. Pestell, 'Kindly Terror and Civic Fury: *Eumenides* and the Language of Myth', *Comparative Literature Studies* 54 (2), 305–328.

38 Hesiod, *Theogony*, in *Theogony, Works and Days, Testimonia*, tr. G.W. Most, Cambridge, MA: Harvard University Press, 2010, pp. 2–85 (pp. 74–75, ll. 886–900).

39 Aeschylus, *The Oresteia*, tr. Thomson, p. 118, *Eumenides* l. 739 (p. 118) = Greek l.736. For a psychoanalytical account of this aspect, see A. Jacobs, *On Matricide: Myth, Psychoanalysis, and the Law of the Mother*, New York: Columbia University Press, 2007.

40 Trousdell, 'Tragedy and Transformation', p. 33.

41 R.G.A. Buxton, *Persuasion in Greek Tragedy: A Study of Peitho*, Cambridge: Cambridge University Press, 1982, p. 111, citing *Eumenides*, l. 886.

42 Trousdell, 'Tragedy and Transformation', p. 6.

43 Trousdell, 'Tragedy and Transformation', p. 15. On the 'boring' work, it is true that the parts of *Choephoroi* concerned with mourning and moral quandary can seem flat on the page, but the text was written to be augmented with choreography and music which a successful production can employ to render the scenes compelling.

44 C.G. Jung, 'The Relations Between the Ego and the Unconscious' [1928; 1935], in *Two Essays on Analytical Psychology* [*Collected Works*, vol. 7], tr. R.F.C Hull, London: Routledge & Kegan Paul, 1966, §202–§406 (§269).

45 Jung, 'The Relations Between the Ego and the Unconscious', §245; original emphasis.

46 Jung, 'The Psychology of the Child Archetype', p. 100; original emphasis.

47 Jung, 'The Psychology of the Child Archetype', p. 99.

48 Jung, 'The Psychology of the Child Archetype', pp. 101–104.

49 Jung, 'The Psychology of the Child Archetype', p. 102.

50 C.H. Kahn, *The Art and Thought of Heraclitus: An Edition of the Fragments With Translation and Commentary*, Cambridge: Cambridge University Press, 1979, fragment 49 (= Diels-Kranz 126, Marcovich 42).

51 R. Seaford, *Cosmology and the Polis: The Social Construction of Space and Time in the Tragedies of Aeschylus*, Cambridge: Cambridge University Press, 2012, p. 273.

52 Seaford, *Cosmology and the Polis*, pp. 281 and 293–296.

53 R. Seaford, 'Aeschylus and the Unity of Opposites', *The Journal of Hellenic Studies* 123, 2003, 141–163 (p. 161).

54 Seaford, *Cosmology and the Polis*, p. 270.

55 Seaford, *Cosmology and the Polis*, p. 273.

56 It later transferred to Trafalgar Studios in the West End, and Icke won the 2016 Laurence Olivier Award for Best Director for the production. The other two productions of the *Oresteia* were at the Globe in London and Home in Manchester.

57 Euripides, *Iphigeneia at Aulis*, in *Bacchae and Other Plays*, tr. J. Morwood, Oxford: Oxford University Press, 1999, pp. 84–132 (p. 112, ll. 902–14).

58 For example, *Les Atrides* (1990–1991), directed by Ariane Mnouchkine, which consisted of four parts: *Iphigénie à Aulis* (tr. J. Bollack), *Agamemnon*, *Les Choéphores* (both tr. A. Mnouchkine), and *Les Euménides* (tr. H. Cixous). Information from Archive of Performances of Greek and Roman Drama (APGRD) database. Available online from: www.apgrd.ox.ac.uk/productions/production/2235. Accessed 22 September 2016.

59 He explained, 'The reason I added the first play, the Iphigeneia play, which of course is not a Euripides rewrite but a dramatization of Aeschylus' Chorus – is because the fifth-century Athenians would have known that story from Homer'; Robert Icke quoted in interview with Emma Bridges, *Practitioners' Voices in Classical Reception Studies* 6, 2015. Available online from: www.open.ac.uk/arts/research/pvcrs/2015/icke. Accessed 12 November 2015. There are some structural similarities between Icke's first act and

Iphigeneia at Aulis, for example, the prologue of Agamemnon consulting with wise counsel (the old man in Euripides, Calchas in Icke), and Agamemnon's moral argument with Menelaus. But Icke's differs profoundly by not mirroring Iphigeneia's speech in which she voices her willingness to die for Hellas (*Iphigeneia at Aulis*, ll. 1368–1401).

60 Transliterations of the names here are as given in Icke's text; see R. Icke, *Aeschylus: Oresteia: A New Adaptation by Robert Icke*, London: Oberon, 2015.
61 Icke, *Aeschylus: Oresteia*, p. 100.
62 Icke, *Aeschylus: Oresteia*, p. 126.
63 Icke, *Aeschylus: Oresteia*, p. 126.
64 G. Thomson, *Æschylus and Athens: A Study in the Social Origins of Drama*, 4th edn, London: Lawrence and Wishart, 1973, p. 277.
65 I. Lada-Richards, 'The Subjectivity of Greek Performance', in *Greek and Roman Actors: Aspects of an Ancient Profession*, ed. P. Easterling and E. Hall, Cambridge: Cambridge University Press, 2002, pp. 395–418 (p. 403).
66 Lada-Richards, 'The Subjectivity of Greek Performance', p. 403.
67 Lada-Richards, 'The Subjectivity of Greek Performance', p. 410.
68 B. Snell, *The Discovery of the Mind: The Greek Origins of European Thought* [1948], tr. T.G. Rosenmeyer, New York: Dover, 1953, p. 91.
69 C. Segal, *Dionysiac Poetics and Euripides' 'Bacchae': Expanded Edition*, Princeton, NJ: Princeton University Press, 1997, p. 215.
70 Lada-Richards, 'The Subjectivity of Greek Performance', pp. 418.
71 Trousdell, 'Tragedy and Transformation', p. 26.
72 Trousdell, 'Tragedy and Transformation', p. 32.
73 S. Freud, *Totem and Taboo: Some Points of Agreement Between the Mental Lives of Savages and Neurotics* [1913], tr. J. Strachey [1950], London: Routledge, 2001, p. 105.
74 Jung, 'The Relations Between the Ego and the Unconscious', §293.
75 Interplay between mythic thought and political reality is examined at greater length in Pestell, 'Kindly Terror and Civic Fury'.

7

MONETISED PSYCHE AND DIONYSIAC ECSTASY

Richard Seaford

I propose in this chapter to provide (a) a new perspective on the origin of the Greek idea of the (bounded and unified) inner self (*psuchē*), and (b) an example of how the tradition of Dionysiac ecstasy might be adapted to express reaction to this new reality.

I begin with a Jungian account of the earliest (Presocratic) Western 'philosophy', by the analyst Edward Edinger (1922–1998).[1] In two respects his account deserves appreciation. Firstly, he claims that ideas from the remote past are relevant to understanding our own psyches. Secondly, he asks the question that is almost never asked (and never properly answered) by scholars of Presocratic philosophy: given that the world around us is obviously multiple, why do the earliest philosophers concur in imagining that it is in fact composed of a single substance (monism)? Most scholars treat Presocratic philosophy as the purely intellectual activity of 'philosophy', the use of reason to understand the world, and are accordingly relatively uninterested in preconceptions and their source. But Edinger is right to suppose that monism derives neither from observation nor from reason, but from preconception.

So far, so good. But what is the nature and the source of the preconception? His answer is that Presocratic monism is a projection of the 'unity of the psychic Self' (p. 17). In fact, for Edinger Greek metaphysics is always a 'projection of the reality of the psyche, which lies behind sensible, concrete existence' (p. 10). Greek metaphysics varies greatly. For instance, Heraclitus maintains that everything is constantly changing; whereas for his contemporary Parmenides all change is an illusion, and what truly exists is invariant in time and space. For Edinger, the Heraclitean metaphysic represents the constantly changing ego, whereas the Parmenidean metaphysic represents the transpersonal Self, which 'transcends time' (pp. 34–35). Further, Edinger identifies as 'the fundamental insight of Jungian psychology' Heraclitus' doctrine of the unity of opposites (p. 37).

Edinger is right to insist on the close interconnection between the unities of psychic self and of the cosmos. The first account of the *psuchē* as an organ of unified consciousness is in the fragments of Heraclitus (born *c.* 550 BCE), who is also an early proponent of monism (everything is fire). But two centuries or so earlier, in Homer, there is no monism, and no word for the unified inner self.

However, this also indicates that the unity of the psychic self, and the timelessness of the transpersonal self, have only limited explanatory power. The unified inner self and monism go together. But why do they appear only from the sixth century BCE, and first in Ionia? And why do they appear as part of an intellectual revolution in which—in the minds of an elite, at least—polytheism is replaced by a single, impersonal, all-powerful, semi-abstract substance that is transformed from and into everything else? These questions, and this revolution, cannot be explained in Jungian terms.

In general, we are condemned to imagine the unknown in terms of the known. Premodern societies generally imagine power over the world in terms of power over society. Zeus is a patriarchal monarch with beard and sceptre: transcendent monarchical power over society is projected as transcendent power over the whole world. But Ionia in the early sixth century BCE had ceased to be monarchical. Moreover, it is the first known society in history to be pervaded—as a result of the invention and rapid spread of coinage from about 600 BCE—by money. And its commercial centre is Miletos, the first city in history to produce 'philosophers', each of whom maintained that the universe is subject to a single impersonal power-substance that is transformed from and into everything else. When Heraclitus of nearby Ephesos then says that 'all things are an exchange for fire and fire for all things, like goods for gold and gold for goods' (Diels-Kranz B90), this is not simply a metaphor: it is imagining the unknown in terms of the known. Impersonal monism derives from the impersonal universality of money. The first 'philosophy' in history is produced at exactly the same time and in exactly the same place as the first pervasively monetised society in history. Transcendent power is no longer monarchical, it is monetary—as I have argued in detail in my *Money and the Early Greek Mind* (2004).

My specific concern here, however, is the psyche. The Homeric world is not the only one that lacks the concept—familiar to the modern West—of a bounded, comprehensive, individual inner self:

> The western conception of the person as a bounded, unique, more or less integrated motivational and cognitive universe; a dynamic centre of awareness, emotion, judgement and action organised into a distinctive whole and set contrastively against other such wholes and against a social and natural background is, however incorrigible it may seem to us, a rather peculiar idea within the context of the world's cultures.[2]

Ethnography also provides an indication of what may be the social change promoting the emergence of the concept. For instance:

An implicational logic runs from the appearance of the tradestore to the emergence of the individual aspect of personhood. The tradestore implies the right of private property, exemplified by a decline in the obligation to share, and private ownership is in turn a metaphor for privacy, or the self-containment of the person that is an index of individuality.[3]

Compare with a development in seventeenth-century England, where 'its conception of the individual' was 'as essentially the proprietor of his own person or capacities, owing nothing to society for them':

> The individual was seen neither as a moral whole, nor as part of a larger social whole, but as an owner of himself. The relationship of ownership, having become for more and more men the critically important relation determining their actual freedom and actual prospect of realizing their full potentialities, was read back into the nature of the individual.[4]

Equally instructive is a debate within recent English analytical philosophy. To the claim that 'we cannot deduce, from the content of our experiences, that a thinker is a separately existing entity [. . .] we could fully describe our thoughts without claiming that they have thinkers',[5] it is responded that 'a person is something that has psychological states and does things; for short that *owns* psychological states and action'.[6]

Both these philosophical claims are made as if they apply to all cultures. And in the latter, it is unclear what 'owning' (presumably meant as a metaphor) is a metaphor for. We should rather again say that the unknown is imagined in terms of the known. The debate ignores what is crucial: individual ownership of property, which is culture-specific, is one of the elements out of which the idea of the person (or inner self) is constructed.

Turning back to Greece, I note that there is evidence in the archaic period for the development of the institution of individual property, and propose the hypothesis that this socio-economic development was a factor in the development of the idea of the individual inner self. Moreover, individual property creates the conditions for—and is in turn promoted by—monetisation. Accordingly, I also propose the more specific hypothesis that the idea of the individual inner self was shaped—in part—by monetisation.

In Homer, there is no monism, no comprehensive inner self, and no money. Goods and services are exchanged in part through centralised redistribution (by the king) and in part through gift-exchange. The reciprocity of gift-exchange (and—at least initially—of centralised redistribution) works through creating good will (and the moral obligation to reciprocate) in the recipient. In Homer, this reciprocity breaks down, but what replaced it historically—commerce—is as yet merely marginal. The subsequent monetisation of the *polis* is revolutionary, in promoting a new conception not only of the universe (as we have seen), but also of the self: precious metal money is unprecedented not only in its power to acquire all goods and services, but also in the ease with which it is individually owned (and exchanged, stored, hidden, and moved). The individual with money can in principle dispense with the relationships by which the premonetary individual is sustained and constituted, notably kinship and reciprocity. Monetisation tends to isolate the individual, creating boundaries around the inner self. Moreover, because the effectiveness of money does not depend on creating good will in others, it seems rather to be immediate, and so is easily identified with the will of its owner. The invisible (abstract) universal power of money is easily introjected as the power of the invisible inner self over itself and over others. In Greek texts, people are often identified with coins, and conversely money is often imagined as having a will.[7] Philo of Alexandria, for instance, calls the soul *nomisma* (currency), its mark the eternal *logos* impressed by the seal of god.[8]

It is against this background that we should understand the co-existence in the Heraclitean fragments of (monetised) monism with the earliest extant focus on the *psuchē* as comprehensive inner self.[9] The cosmos is an ever-living fire (Diels-Kranz B30) that undergoes a cycle of transformation into water and earth (B31). The *psuchē*, which is composed of fire,[10] undergoes the same cycle, in which its transformations are 'death' (B36). The cycle is, we saw, a projection of the monetary cycle. The idea of death as expenditure of *psuchē* is frequent in early Greek texts.[11] In a fragment of Heraclitus, what *thumos* (anger, spirit) wants 'it buys at the price of *psuchē*' (Diels-Kranz B 85), i.e., as if *psuchē* were money. For Heraclitus, everything happens according to the communal *logos*,[12] a numerical formula[13] that is somehow embedded in fire[14] (and could at this time refer to a monetary account).[15] Accordingly, the *psuchē*, consubstantial with the (fiery) cosmos, contains *logos*: 'the boundaries of the *psuchē* you would not find out, even by travelling along every path: so deep a *logos* does it have' (Diels-Kranz B45). Money is, as *logos*-embodying fire, both projected (onto the cosmos) and introjected (into the inner self). Or rather, to be more specific, it is the (communal) circulation of money that is projected and introjected. Circulation, regulated by the *logos*, is constant and unlimited, and connects individual with society, with the result that (from the communal perspective) the limits of the (*logos*-endowed) *psuchē* are so remote. I must add—without going here into detailed explanation[16]—that it is from the same socio-economic perspective that we can best understand the origin of the Heraclitean doctrine of the unity of opposites (whatever the usefulness of the doctrine for psychology).

Essential to money is circulation, without which—from a communal perspective—it does not function as money. But money must also be imagined as having value that does not vary according to time and place. This is the other essence of money, from the perspective of individual possession.

It is this other essence of money that is projected onto the universe by Heraclitus' younger contemporary, Parmenides. All that exists (Being) is eternal, one, unchanging, abstract, continuous, limited, self-sufficient, inviolate, and held in place by Justice (Diels-Kranz B7, B8). This entirely counter-intuitive conception derives neither from observation nor from reason but from preconception:

more specifically, it is a projection of individually possessed (and so limited, just, and inviolate) of the (ideal) invariance (in time and space) of all-pervasive abstract value, separated entirely—not least by the aristocratic ideology of self-sufficiency—from circulation. Once again, I have argued this in detail elsewhere.[17] What then of the inner self? There are in the fragments various indications of assimilation between the inner self and Being.[18] Here I have space only for the most substantial of them. The goddess tells the solitary initiate Parmenides: 'Look equally at absent things that are firmly present to the mind. For you will not cut off for yourself what is from holding to what is, neither scattering everywhere in every way in order nor drawing together' (Diels-Kranz B4).

What is (Being) is seen by imaginative introspection to be unitary and (temporally and spatially)[19] continuous, as it is said to be in, for example, fragment B8.6 ('one, continuous') and in fragment B25 ('so it is all continuous; for what exists draws near to what exists').[20] The mind (*nous*) sees absent things, and so is clearly distinguished from perception, as is the Platonic soul when it withdraws into itself and trusts nothing except itself and its thoughts in itself of what is real in itself, and sees what is invisible and intelligible.[21]

The mind may indeed imagine its contents as an indivisible whole. But may not the mind may also imagine its contents as diverse and changeable? Yes. But introspection discovers what it is predisposed to discover—and this particular predisposition (presented as a revelation by the goddess) expresses the historical newness of the self-conscious abstract unity of the bounded individual mind. The revelation creates a premise from which is then deduced the abstract continuity (and so unity) of what exists: the abstract Being of money both introjected and projected.

The fourth-century BCE Derveni papyrus, discovered in 1962 and adequately published only in 2006,[22] provides an interesting example of the introjection of all-pervasive value. It is a 'philosophical' commentary on an earlier mythical theogony:[23] new meaning is given to a traditional narrative. The narrative contains the words, 'Into [or onto] him [Zeus] all the immortals grew, blessed gods and goddesses and rivers and lovely springs and everything else that had then been born; and he himself became the sole one.' This is interpreted by the commentator as follows: 'And as for the phrase "and he himself became the sole one", by saying this he makes clear that Mind being alone is always worth everything, just as if the other things were nothing.'[24] The universal power of the monarch (Zeus) is in the theogony physically individualised (everything is absorbed into Zeus), and then mentally individualised, introjected into the mind as universal value (mind is all, and worth everything).

Because an especially influential account of the comprehensive bounded *psuchē* is Plato's, I will conclude this section with two examples of the Platonic introjection of money. The first is from the *Phaedo*. The *psuchē* is invisible and separable from the body, but may be 'dragged by the body into things that are always changing, and itself wanders about and is agitated [. . .]'. It succeeds in being by itself by gathering itself from all parts of the body (67c, 80e, 83a). And '*phronēsis* is the only right currency (*nomisma*), for which all those things [pleasures, pains, fears] must be exchanged' (69a). The second example is from the *Republic* (416e). The guardians of the ideal state are to be told that they have from the gods always in their *psuchē* divine gold and silver money (*chrusion* and *argurion*), which is pure and not to be contaminated by the polluting mortal coinage of the multitude. As in Parmenides, abstract value is separated from circulation, sublimated, and introjected. Wealthy individuals such as Parmenides and Plato[25] control a variety of concrete goods and services by means of unitary abstract value, which as philosophers they both project (as Parmenidean Being and the Platonic 'form of the good')[26] and introject[27]—through the 'currency' (wisdom) by which the variety of pleasures, pains, fears, etc., are controlled.

I conclude this section. The advent of monism and of the idea of the unified inner self cannot be explained from the Jungian perspective adopted by Edinger. Rather, they owe much to (respectively) the projection and introjection of money, the advent of which by contrast can be explained (in terms of a combination of various historical factors).[28]

****

The second part of this chapter is an (inevitably selective) account of the Greek reaction to the advent of the monetised inner self. My focus is on tragedy. Greek tragedy is as a genre unique, in being invented at a particular time and in a particular place (rather than a traditional kind of performance eventually committed to writing, as were all the other 'literary' genres). Why did tragedy rapidly come into being in Attica in the last quarter of the sixth century BCE? What was happening at the same time (perhaps from as early as the middle of the century) was the monetisation of Attica promoted by the arrival (from across the Aegean) of coinage. This is the most important single fact I know about Greek tragedy—to use a rhetorical hyperbole prompted by the complete absence of the fact from the entire vast body of writing about Greek tragedy. Tragedy, invented in the wake of the monetary revolution, provides much untapped evidence for its impact.

The various respects in which monetisation was a precondition for the invention of tragedy I have set out in detail elsewhere.[29] My focus here is on the monetised individual at the heart of tragedy. This individual is sometimes oddly called the 'tragic hero', despite the fact that the tragic individual is never called hero (ἥρως) in any ancient text:[30] the normal word is *turannos* (autocrat). The themes of Greek tragedy are taken from myth, which is pre-*polis* and pre-monetary in origin, but in tragedy is heavily influenced by fundamental recent developments: of the *polis* and of money. The biography of the *turannos* in historical and philosophical texts tends to have three characteristics: obsession with money, killing within the family, and profaning the sacred; the same combination also characterises the *turannos* of tragedy.[31] I select for discussion three such tragic *turannoi*, all of Thebes: Oedipus, Creon, and Pentheus.

The tragic *turannos* is isolated not only by his obsession with money (for the reasons described above), but also by the other two characteristics of the *turannos*:

bloodshed alienates him from his family, profanation from the gods. There is nobody in earlier literature as isolated as the tragic individual. Even the ship-wrecked Odysseus in the *Odyssey*, his companions drowned and himself almost drowning, has the support of Athena and will return to the bosom of his family. But Oedipus, Creon, and Pentheus are each completely and irreversibly isolated both from the gods (by transgression) and from his entire family (by killing or self-killing). I suggest that a crucial factor in this unprecedented isolation of these and other tragic individuals was the unprecedented recent process of monetisation.

Tragedy originated in a Dionysiac choral song (the dithyramb),[32] its earli-est themes involved the god Dionysus, and it continued to be performed in a Dionysiac festival. The opposition in tragedy between the individual *turannos* and the anonymous chorus goes back—I have argued—to the beginnings of tragedy in Athens at the very time at which the *turannos*, whose power depended largely on money, was replaced by democracy.[33]

The only extant tragedy on a Dionysiac theme is Euripides' *Bacchae* (written at the end of the fifth century). The *turannos* Pentheus, opposing the arrival of Dionysus in Thebes, accuses the seer Teiresias of being motivated (in his adher-ence to the new Dionysiac cult) by money (257). The same accusation is made against Teiresias (and others) by Oedipus in Sophocles' *Oedipus Rex* and by Creon in Sophocles' *Antigone*. When Creon does it, Teiresias replies by implying that Creon is as a *turannos* projecting his own love of money onto him (Teiresias)[34]—an example of the extraordinary psychological acuteness of Greek tragedy (despite the lack of terms such as 'projection').

Central to *Bacchae*, I suggest, is the contrast between the psychic boundedness and isolation of Pentheus on the one hand and on the other the psychic unison of the Dionysiac choruses (one chorus in the theatre, the other imagined on the mountainside). This opposition, which pervades the play, can be discussed only briefly here.

First, the bounded isolation of Pentheus. 'The whole *polis* was put into a bacchic frenzy' (1294) which, however, Pentheus vehemently excludes from himself, fear-ing to be infected with folly by the touch of his bacchant grandfather (343–344), rejecting all advice, and failing to register the destruction of his palace by earth-quake, thunder, and lightning invoked by Dionysus. Similar in Antigone is the impermeable obtuseness of Creon, with whom his son Haimon aptly, but vainly, pleas 'do not carry within yourself one ἦθος [mentality] only' (705). Haimon then comments on the emptiness of thinking that one has eloquence or a *psuchē* that nobody else has (708–709), which does not prevent Creon from claiming that he owns the *polis* (738).

Now I give some examples of the psychic solidarity of the Dionysiac choruses of maenads ('raving women'). Mystic initiation involves 'merging the *psuchē* with the *thiasos* [the Dionysiac sacred band]'; θιασεύεται ψυχάν (75). The *thiasoi* on the mountainside are a 'marvel of good order' (693). They move off like a rising flock of birds rising (748). Their unity extends to unity with nature: when they called 'in unison' on the god, 'the whole mountain and wild beasts joined in their bacchic movement' (725–727). They suckle wild animals, and produce water from a rock and wine and milk from the earth (699–710). They unite the basic opposites of human and animal, as well as—for they act like warriors (752–754)—female and male, whereas Pentheus treats Dionysus like a trapped animal (451–452) and disparages his 'female form' (353). The dancing inspired by Dionysus is universal: 'the whole land will dance whenever Bromios [Dionysus] leads the *thiasoi*.'[35] The ecstatic, head-shaking, but seemingly co-ordinated dancing that is central to the drama, practised not only by the maenads but even by the old men Cadmus and Teiresias (184–185), is visible in numerous contemporary Athenian vase-paintings of maenads.

But the psychic isolation of Pentheus and the psychic solidarity of the chorus are not simply juxtaposed. Pentheus, on the point of taking military action against the maenads on the mountainside, is asked by Dionysus (disguised from the beginning as a mortal) whether he would like to see them there. Pentheus replies that he would give an enormous weight of gold to do so (811–812). This expression of internal monetisation marks the turning point of the play. He instantly accommodates opposites by agreeing that he would take pleasure in seeing something unpleasant for him (815–816). He then puts on female clothes (to be disguised as a maenad),[36] sees Dionysus as a bull (920–922), and is eventually on the mountainside taken to be an animal, and torn apart, by the maenads (1108–1278). There is only one sun, and one city of Thebes, but—once dressed as a female—Pentheus sees two of each (918–919).[37] The catastrophes of Oedipus and Creon in Sophocles are also represented as the confusion of basic distinctions, in the case of Oedipus between family members,[38] in the case of Creon between areas of the cosmos.[39]

Whereas the bounded *psuchē* of the tragic *turannos* is Parmenidean in its individual self-sufficiency, the communal solidarity of the choruses, their merging of the *psuchē* into the group, and their embodiment of the unity of opposites, is Heraclitean. The new Dionysiac cult is like a 'a fire blazing up close' (778–779). In tragedy, a communal event organised by the *polis*, Parmenidean self-sufficiency is generally destroyed (or destroys itself), and the communality that is central to Heraclitus' vision generally prevails.[40] In *Bacchae*, for instance, the failure to accommodate opposites[41] that we noted in Pentheus is eventually replaced by their overwhelming introjection, and the play ends with the founding of the *polis* cult stated by the god at the beginning of the play to be his reason for coming to Thebes.[42]

The extreme Parmenidean individual of myth is Midas.[43] And he, too, is set against the values represented by Dionysus. Silenus (an immortal, animal-like follower of Dionysus) reveals to Midas wisdom that consists of 'natural and ancient things', calls Midas 'ephemeral', and states that the best thing for humankind is never to have been born, the second best to die as soon as possible. Offered by Dionysus the fulfilment of any wish, Midas chooses the power to turn all things by his touch into gold, which he subsequently regrets when his food is turned to gold. He is initiated into the Dionysiac mysteries, and saved from his monetary power by

Dionysus. The same opposition—between money held to be the best of all things and the permanent salvation conferred by Dionysiac initiation—is expressed by the chorus of Bacchae while Pentheus is dressed as a female.[44]

As a postscript, I note that the same intellectual shift that we identified between Homer and the Presocratics—from (a) polytheism with no comprehensive inner self to (b) impersonal monism and the centrality of the comprehensive inner self—occurred (also along with autonomous monetisation) in the Indian transition from the Rgveda to the Upanisads. For Greece, my suggestion is that traditional Dionysiac cult became a site for reaction to the new monetised individual. In India, a different kind of reaction is, I suggest, represented by the Buddhist doctrine of non-self, *anatta*. But that is a theme for another publication.

Notes

1 E.F. Edinger, *The Psyche in Antiquity*, book 1, *Early Greek Philosophy*, Toronto: Inner City Books, 1999. Further references to this text are in the text in parentheses.

2 C. Geertz, '"From the Native's Point of View": On the Nature of Anthropological Understanding', in *Local Knowledge: Further Essays in Interpretive Anthropology*, New York: Basic Books, 1984, pp. 55–70 (p. 59).

3 E. LiPuma, 'Modernity and Forms of Personhood in Melanesia', in M. Lambek and A. Strathern (eds), *Bodies and Persons*, Cambridge: Cambridge University Press, 1998, pp. 53–79 (p. 74).

4 C.B. Macpherson, *The Political Theory of Possessive Individualism: From Hobbes to Locke*, Oxford: Oxford University Press, 1962, p. 3.

5 D. Parfit, *Reasons and Persons*, Oxford: Oxford University Press, 1984, p. 225.

6 R. Sorabji, *Self: Ancient and Modern Insights about Individuality, Life, and Death*, Oxford: Oxford University Press, 2006, p. 265, emphasis in the original.

7 R. Seaford, *Money and the Early Greek Mind*, Cambridge: Cambridge University Press, 2004, pp. 297–298.

8 See Philo of Alexandria, *De Plantatione*, §18; and *Legum Allegoriae*, book 3, §95.

9 Its comprehensiveness is indicated by, for example, Diels-Kranz fragment B109: 'eyes and ears are bad witnesses for men having barbarian souls (ψυχάς)'.

10 See Diels-Kranz fragments B36 (cf. B31), B118, B117; in G.S. Kirk, D. Raven, and M. Schofield, *The Presocratic Philosophers: A Critical History with a Selection of Texts*, 2nd edn, Cambridge: Cambridge University Press, 1983, pp. 198–199 and 203–208.

11 This is prefigured already in the passage in Homer in which the living *psuchē* is most valued (*Iliad* 9.378–409); see also Pindar, *Isthmian* I.68–70; Euripides, *Suppliants*, 775–777; *Medea*, 968; *Phoenician Women*, 1228. Cf. Aeschylus, *Agamemnon*, 437–441; *Psychostasia*; Isocrates, 6.109; Xenophon, *Cyropaedia*, 3.1.36; and *Anthologia Graeca*, 7.622.6. Human life involves a *debt* to death, see Euripides, *Alcestis*, 419 and 782; *Andromache*, 1272; Plato, *Timaeus*, 942e–943a; and *Anthologia Palatina*, 10.105.

12 See Diels-Kranz fragments B1 and B2.

13 Diels-Kranz fragment B31; cf. fragment B30.

14 Kirk, Raven, and Schofield, *The Presocratic Philosophers*, pp. 177–178 and 199–220; see R. Seaford, *Money and the Early Greek Mind: Homer, Philosophy, Tragedy*, Cambridge: Cambridge University Press, 2004, p. 233, n. 12.

15 Seaford, *Money and the Early Greek Mind*, p. 231.

16 For which see for which see Seaford, *Money and the Early Greek Mind*, pp. 236–240 and 281.

17 Seaford, *Money and the Early Greek Mind*, pp. 242–265.

18 Seaford, *Money and the Early Greek Mind*, pp. 227–279 and 252.

19 Some commentators would exclude a temporal sense, citing B.8.25; but this is to ignore the thought experiment (look!), in which what is imagined (absent) is obviously not restricted to simultaneity.

20 See also Diels-Kranz fragments B8.33 and B8.47–48.

21 Plato, *Phaedo*, 83b1-4; also 81a; and *Phaedrus*, 248c–249d.

22 T. Kouremenos, G.M. Parássoglou, and K.Tsantsanoglou, *The Derveni Papyrus: Edited with Introduction and Commentary*, Florence: Olschki, 2006.

23 West dates the theogony to a generation either side of 500 BCE; see M.L.West, *The Orphic Poems*, Oxford: Oxford University Press, 1983, pp. 108–110.

24 Column xvi. I reproduce the translation of Kouremenos et al. (2006), based on their authoritative edition of the fragmentary Greek.

25 Diogenes Laertius, *Lives and Opinions of the Great Philosophers*, 3.41–43; and 9.21.

26 Plato, *Republic*, 505a; *Republic*, 508a–e, 532b1, *Laws* 965b–966b.

27 Plato, *Phaedo*, 83b1–4; also 81a; and *Phaedrus*, 248c–249d.

28 For one such explanation, see Seaford, *Money and the Early Greek Mind*, part one.

29 For further discussion, see R. Seaford, *Cosmology and the Polis*, Cambridge: Cambridge University Press, 2012.

30 The exception (Euripides, fragment 446) proves the rule: Hippolytus is called ἥρως once he is *dead*.

31 See R. Seaford, 'Tragic Tyranny', in K. Morgan (ed.), *Popular Tyranny: Sovereignty and its Discontents in Ancient Greece*, Austin TX: University of Texas Press, 2003, pp. 95–116.

32 See Aristotle, *Poetics*, §4.

33 For further discussion, see Seaford, *Cosmology and the Polis*.

34 I discuss all these passages in R. Seaford, 'Tragic Money', *Journal of Hellenic Studies* 118, 1998, 119–139.

35 114–155; see also 206–209, in R. Seaford, *Euripides: 'Bacchae'*, Warminster: Aris and Phillips, 1996.

36 We are reminded of the Jungian principle that 'all consciousness, perhaps without being aware of it, seeks its unconscious opposite, lacking which it is doomed to stagnation, congestion, and ossification' (C.G. Jung, *The Psychology of the Unconscious*, in *Two Essays on Analytical Psychology* [*Collected Works*, vol. 7], tr. R.F.C. Hull, Princeton, NJ: Princeton University Press, 1996, §78 (p. 53).

37 This derives from the use of the mirror in Dionysiac initiation; see Seaford, *Euripides: 'Bacchae'*, pp. 223–224.

38 Sophocles, *Oedipus Tyrannus*, 425, 457–60, 1207–1210, 1215, 1250, 1256–1257, 1358–1362, 1403–1407, 1481, 1485, 1497–1498.

39 *Antigone*, 1015–1022, 1040–1044, and 1068–1073.

40 See Diels-Kranz fragments B2, B44, B89, B113, B114, and B116.

41 This has been connected with the psychological phenomenon of 'splitting'; for further discussion, see Seaford, *Euripides: 'Bacchae'*, p. 170.

42 The occasional doubts expressed about this (arising out of a large gap in the manuscript) are absurd; see Seaford, *Euripides' 'Bacchae'*, pp. 252–253.

43 For the source references in this paragraph, see Seaford, *Money and the Early Greek Mind*, pp. 305–307; and R. Seaford, 'Dionysos, Money, and Drama', *Arion: A Journal of the Humanities and the Classics*, series 3, 11 (2), Fall, 2003, 1–19.

44 Seaford, *Euripides: 'Bacchae'*, pp. 218–219.

PART III

Ancient ecstatic in other worlds

8

HISTORY, PHILOSOPHY, AND MYTH IN LUO GUANZHONG'S *THREE KINGDOMS*

Terence Dawson

Three Kingdoms is often described, somewhat misleadingly, as the *Iliad* of Chinese literature. It is a very long historical novel set during the protracted and troubled fall of the Han Dynasty, a period which corresponds almost exactly with the beginnings of the decline of the Roman Empire.[1] It was distilled and adapted by Mao Lun and his son, Mao Zonggang, from an early sixteenth-century history of the period. And it was first published in 1679—that is, one year after the publication, in Paris, of a very different kind of historical novel.[2] *La Princesse de Clèves* is a short romance, set in the French court of Henri II between late 1558 and late 1559. Although published anonymously, it has long been attributed to Madame de Lafayette.[3] Within their respective traditions, both works mark the beginning of a new kind of prose fiction: the novel.

The focus of their respective concerns reveals interesting cultural differences. The setting of *La Princesse de Clèves* is loosely based on history, but the main plot is entirely fictional. It begins with the young heroine's marriage to a man she respects. She then meets the handsome duc de Nemours who falls passionately in love with her, as she does with him. But instead of enjoying an affair with him, as the novel insists any other woman would do, she determines to resist the love she feels for Nemours and remain true to her husband. If *La Princesse de Clèves* is widely regarded as the first modern novel in the European tradition, it is because the novelist has made a new kind of connection between the concerns of the minor characters and the main plot and given a new depth to the moral dilemma facing the heroine. It paves the way for the further exploration of the inner experience of a main character.

Three Kingdoms is a prose epic, with occasional verse. It is fictionalised history. All the main characters are based on historical originals, even if sometimes considerable license has been taken with what is known about them.[4] The three most important are Liu Bei (Xuande), his advisor Zhuge Liang (Kongming), and the man whom they seek to oust from power, Cao Cao (Mengde).[5] Their personal concerns only rarely intrude. The novel focuses on their actions, on how they each respond to changing circumstances. It explores the sweeping momentum of political intrigues, their military consequences, and the tension between the dictates of Heaven and the erratic and unpredictable behaviour of human beings, and how even the best can be misled by their own tendencies and psychological blind spots. If *Three Kingdoms* is widely regarded as the first novel, it is not only because it is the first long Chinese prose fiction to be divided into chapters, each of which ends in carefully managed suspense, but also because it examines the human and moral qualities needed to hold a very diverse nation together.

Both works explore narrative structures and concerns first formulated in a 'mythic' or 'archaic' past. In *La Princesse de Clèves*, the heroine's dilemma is characterised by the disturbance (or, in French, *trouble*) which the duc de Nemours causes both in her heart and her mind. Whenever she sees him, she is thrown into confusion and agitation. She doesn't experience Nemours as just another man whom she happens to meet at court. She experiences him as someone with 'a natural brilliance' about him, as a numinous *image*, someone from whom she instinctively feels she must flee if she does not want to be burned by her experience.[6] The effect he has on her can be compared with that which Apollo has on Daphne. Just as Daphne tries to escape Apollo, so the young princesse de Clèves tries to distance herself from Nemours.[7] The dilemma at the heart of the novel represents an intriguing elaboration of a pattern of behaviour associated with an ancient myth. Jung would have called such a pattern *archetypal*, by which he meant one that impresses itself on consciousness because it encapsulates a tendency which requires the subject's attention.

In *Three Kingdoms*, the two pivotal heroes (Liu Bei and Zhuge Liang) are equally obsessed—but *not* with an image, and least of all with an image experienced only by themselves. They are obsessed with an *idea* or, perhaps more accurately, with a number of interrelated *notions*. And they regard these notions as harbouring so much greater importance than themselves that they willingly subordinate themselves to them. The novel, however, is not about their personal desire or their personal ambition; it is about a complex of abstract collective issues including loyalty to the Han Dynasty, responsibility to those under their command, and the integrity which links the individual to the community and fosters civic harmony.[8] And these notions rest on deeply ingrained convictions derived from ideas first articulated in 'archaic' times, notably by Confucius and Sun Tzu. And the resonance these notions harbour can also be defined as archetypal. The reader grasps instinctively that they represent some of the most deeply felt values of both ancient and modern China.

It is customary to distinguish between myth, history, and philosophy. This chapter argues that, in psychological terms, they often overlap. It seeks to demonstrate that, under certain circumstances, both history and even philosophy can be described as 'archetypal'. And *Three Kingdoms* illustrates this.

Myths are fantasy, narrative structures which harbour archetypal issues that resonate intensely for the society in which they emerge. They invite repeated reformulation and reinterpretation. As both myth criticism and Jungian approaches to literature have shown, many of the great texts of Western literature either represent or include intriguing adaptations of the narrative structures and concerns of classical and other myths. It is unlikely that Madame de Lafayette intended her work to elaborate on the concerns at the heart of the myth of Daphne and Apollo. If it does so, it is because, while thinking about how to explore romantic love—an emergent concern at the time—the basic structure of the myth proposed itself to her. And inevitably, her adaptation of this structure reflects concerns pertinent both to her age (the age of Louis XIV) and to herself.[9]

History purports to be objective. The claims advanced by historians may rest on facts, but they are *not* synonymous with those facts. Every historical 'fact' is open to interpretation. We tend to think of the past in causative and material terms: hence, every new historical study claims to be revealing the truth about a person or a period for the first time. In psychological terms, however, such claims are naïve. As Schopenhauer reminds us in *The World as Will and Representation*, 'materialism is the philosophy of the subject who forgets to take account of himself'.[10] We can only contemplate the past from the perspective of our own present situation and circumstances. Every claim about the past is a construct coloured by tendencies pertinent not only to the age in which the claim is made, but also to the historian who makes it. History is much less objective than historians would have us believe.

Every nation has periods to which historians return repeatedly, because these periods encapsulate issues that carry the same archetypal intensity for its people as those found in myth. In Britain, such periods include the Tudor age and the Civil War; in France, the Wars of Religion and the French Revolution, and in China, the Warring States and the Han Dynasty. These pages outline the gradual transformation of the *history* of the fall of the Han Dynasty into a *prose epic* as powerful and resonant as any myth.[11]

The popular idea of philosophy is that it is a dry, intellectual activity practised only by those with a disposition to quibble endlessly. But in psychological terms, this lazy assumption is equally naïve. In the same way as the historian seeks the truth about a past event, so the philosopher seeks the truth about the way we think. By extension, philosophy suggests that we should act in accord with the truth about our way of thinking. It reminds us to expect the best of ourselves in the way we understand and relate to the world. Ever since the time of Plato, every age of Western history has sought to reinterpret for itself the phrase attributed to Socrates at his trial: 'the unexamined life is not worth living' (*Apology*, 38a).[12] If myth can be defined as the *imaginal* expression of concerns central to a given culture, then philosophy can be defined as the *verbal* expression of notions central to the culture. And the older a philosophical claim is, the more likely it is to harbour archetypal implications.

The archaic is, in Paul Bishop's felicitous phrase, 'the past in the present'.[13] The culture of a nation rests on the ideas, and especially the archaic ideas in which it finds its deepest meaning. In the course of the first millennium of the common era, most European countries gradually adopted Christianity. In spite of the upheavals of the twentieth century, Chinese culture still rests on the claims advanced by three much earlier thinkers whose ideas began to flourish in China during the Han Dynasty. Gautama Buddha came from Nepal and India. The other two were native to China: Confucius (Kongzi) and Laozi (Lao Tse), the reputed author of the *Dao De Jing* (= The Way of Virtue Book), which is the classic expression of Daoist thought.

This chapter explores the importance given to the ideas of Confucius and his near contemporary, Sun Tzu (Sunzi), author of *The Art of War*, during the Han Dynasty—ideas that were central to every history of its gradual decline, including the much-loved novel of 1679. *Three Kingdoms* is not just a fictional account of factual events which have had a lasting impact on Chinese culture. It is the expression of deep-rooted archetypal notions, and its subsequent impact stems from the sophisticated way in which its narrative harnesses these archetypal notions to very powerful effect.

Jung was predominantly interested in the relation between image and experience. Scholars working with his various theories have tried to extend them into domains such as culture and politics.[14] Astonishingly, the archetypal nature of our ideas about history and what we remember from philosophy has received little attention. The following pages contend that history and philosophy harbour powerful archetypal notions, and that these notions are just as resonant as those harboured by imagery and myth.

Western assumptions, Chinese values

Three Kingdoms begins by placing primary responsibility for the decline of the Han Dynasty on the corruption of the palace eunuchs, who took advantage of a succession of very young emperors to seize effective control of the nation. It then briefly describes the Yellow Scarves rebellion, which broke out in 184 CE. Eighty of the one hundred and twenty chapters then focus on the diplomatic and military wrangles between three loosely defined and ever shifting regions: Wei (Northern China), Shu (South-western China), and Eastern Wu (South-eastern China). Each of these falls into the hands of a powerful warlord: Cao Cao, who keeps the Emperor firmly under his control, governs Wei; Sun Jian and his successors Sun Ce and Sun Quan have command of Wu, while Shu falls into the hands of Liu Bei. All three leaders seek legitimacy and total control of the Empire. The last forty chapters depict the inevitable consequences. In 220, China finally splits, but not into three kingdoms: each of the warlords declares himself *emperor*.[15] The struggles continue through a second generation. The novel ends forty-five years later, when Sima Yan seizes the imperial throne for himself, reunifies the nation and establishes the Jin Dynasty.[16] *Three Kingdoms* is one of the great works of world literature, grander in its scale even than the *Iliad*: it has a great many equally memorable scenes, and its outcome is just as overwhelming.

The opening chapters of *Three Kingdoms* describe how Liu Bei meets two other men who are keen to defend the Han Dynasty against the threat posed by opportunist warlords. As soon as they discover their common cause, they swear to treat each other as 'brothers'. This involves them agreeing to live and to die together. They are well differentiated: indeed, so different are they that it is sometimes difficult to imagine they would have had much to say to each other. In *La Princesse de Clèves*, all the main characters are aristocrats. What the three brothers have in common is that they are all firmly placed in the lower rungs of society and they have a burning loyalty toward the Han. None of them is either glorified or idealised. They are all presented as having their own mix of appropriate attitudes and all-too-human weaknesses.

The oldest is Liu Bei, whose family have fallen on hard times. Prior to the events of the novel, he made straw sandals and mats for a living. He has struggled to give himself a passable education. Guan Yu (Yunchang) belongs to a significantly higher level of society: he reads the Chinese classics regularly. But having killed a local bully, he is an outlaw. The third of the brotherhood and, somewhat ironically, the most successful, is Zhang Fei (Yide), an easy-going, hard-drinking, but virtually illiterate wine merchant and butcher.

Early in the novel, Dong Zhuo, a coarse and brutal warlord, seizes control of the Emperor. A number of regional leaders who want to restore the Han Emperor to power set up a camp and make a call to arms. The three 'brothers' promptly make their way to the camp and ask to see the leaders. They are shocked by what they find. Instead of being united by their cause, the leaders are squabbling amongst themselves, each seeking their own advantage or profit. And they are indignant that such lower-order individuals should seek inclusion in their meeting.

Meanwhile, at the gates of the camp, one of the usurping strongmen, Hua Xiong, is challenging any of the Han supporters to single combat. Yu She volunteers to meet the challenge. No sooner has he left than the news returns that he has been killed. Pan Feng meets the same fate, and as quickly. The leaders begin to panic. Guan Yu then volunteers. The leaders are irate at the presumption of this mere archer. He leaves. And, as he had said he would, before the wine poured for him has gone cold, he returns with the head of the rebel champion. Yuan Shu, brother of the commander-in-chief of the Han supporters, is outraged: he wants all three brothers sent packing. Cao Cao intervenes to calm the assembly.

The scene is familiar to every Chinese reader. Guan Yu has distinguished himself. His feat of arms might well have been the focus of the novelist's attention. It isn't: all three encounters take place outside. The author's attention is on the bickering of the leaders which so evidently undermines their cause and contributes to the instability of the nation. The implication is clear. In uncertain times, each seeks his own *individual* opportunity, his own *individual* advantage, his own *individual* gain, his own *individual* profit. Western nations regard individualism as an advance on collectivism. *Three Kingdoms* illustrates its negative tendencies and the price a nation pays for it.

Western literature privileges myth, which is based on narrative structure, imagery and the personal concerns of a main character. And so too does Jungian psychology. Although Chinese literature is rich in imagery (the Chinese language ensures this), it privileges abstract notions and the collective concerns of a community or nation. This distinction requires illustration: two examples must suffice. The first foregrounds a very minor character, but for all her unimportance, she plays a truly memorable role and continues to be widely admired for her action.

Early in the novel, Dong Zhuo has seized power. One evening, Wang Yun, who is Minister of the Interior, is racking his brain to find a way to overthrow Dong Zhuo and return the Han to power. He is weeping with frustration at his inability to come up with a plan when he hears his sixteen-year-old ward, Diaochan, also weeping. When he asks her why, she replies that she is crying because she cannot think of a way to be of help to him: 'But if there is any way I can serve you,' she tells him, 'I would welcome death ten thousand times before declining.'[17]

Wang Yun suddenly realises how she might save the Han Dynasty. He gets down on his knees and kowtows to Diaochan, a gesture which signals highest respect. She is shocked by his action. He pleads that she accept his plan. She is taken aback: she thought she had already made it clear that she would do whatever he asks. He tells her his plan. He will find a way to persuade Dong Zhuo's adopted son, Lü Bu, the best warrior of his age, to fall in love with her, while also secretly offering her to Dong Zhuo. He will then tell Lü Bu that Dong Zhuo stole her for himself, in the hope that Lü Bu will be so enraged with his foster-father that he will kill him. The plan works.

For a Western reader, what is of note is that neither Wang Yun nor Diaochan hesitate. The monstrosity of his suggestion does not occur to him; more surprisingly, it does not occur to her. She feels she owes a debt to Wang Yun—to Wang Yun, not as an individual, but as a guardian who has always loved her—and now this debt must be repaid. He hands over a beloved foster-daughter to a monster of a man whom he hates, and she willingly embraces her fate. Personal feelings have no place in their decisions. Diaochan wants to repay her foster-father for his kindness; he wants to take a first necessary step toward reviving the Han.[18] The second example might also shock the Western reader. But once again, it illustrates the smallness of personal interest when weighed against collective concerns.

Cao Cao, who tried to help Liu Bei when they first met at the ill-fated assembly of leaders, subsequently seizes control of the Emperor, effectively imprisoning him. He has slowly gained in power. Liu Bei has turned to Zhuge Liang for advice. But because this advice strikes him as immoral, he hesitates to act on it. As a result, he and his supporters soon fall into disarray and headlong retreat. Their retreat is slowed dangerously because, rather than submit to Cao Cao, the people of the towns of Fan and Xinye have preferred to follow Liu Bei and he, against all advice, will not abandon them.

At a particularly difficult moment, Liu Bei entrusts Zhao Yun (Zilong), one of his bravest generals, with his two wives (Lady Gan and Lady Mi) and his baby son (Ah Dou). Cao Cao presses hard on all Liu Bei's forces and various groups become scattered. Liu Bei is told that Zilong has defected. He refuses to believe it. Zhang Fei, furious, sets off to find out. In the fighting, Zilong had been separated from his charges, and is trying to find them. He finds Lady Gan and sends her back to

Liu Bei. He then sets off in search of Lady Mi and Ah Dou. He finds her limping badly. She begs him to take her son back to Liu Bei, but without her, as she would only slow their progress. He hesitates. To force him to do as she asks, she throws herself down a well. Zilong then straps the baby to his chest and single-handedly fights his way back through several groups of enemy strongmen in order to reach Liu Bei. His determination is extraordinary. At last, he is glad to be able to return Ah Dou to his lord.[19]

A Western reader will understand Lady Mi's sacrifice, but might have considerably more difficulty with Liu Bei's reaction on being handed back his son. He throws the 'suckling' to the ground in a rage, not, as one might guess, because he would rather have lost his son than his wife.[20] He does so because he knows Zilong's worth: wives and babies can be replaced, but generals with the loyalty and courage of Zilong are irreplaceable. Liu Bei is furious with Zilong for having risked his life for the sake of a baby.[21] The great cause must come first: which is to do all one can to overthrow Cao Cao and restore the Han.

In both scenes, personal considerations have no place when weighed against collective concerns. Moreover, the resonance of these two episodes comes not from an image, but from an *idea*. *Three Kingdoms* is not about heroes engaging with an 'image' which represents an implicit challenge. It is about a mix of psychological integrity and moral philosophy.

The Han Dynasty: history and Confucius

China stretches over a vast and very varying terrain, and each geographical region harbours distinct peoples with distinct cultural traditions. Each of these local tribes and cultures worried constantly about one or more of its neighbours becoming too powerful, and this suspicion increased when the neighbours in question belonged to an emphatically foreign culture. China can boast a cultural history of some 5,000 years or more, but its borders have grown and shrunk, and taken in or excluded a great many different tribes and people in the course of these years. On at least four occasions, powerful neighbours to the north or to the east have invaded and occupied either a part or the whole of its heartland.[22] The Chinese have often lost what they thought they had gained, and foreign occupation has been a frequent experience. This may help to explain their interest in history.

The Chinese word for *history* suggests a record, or the recording of (past) events or experiences.[23] In contrast to the Greek word *historiê*, it does not suggest that there might be more than one view about an event, nor that the process of recording an event or its interpretation might be intrinsically problematic.[24] And yet the Chinese very quickly realised that a historical record can be harnessed to a specific purpose. It can comment on an era. It can manipulate opinion. It can explore the consequences of ill-judged action. It can revitalise views which promote collective well-being. *Three Kingdoms* is a product of this awareness.

The novel is challenging for Western readers, because it assumes familiarity with at least five periods of China's early history—and each of them harbours different characteristics. The Spring and Autumn period corresponds to the pre-classical period in Greek literature, from Homer through Hesiod to Pindar. Its dates are derived from *The Spring and Autumn Annals*, a year-by-year chronicle of somewhat random events pertinent to the state of Lu between the years 722 and 481 BCE. (Other states kept comparable annals; none has survived.) These annals are of only specialist historical interest, but later scholars attributed them to Confucius and so they became one of the five classics of Chinese literature.[25]

The importance of the period is that it produced three of the most influential Chinese philosophers—and the ideas of Confucius, Laozi, and Sun Tzu could hardly be more different. Although very little is known for certain about any of them, their ideas gradually became central to Chinese culture, not least because they are central to the history of the decline of the Han Dynasty.

The Warring States (*c.* 475–221 BCE) was a period of unbridled ambition and shifting allegiances, of regional power won and lost, and of the carnage and turmoil that came in their wake.[26] But it was also an age of extraordinary intellectual searching and experimentation, an age every bit as remarkable as the early Hellenistic period in the Mediterranean with which it is contemporary. It boasted a 'Hundred Schools of Thought', and even if this number is somewhat exaggerated, it nonetheless suggests the extraordinary variety of ideas which emerged during this period. For it was about one hundred and fifty years *after* the death of Confucius that two philosophers began to develop an interest in his ideas. And by doing so, Mencius (Mengzi, *c.* 370–295) and Xun Kuang (Xunzi, *c.* 310–225) laid the foundations of a wide-ranging Confucian cultural philosophy.

Meanwhile, a very different political philosophy was beginning to enjoy more visible success. The ideas behind the reforms made by Shang Yang (390–338 BCE) came to be known as Legalism. They revitalised administrative practices, and placed an emphasis on efficiency and equality before the law. These soon led to the rise of the state of Qin. The period known as the Warring States was brought to an end when King Zheng of Qin united the neighbouring regions and appointed himself Shi Huang, First Emperor of the Qin Dynasty.

The reign of the First Emperor lasted only a decade, but in the course of this decade so much was achieved, and on such a scale, that one can only wonder how it was managed. Li Si, a visionary minister, weakened the feudal traditions in order to unify the country; he also oversaw the standardisation of weights, measures, currency, and the Chinese script. Meanwhile, followers of Shang Yang's legalism established a nationwide system of administration and military command. The changes they brought about were designed to foster equality both of opportunity *and* before the law—but they very soon revealed an unanticipated shadow. Legalism became associated with both judicial harshness and authoritarian excess. The most obvious examples of the latter were the linking of a number of existent walls to form the 'Great Wall' and the construction of Shi Huang's tomb, with its thousands of terracotta soldiers. These and other ambitious projects soon led to bribery and corruption. Dissent began to be expressed, and views and books which fostered earlier traditions were banned.[27] Inevitably, soon after the death of the First Emperor, revolts began to erupt. Liu Bang was a rebel leader from the peasant class. Somewhat unexpectedly, he quickly won sufficient support to become emperor of a new dynasty: the Han Dynasty (206 BCE–220 CE).

There are good reasons why the Chinese came to regard the Han Dynasty as a golden age and to define themselves as Han Chinese. In spite of constant political turmoil, it also witnessed considerable advances in almost every aspect of life. Legalism had promoted efficient administrative systems, but these often fell into the hands of individuals who quietly sought their own advantage. Somewhat ironically, this led to the most lasting development of the Han Dynasty. In order to check the harshness and corruption associated with legalism, Confucian practices were gradually introduced into government and, from there, they moved into the mainstream of Chinese culture. The emphasis of Confucianism on ritual and tradition promoted a much-needed social stability, and the moral rectitude it expected of its adherents helped to ensure that legalist systems functioned with both integrity and compassion.[28]

Confucius held a highly idealised view of the distant past, especially of the early semi-mythical Xia Dynasty (2070–1600 BCE). This obsession with the past stirred his later followers to develop a fascination with history, which soon became a fundamental characteristic of Chinese culture permeating all levels of society. Whilst it is extremely unlikely that Confucius had anything to do with *The Spring and Autumn Annals*, later Confucian scholars were quick to attribute it to him and to produce 'commentaries' on it. And these commentaries are amongst the first histories. History soon became the sounding board for all moral and political views.[29]

The parallel with Western neoclassicism is evident. Just as the Renaissance brought about an idealisation of ancient Greek and Roman models, so Confucianism fostered not only a respect for Confucius and other thinkers of his age (the Warring States period), but also for the practices attributed to the much earlier and semi-mythical Xia Dynasty. Western admiration of classical culture gradually faded, but Chinese thought continued to be influenced by Confucius until the mid-twentieth century—indeed, albeit less obviously, it continues to be so.

Each new dynasty produced more or less official accounts of the preceding dynasty. Later, each would write its own history. And independent scholars wrote their own accounts. The Chinese may have come to history later than the Greeks, but once they discovered it, they very quickly grasped the various purposes to which it can be put. History can validate the present, it can legitimise an ideology, it can disguise a blunder, it can provide the cornerstone of nation making. It can also identify both corruption and tyranny, it can analyse their cause, and it can propose an alternate and better course of action. History is everything and anything but an objective study of past events. Chinese historians used history both to justify *and* to challenge government actions in the present.

When the Han Dynasty fell into decline, scholars were quick to write their version of the events, and the events of this period very quickly became the test case for discussion about the nature of moral rectitude and good government. The 'history' of the collapse of the Han Dynasty fascinated all strata of Chinese society for some 1,300 years *before* it became the subject of the novel attributed to Luo Guanzhong. And each successive history tacitly reflected the political conditions of the time in which it was written.

History as myth

'Here begins our tale. The empire, long divided, must unite; long united, must divide. Thus it has ever been.'[30] This justly famous opening of *Three Kingdoms* was written during the Qing Dynasty. It encapsulates the cyclical course that the history of China has taken. The desire of individuals for greater autonomy has often been accompanied by a desire for greater power; and the seizure of great power has always led to concerns about the exercise of excessive authority over individuals. Without the text actually asserting this, every reader in 1679 would have known that the most recent years of *unity* were those of the Ming Dynasty, a golden age ruled by Han Chinese, and that the *divisions* led to China once again falling into the hands of foreign rulers: the Manchurians. *Three Kingdoms* is a novel about foreign occupation and the political oppression this signals.

Three Kingdoms, the novel, emerges from a long line of histories about the decline and fall of the Han Dynasty. And in each case, the thrust of the argument reflects situations pertinent to the writer's time. The events were a recent memory when Chen Shou combined the official histories for each of the so-called Three Kingdoms into a single text: *Records of the Three Kingdoms* (*Sanguozhi*) from 184 to 280. His focus was on the moral character of the main players: in Western terms, he was closer to Plutarch than to Thucydides. His study was much admired. About one hundred and thirty years later, Pei Songzhi (372–451), working from archival documents, produced an extensively revised and annotated edition.

The emphasis on the biography and character of the major protagonists of the period lasted for five hundred years before finally giving way to an interest in the moral implications of the over-arching narrative itself. Two famous—and very different—accounts of the Song Dynasty (960–1279) illustrate this. The first was by Sima Guang (1019–1086), a political conservative of the Northern Song who fiercely resisted the liberal reforms proposed by Wang Anshi. He is most famous for being the author of the *Comprehensive Mirror in Aid of Governance* (*Zizhi Tongjian*, 1084), which is an epic chronicle of Chinese history from 403 BCE (the beginning of the Warring States period) to 959 CE (the end of the Five Dynasties and Ten Kingdoms period and the beginning of the Song Dynasty).[31] It runs to 294 volumes and totals some three million characters (that is, about four times longer than the later novel). It was written when the Song Dynasty was at its peak and its capital was in Bianjing (Kaifeng). As one would expect, Sima Guang held a positive opinion of Cao Cao, the northern warlord of Wei who acted as the Emperor Xian's prime minister.

The *Zizhi Tongjian* was much admired, and various shorter adaptations of it soon appeared. The most important was the *General History for the Aid of Government* by the equally conservative Song philosopher Zhu Xi (1130–1200). But he was writing under very different political conditions from Sima Guang. Soon after the latter finished his work, the Jurchen invaded and seized control of the northern half of the Chinese empire, where they established the Jin Dynasty (1115–1234). This forced the Song government to retreat south of the Yangtze, where Lin'an (Hangzhou) became their new capital. Writing *while the Jurchen occupied the Chinese heartland*, one can readily understand why Zhu Xi cast Cao Cao as the villain, thereby tacitly transforming Liu Bei, warlord of the southern Shu, into the hero. Zhu Xi presents Liu Bei as someone fighting to reunify the empire. And inevitably, Chinese storytellers in occupied Kaifeng quickly began to adjust their accounts of the events accordingly. The history of the period of Three Kingdoms had become a narrative about resistance to foreign occupation.

The Jurchen empire did not last long. Pushed back by the Chinese, the Jurchens were then invaded by the Mongols. In Europe, Genghis Khan is most famous for the rapid westward expansion of his empire. In East Asia, he is most famous for his conquest of much of the territory then controlled by the Jurchen Jin Dynasty. His third son, Ögedei Khan, took possession of much of northern China, and his nephew continued the conquest south. In 1271, Kublai Khan proclaimed himself Emperor of China, thereby establishing the Yuan Dynasty. The Mongol occupation lasted almost a hundred years—and it left a profound mark on China.

The Mongols may have insisted on the subservience of the Chinese, but they held a high regard both for their skill in administration and for their culture. As a result, under the Yuan, China prospered. Khanbaliq (present-day Beijing) became the new capital of the Mongol empire. Trade through the Silk Road increased (promoting, for example, the development of the blue and white ceramic ware, which later became identified with China even though the cobalt came from Persia). Several Mongol leaders, notably Jayaatu Khan, patronised Chinese literature thus helping its drama and prose to flourish. And perhaps inevitably, both sophisticated and popular retellings of the stories associated with the period of the Three Kingdoms became increasingly coloured by fictional embellishments, some of which contained cleverly disguised protests at Mongol rule. The most important of these was *Three Kingdoms: A Historical Novella*, written in the 1320s, which anticipates many of the main directions of the later novel.

In the late fourteenth century, the Mongol overlords were finally defeated, and the Yuan Dynasty gave way to the Ming Dynasty (1368–1644). Even so, the story of the collapse of the Han Dynasty lost none of its resonance. The first printed edition of yet another history of this turbulent period was published in 1522. Somewhat incongruously, its preface, dated 1494, is attributed to a *fourteenth*-century writer, Luo Guanzhong. *Historical Novel for Popular Reading Based on the Annals of the Three Kingdoms* is long: it is composed of some 900,000 Chinese characters and incorporates extensive quotations from historical documents as well as a great many poems. It enjoyed enormous popularity, and even today, many Chinese scholars and readers regard it as the definitive account of the events.

About one hundred and forty years after the publication of the 1522 text, the Manchurians overthrew the Ming Dynasty. In 1644, they established the Qing Dynasty and, once again, China was an occupied nation; once again, the overlords took advantage of the Chinese skill at administration, and once again, they showed respect for Chinese culture. In 1673, during the reign of the Kangxi Emperor, a serious rebellion—the revolt of the three feudatories—broke out in the south and rumbled on until 1681.

It was in the midst of this instability that Mao Lun and his son, Mao Zonggang, produced a significantly and cleverly edited version of the 1522 text. They shortened the work to some 750,000 characters. They removed much of the historical documentation and half of the incorporated poems, especially those from popular traditions. And they added sections of their own, including the famous opening. They also removed several passages praising Cao Cao and his generals, thereby further emphasising the sympathy for Liu Bei initiated by Zhu Xi five hundred years earlier. Their formal contributions were equally great. The 1679 text is a very great work of literature. It deserves its place as one of the four great Chinese novels.[32]

Ever since its first publication, the version of *Three Kingdoms* edited by Mao Lun and his son, Mao Zonggang, has been widely read by all levels of society. It too has generated a great many retellings, most recently in comic books, films, and television adaptations.[33] Such widespread and lasting interest in the collapse of the Han Dynasty suggests that it crystallises concerns of deep significance to Chinese society—and this invites us to return to our premise.

History does not, and cannot tell us the truth about what happened in the past. Every historical study is coloured by the concerns both of the age and of the historian. In other words, there is much less difference than one might assume between the latest narrative history and the latest adaptation of a myth. The common denominator is that history and myth both provide basic narrative structures, and these narrative structures invite constant adaptation and reformulation. A myth is a narrative structure which invites astonishingly different adaptations. And the Chinese were very quick to understand that *history*—whether of a defined period, of an artefact, or of a person—also invites constant reformulation to reflect the changing concerns of a society and its individuals.

In short, just as the princesse de Clèves finds herself confronted by a man to whom she responds *as if* he were Apollo, so Mao Lun and Mao Zonggang were fascinated by the history of the decline of the Han Dynasty. And just as Madame de Lafayette produces a variant of the mythic pattern for an age interested in irresistible desire, so the Chinese father-and-son team produce a variant of the story of the three kingdoms which reflects China's need to recover its independence—and its unity. *Three Kingdoms* is a novel about 'paradise lost'—and an account of those who seek to 'regain' it.

Philosophy as psychology

History is written from a present moment—that is, it looks 'backward'. And the farther the historian looks back into the past, especially if it is an archaic past about which most of what we know is conjectural, the more likely one is to find ideas and notions that have an archetypal resonance.

The driving concern of *Three Kingdoms* is the desire to recover political unity: that is, for the whole of China to have once again an Emperor of the Han Dynasty—for this would signal a return to the Mandate of Heaven. In 1679, for Han Dynasty, read anyone who is Han Chinese. In the novel, this desire for national unity has the intensity and resonance of an archetypal notion. Today, as the call for 'One China', it continues to be felt. As 'One Nation', it is an archetypal motif which can also be found elsewhere: for example, in Spain, Germany, or the United Kingdom—or even in the European Union. The call for 'One Nation' does not rest on an 'image'. It rests on an 'idea', a word whose etymology embraces both 'form' and 'abstract concept'.

In *Three Kingdoms*, the depiction of the political and military events is determined by a concern with righteousness and moral government. And this concern rests on a running tension between two contrasted ways of thinking. The first is between legalism and Confucianism: between a rule of law which is necessarily subject to human whim, and a rule of righteousness which is always guided by benevolence and compassion. The second is between the strategies and objectives of Sun Tzu and those of Zhu Xi: in other words, between strategies that foster self-interest and individualism and strategies concerned not with an objective, but with appropriate behaviour.

Cao Cao is the ostensible villain of the novel. He is highly intelligent and a brilliant administrator and military strategist. He surrounds himself with talented men, both administrators and intellectuals. His positive qualities, however, are undermined by weaknesses. He vividly represents how the rule of law can take a wrong turning. He understands human nature, and it is often an unnecessary fear of this which leads him to ruthlessness. Although he suffers from debilitating migraines, which might suggest a guilty conscience, he remains unrepentant to the end.

Liu Bei embodies various forms of righteousness including loyalty to the state, loyalty to his family, loyalty to his sworn brothers, and concern for the common people. But he is also vain and self-righteous: for example, he always introduces himself to others as a distant relative of the Emperor. He forgets to mention that the sixth Han Emperor, from whom he is descended, died some three hundred and twenty years previously. Following Liu Bei's marriage to Sun Quan's sister, Zhou Yu is quick to realise that Liu Bei's weakness.[34] Even more pertinently, he always assumes that his definition of moral conduct is the only one possible. He seems to know that Heaven has decreed that the Han Dynasty is doomed and yet he seeks to reverse this. In this, the extraordinarily gifted Zhuge Liang may be at even greater fault, for he understands the will of Heaven better than Liu Bei, and yet he too wants to see if he can reverse its decision: it is a kind of hubris. After Liu

Bei's death, Zhuge Liang continues stubbornly to pursue Liu Bei's goal, with fatal consequences both for himself and for the cause he serves.

Liu Bei's sworn brothers are equally flawed. Guan Yu is the model of honour and loyalty, but he is arrogant.[35] The youngest of the brothers is Zhang Fei. He is a good man, courageous, and the personification of loyalty; but he is coarse, and when drunk becomes such a mindless thug one can hardly think of him as a hero. All three brothers have their individual tragic flaw, and in each case, their flaw is responsible for their respective setbacks, including their death.

The contrast between Liu Bei and Cao Cao is self-evidently moral; but it is also psychological. Even the theme of military strategy has its psychological implications. For example, *Three Kingdoms* makes frequent references to *The Art of War*. Sun Tzu knew that military action always has a price. As he writes: 'Raising an army / Of a hundred thousand men / [. . .] keeps seven hundred thousand families / From their work.'[36] His highest value may be the obligation to fulfil one's duty to the nation, but he would much rather that his soldiers had been left to fulfil their obligations to their family. His work might just as well have been entitled 'The Way to Peace'. More surprisingly, however, the strategies that he advocates for war are not only strategies for military advantage; they are strategies for self-understanding. The military application of his most famous aphorism is obvious: 'Know the enemy, / Know yourself, / And victory / Is never in doubt, / Not in a hundred battles.'[37] But the aphorism is just as applicable to oneself: the 'enemy' are those self-destructive aspects of one's own personality of which one is largely unaware, and 'know yourself' implies learning to come to terms with these. And this, of course, reflects a primary concern of Confucius.

Confucius realised that the problems of his time were the inevitable consequence of human nature. He realised that people tend to think themselves better than they are—and their neighbours worse than they are. He argued that, rather than making war on one's neighbours, one should concentrate on overcoming one's own negative tendencies: 'Attacking one's own bad qualities and avoiding attacks on other people's bad qualities—is not this the way to reform wickedness?'[38] Or again: 'What the gentleman seeks in himself the small man seeks in others.'[39] The Confucian gentleman is not necessarily someone of privileged birth: he is someone who always behaves with self-understanding, modesty, compassion, and benevolence.

Confucius saw that people are always blind to their faults. He sought to persuade them that the world would be a better place if they learned to overcome their own worst tendencies. As he writes, 'I have never come across anyone capable of discerning his errors and inwardly bringing himself to justice.'[40] Some two thousand three hundred years later, Goethe makes the same point: 'We are willing to acknowledge our shortcomings, we are willing to be punished for them, we will patiently suffer much on their account, but we become impatient if we are required to overcome them.'[41] For Confucius, there could be no improvement in the political situation until such time as individuals learned to come to terms with their own negative tendencies and actively sought to develop their positive qualities. As he writes:

> My failure to cultivate virtue, my failure to put into practice what I have learnt, my knowing what is right and my inability to move towards it, and my powerlessness to change what is not good in myself—these are my worries.[42]

His driving concern was neither ritual nor filial piety. It was to persuade individuals, whatever the temptation to do otherwise and whatever the occasion, to choose the path of moral rectitude.

It fell to one of his later followers to explain this process in philosophical-cum-psychological terms. Zhu Xi (1130–1200) was the first to emphasise Liu Bei's virtue, thus making him the hero of the history. He was a Confucian scholar who believed that outer and inner nature is fundamentally one: he called this unity *li*, and he regarded *li* as fundamentally good. But he also recognised that everything natural also harbours *qi*, a force which explains how *li* can be diverted from its purpose. As a result, in all that human beings do they have to control their *qi* so as to allow their *li* to attain its natural purpose. They must overcome their *qi* in order to become the individuals that their *li* intends them to become.

This, in effect, distils the moral concern of the novel. For in *Three Kingdoms*, there are no 'evil' men: there are only good men who become, to greater or lesser extent tainted by their love of self-interest. The most important psychological concern of the novel is the contrast between the tragic flaws of the two central protagonists. Why, it asks, can Cao Cao not overcome the *qi* which corrupts his Cao Cao nature? And why can Liu Bei not get the better of his *qi* which taints his Liu Bei nature?

'The empire, long divided, must unite; long united, must divide.' Maybe, but the empire is not only the vast and varied terrain of the Chinese subcontinent and the government responsible for it at any given moment. It is also the human nature of the leaders of this empire. They must prevent their *qi* from misleading them; they must want to live in accord with *li*. And it is also the individual reader, who can learn from the lesson implicit in the novel. Unless one can overcome one's *qi*, one will never be in accord with one's *li*—that is, with oneself. The dream of One China is very closely related to a yearning for individual integrity and wholeness—and it stems from concerns first articulated by Confucius, concerns which are archetypal in nature and thus belong to the domain not only of philosophy, but also of psychology.

Conclusion

Three Kingdoms is a devastating indictment of unchecked individualism. It is an account of the various ways in which the figures who defined an age are led astray by the combination of their individual ambitions and their psychological blind spots. Liu Bei and Cao Cao are characterised by their separate attitude toward notions which became central to Chinese thought during the Han dynasty, but which were first articulated in much earlier times. Albeit in somewhat abstract terms, Zhu Xi's explanation of human nature not only develops the central concern of Confucius, it also, and more surprisingly, anticipates a primary concern of Jungian psychology: the difficulty of coming to terms with one's inferior tendencies. The driving concern in *Three Kingdoms* is not only the recovery of political unity and righteous government; *it is also* the importance of identifying and discarding every aspect of one's *qi* in order to allow one's authentic *li* to guide one toward achieving the perfect moral rectitude of a Confucian gentleman.

The cumulative impression left by *Three Kingdoms* is of an overwhelming tragedy every bit as shattering as the *Iliad*, the *Oresteia*, or *King Lear*—and this, not just because of the novel's cleverly interlocking themes, but because of its moral vision. (Earlier accounts spend less time on the process of division, which their authors clearly found painful, and far more time on the process of reunification and the struggles of the heroes who sacrificed for it.)

Confucius was not a stuffy traditionalist. He was the first philosopher to analyse seriously not only his actions, but also his motivations. He found his unconscious in all those aspects of his personality which seemed to escape his control. Long before either Epicurus or Jesus Christ, he understood the importance of coming to terms with his unconscious or 'shadow' tendencies. And—long before Freud or Jung—he realised that history and ethics, psychology and politics are all inextricably related.

Notes

1 *Three Kingdoms* is considerably longer than Tolstoy's *War and Peace* (1865–1867), and almost as long as Richardson's *Clarissa* (1748). Cassius Dio (*c.* 155–235) described 180 (the year in which Commodus becomes emperor) as the beginning of the decline of the Roman Empire: as marking the descent 'from a kingdom of gold to one of rust and iron' (72.36.4). Edward Gibbon famously concurred (see *The Decline and Fall of the Roman Empire*, ed. Hugh Trevor-Roper, 6 vols, New York: Everyman, 1993–1994, vol. 1, chapter 4, pp. 95–116).
2 The long early sixteenth-century history was first *printed* in 1522, with a preface, dated 1494, attributed to Luo Guanzhong, a *fourteenth*-century writer. Some argue that this history was the product of several hands; Moss Roberts argues that the artistic coherence of the work suggests a single authorship: that of Luo Guanzhong. Some hold it in higher esteem than the later and more widely read adaptation published in 1679. In spite of the extensive changes made by Mao Lun and Mao Zonggang, they continue to be regarded as 'editors'. Their text continues to be attributed to Luo Guanzhong, who may not even be responsible for the earlier history.
3 See, for example, J. Campbell, 'Madame de Lafayette', *French Studies* 65, 2011, 225–232.
4 For example, the historical Cao Cao was a talented poet and nowhere near as devious as the novel suggests; and although Guan Yu was a much less significant figure in history than in the novel, his early deification suggests that stories about him grew up very soon after his death.
5 A brief note on Chinese names: the first name is the family name; the second name is the given name. The bracketed name is the courtesy or style name. In ancient times, the latter

was given to a male upon reaching adulthood, and to a female upon marriage. It was used by those of the same generation as the individual, both by friends and more formal acquaintances. In this article, the family and given name are used; in the novel, most of the characters refer to each other by their courtesy name. As in a Russian novel, the form used is always significant.

6 Madame de Lafayette, *The Princessse de Clèves*, tr. R. Buss, London: Penguin, 1992, p. 43.

7 For the story of Daphne and Apollo, see Ovid, *Metamorphoses*, book 1, lines 452–567.

8 Liu Bei enjoys 'the allegiance of men' (Luo Guanzhong, *Three Kingdoms: A Historical Novel*, 4 volumes, tr. M. Roberts, Beijing: Foreign Language Press, 1995, vol. 2, chapter 38, p. 680). I am grateful to Kevin Goh Ke Min for his comments on this and other points.

9 See T. Dawson, 'Catherine de Médicis and *La Princesse de Clèves*', *Seventeenth-Century French Studies* 14, 1992, 191–210.

10 Schopenhauer, *The World as Will and Representation*, vol. 2, chapter 1, in *The World as Will and Representation*, tr. E.F.J. Payne, 2 vols, New York: Dover, 1966, vol. 2, p. 13.

11 In Western literature, one thinks of Schiller's history plays, which transformed relatively little-known stories about historical figures into national myths, i.e., *Mary Stuart* (1800), *The Maid of Orleans* (1801), and *William Tell* (1804).

12 Plato, *Euthyphro, Apology, Crito, Phaedo, Phaedrus*, tr. H.N. Fowler, Cambridge, MA: Harvard University Press, 1914, p. 133.

13 P. Bishop (ed.), *The Archaic: The Past in the Present*, Hove: Routledge, 2012, p. 38.

14 V.W. Odajnyk, *Jung and Politics: The Political and Social Ideas of C. G. Jung*, New York: New York University Press, 1976; J.L. Henderson, *Cultural Attitudes in Psychological Perspective*, Toronto: Inner City Books, 1993; A. Samuels, *The Political Psyche*, London: Routledge, 1993; and *Politics on the Couch: Citizenship and the Internal Life*, London: Profile Books, 2001; and T. Singer and S.L. Kimbles (eds), *The Cultural Complex: Contemporary Jungian Perspectives on Psyche and Society*, Hove: Brunner-Routledge, 2004.

15 Historians sometimes identify the three kingdoms as Cao Wei, Shu Han, and Dong (or Eastern) Wu.

16 It may be compared with the slightly earlier Japanese verse epic, *The Tale of the Heike*, which recounts the struggle by two clans for control of Japan in the Genpei War of 1180–1185.

17 *Three Kingdoms*, vol. 1, chapter 8, p. 127. Much of my information comes from Moss Robert's 'Introduction' and 'Afterword' to his edition.

18 In spite of Lü Bu's protestations of love for her, there is a chilling moment later in the novel when the reader learns that Diaochan has become not his wife, but only another mistress.

19 *Three Kingdoms*, vol. 2, chapter 41, pp. 731–740.

20 As Liu Bei chides Zhang Fei with an old saying: 'Brothers are like arms and legs; wives and children are merely garments that can always be mended' (*Three Kingdoms*, vol. 1, chapter 15, p. 243).

21 *Three Kingdoms*, vol. 2, chapter 42, pp. 741–742.

22 In 1115, the Jurchen, a people from what is today north-eastern China, founded the Jin Dynasty, which lasted until 1234. In 1271, the Mongols established the Yuan Dynasty, which lasted until 1368. In 1644, the Manchurians set up the Qing Dynasty, which lasted until 1911. And in 1931, most of eastern China fell to the Japanese, who remained until 1945.

23 The Chinese word for history is 历史 (lì shǐ). The first character, 历, comes from the word 经历 (jīnglì), which means 'to experience' or 'to go through' something. The second character, 史, means both 'annals' and history, and is the title of the official historian in ancient China. My thanks to Helena Huang Yixin for this information.

24 The Greek word *historiê* means 'inquiry' or 'investigation'. This assumes that *history* means finding a path between different, and possibly even contradictory accounts in order to arrive as close as one can to a fact or truth. It implies that whatever is said about the past

is only one of many possible narratives as imagined by one person in one place and at a given time.

25 The Five pre-Qin Classics subsequently attributed to Confucius are: *Classic of Poetry*, *Book of Documents*, *Book of Rites*, *Book of Changes* (*I Ching*), and *Spring and Autumn Annals*. A sixth, the *Classic of Music*, was lost during the burning of the books (see note 27).

26 The period derives its name from the *Record of the Warring States*, a work compiled early in the Han dynasty.

27 Shi Huang was accused of having burned classic Confucian texts and buried 460 Confucian scholars alive, in 210 and 213 respectively: the truth of these accusations has been challenged, but the slur has stuck.

28 See, for example, the discussion between Liu Bei and Zhuge Liang in chapter 65: 'The laws of Qin were punitive and harsh, and the people detested them. That is why the Supreme Ancestor's (= Liu Bang, founder of the Han Dynasty's) kindness and leniency won their allegiance' (*Three Kingdoms*, vol. 3, chapter 65, p. 1186). Also, the preceding dialogue, in which Zilong corrects Liu Bei's knee-jerk desire to confiscate the property of defeated officials (p. 1185).

29 According to Moss Roberts, all four of the East Asian nations strongly influenced by Confucius (China, Japan, Korea, Vietnam) developed a strong interest in history; see *Three Kingdoms*, vol. 4, p. 2226.

30 Thus translated by M. Roberts, vol. 1, p. 1.

31 M. Roberts, 'Introduction', *Three Kingdoms*, p. 3.

32 The others are: *Journey to the West*, by Wu Cheng'en; *Water Margin/Outlaws of the Marsh*, by Shi Naian; and *Dream of the Red Chamber/The Story of the Stone*, by Cao Xueqin.

33 Its continuing appeal is testified by two recent and equally successful adaptations. In 1994, China Central Television (CCTV) began to broadcast a very faithful production. One might have thought that 84 episodes of 45 minutes each would be enough for one generation. But in 2010, CCTV produced a fresh dramatisation, which took occasional liberties with the text, but is perhaps the better film. And it had 95 episodes, also of 45 minutes. It is difficult to imagine any single work of European literature holding the attention of a massive audience for so long!

34 *Three Kingdoms*, vol. 2, chapter 55, pp. 944–945.

35 In spite of which, a cult developed around him, perhaps as early as the short-lived but important Sui Dynasty (581–618). A statue of him can be seen outside many Chinese temples, both Taoist and Buddhist. The worship of Guan Yu became more marked during the Song Dynasty (960–1279).

36 Sun-Tzu, *The Art of War*, ed. and tr. J. Minford, London: Penguin, 2009, p. 89.

37 Sun-Tzu, *The Art of War*, p. 19, also p. 68. The passage quoted continues: 'He who knows self / But not the enemy / Will suffer one defeat / For every victory. / He who knows / Neither self / Nor enemy / Will fail / In every battle' (p. 19).

38 Confucius, *The Analects*, tr. R. Dawson, book 12, §21, Oxford: Oxford University Press, 1993, p. 47.

39 Confucius, *The Analects*, book15, §21, p. 62.

40 Confucius, *The Analects*, book 5, §27, p. 19.

41 From Ottilie's Journal, see J.W. Goethe, *Elective Affinities*, II, 4, tr. R.J. Hollingdale, Harmondsworth: Penguin, 1971, p. 181.

42 Confucius, *The Analects*, book 7, §3, p. 24; slightly modified.

9

ENKI AT ERIDU

God of directed thinking

Catriona Miller

A key focus for Jungians and post-Jungians alike has long been the 'interchangeability of mythology and psychology'.[1] C.G. Jung once described mythology as 'the textbook of archetypes', where the unconscious psyche 'is not rationally elucidated and explained, but simply represented like a picture or a story book',[2] and where archetypes can be understood as 'patterns of psychic perception and understanding common to all human beings'.[3] It is interesting to note, however, that in recent times non-Jungian approaches to myth also seem to be reaching towards this way of thinking about the 'interchangeability of mythology and psychology'.

Scholars of Sumerian myth have often felt stymied by the obscurity of the texts they seek to understand—the texts are so ancient that, with very little linguistic and cultural context to go on, translation is a difficult proposition. One publication on Sumerian culture and society, contained this rather striking line: 'Myth is [. . .] imaginative and reflective, rather than analytic or scientific [. . .] yet it remains grounded in the concrete, relying on imagery derived from human life, motivation and experience transferred to the divine sphere.'[4] In another article examining the Sumerian myth *Enki and the World Order*, the author made the point that whilst history is to some extent speculative, it is always anchored in what was believed to have happened. Mythology, he went to on say, is also speculative, but by way of contrast, 'the focus shifts from what happened in the past, to what *continues* to happen, *all the time*'.[5] This is a point also made by Jung to which we shall return below.

These points are striking because they come from authors who do not set out to make a psychological point and yet reach towards a psychological perspective to explain mythological imagery and narrative. An illuminating example of this approach is to be found in the work of Betty de Shong Meador, a Jungian analyst, who worked on translations of material relating to the goddess Inanna and then on a series of temple hymns, relating to a number of the Sumerian pantheon. Her technique of careful analysis of the Sumerian texts and immersing herself in the field of Assyriology, whilst keeping the Jungian model of the psyche in mind, points the way to the mutual benefits available to the study of Sumerian mythology and analytical psychology and has led to a fresh approach to these most ancient of stories.

So this chapter aims to offer some preliminary observations about another important Sumerian deity that has not yet been considered in any great detail from this perspective—the god Enki, but we will begin in an unusual way, with the question of 'where' rather than of 'who'. There is a strong and perhaps unique connection between the city of Eridu, Enki's temple there, called Engur, and the Sumerian cosmological region known as the *abzu*, and when considering the 'interchangeability of mythology and psychology', this conjunction of 'where' and 'who' cannot be regarded as an arbitrary juxtaposition: Eridu, Engur, and *abzu* are all regions closely connected with each other and with the god Enki. They are in fact inextricable because Sumerian belief saw the temple and the city as literally being the home of the god. Thus the *place* of Enki—the city and the temple, which had a tangible reality—were also intimately connected to the *abzu* and the figure of Enki himself. This chapter will consider Enki's city, Enki's temple, and Enki's realm, before circling back round to Enki himself.

Sumer—some context and caveats

The ability of the non-specialist to consider Sumerian texts and their narratives is a relatively fresh development in the field, so I will offer three points of reference and context for the general reader.

First, it is worth noting that the study of Sumer, at least in the Western academic tradition, dates only as far back to 1873 when French Assyriologist François Lenormant began publishing some translations of texts.[6] The Sumerian world has been the preserve of only a few scholars, compared to the history and mythologies of Greece and Rome, which for centuries have been thoroughly embedded in contemporary Western culture and generally very well known both in direct translations of texts and in a whole panoply of retellings.

The first works concentrating on Sumer and Babylon were highly specialised, technical, and very difficult for the non-specialist, whether relating to issues around the translation of cuneiform (the alphabet created in Sumer) or the reporting of archaeological finds. By way of example, merely creating a comprehensive catalogue of tablet fragments from archaeological finds was the important work of several professional careers, most notably that of Samuel Noah Kramer. So, over time, the texts have become more complete, the translations more readable, the historical chronologies clearer and the archaeology has developed a much better context, enough to open up the field to the careful non-specialist, although it is important to remember that the translation of some words and concepts is still not beyond debate. The *abzu* is one such concept.

Secondly, whilst much of the history of this remote time is vague, there are some distinct phases in Mesopotamian history, which is itself a geographical term simply meaning the area between the Tigris and Euphrates rivers. Archaeological finds in the region date back to at least 5000 BCE with traces of the primitive Ubaid culture. The height of Sumerian civilisation, where Sumerian was spoken, cuneiform developed as a writing system, along with urban civilisation in cities such as Uruk, dates to between 3500 and 2350 BCE, which is around the time the first settlement of the Nile Valley was taking place. However, most of the extant texts date from the later Old Akkadian period, where Akkadian replaces Sumerian as a spoken language but Sumerian remains the written language of the educated, and scribal schools lasting into the Babylonian period (1750 BCE till about the sixth century BCE) continue to circulate Sumerian texts.

It is therefore important to keep a note of caution and to remember the very long duration of Sumerian-influenced culture, which lasts some 4,500 years. Many of the texts that have survived were written in Sumerian but by Akkadians who may have had some kind of political point to make by assimilating Sumerian culture and literature, or belong to the even later Babylonian scribal schools which may have also made adaptations. However, fairly complete versions of some of the 'literature' exists precisely because they were copied over and over again at the scribal schools where 'the scribal curriculum was never confined entirely to purely lexical and grammatical texts', for, as Hallo and Simpson point out, 'Sumerian syntax could hardly be learned except from connected prose and poetry, and the schools have preserved for us Sumerian literary works'.[7] Insofar as it is possible, I have kept to Sumerian and Neo Sumerian texts, with regard to consideration of Enki and avoid later Babylonian works except in relation to a cultural shift discussed in more detail below.

The final contextual point relates to the Sumerian pantheon itself, which had about a dozen major deities but somewhere around 5,000 minor deities.[8] It is important to note that, in contrast to the Graeco-Roman and Norse pantheons, the Sumerian pantheon did not have a fixed hierarchy, but study of it has at times suffered from the classical (or biblical) academic backgrounds of the scholars undertaking the early work. Over the 4,500 years of Sumerian culture, the pantheon was organised in a number of ways: genealogically (family relationships); typologically (what they did, powers, areas of influence), and geographically where each city had a special relationship with one god, and the city's political fortunes bound up with the relative dominance of the deity.[9] For example, An is the sky god. His name means 'the Above', and he is regarded as the leader of the gods, so it might be expected that he could be seen as an analogue of Zeus or Odin. Yet An's powers are ill-defined and he appears to have been a distant figure, seldom (if ever) represented.[10] In fact, compared to the rich variety of stories surrounding both Zeus and Odin, there are no surviving texts which feature An as a central character, but there are five major surviving myths and several minor works about Enki. One can also see that the goddesses as a group show a marked decline in prestige over the period of Sumerian culture, with Enki gradually replacing the goddess Ninhursag as one of the top three.

Eridu—the first city

Returning to the 'where' in this exploration of the god Enki, we begin with the city of Eridu, Enki's home and the location of his temple. It is hard to overstate the importance of the 'city' in Sumer. It was the centre of power and the place of civilisation. Renowned Sumerian scholar William Hallo pointed out that the concept itself of 'city' is expressed by a single term—*uru*—throughout virtually all the long history of cuneiform.[11] It was a constant with a fixed meaning.

Yet Eridu, built at the literal boundary of water and earth where the Tigris and Euphrates meet before flowing into the Persian Gulf, had extra significance because it was considered by the Sumerians themselves to be the *first* city. In the Sumerian king list, for example, Eridu is the first city, with the list beginning, 'after the kingship descended from heaven, the kingship was in Eridu'.[12] In fact, Hallo suggested that it is not really a king list *per se*, but rather a city list.[13] It is particularly interesting that the archaeology of Eridu (at the modern site of Tell Abu Shahrein) seems to bear this out—it revealed 18 temples built one on top of each other. The lowest was built on 'clean sand', dating from about 5000 BCE, and was a simple room but with all the standard features of later temples—a niche, two platforms, an alter and offering table.[14]

So although Eridu is never the foremost city in the region politically—which at various times Uruk, Ur, Lagash, and Babylon (with their associated gods) all were—it was revered as the *first*. Even after Eridu was abandoned, Babylonians rebuilt the temple there and named a district of Babylon after it,[15] and in fact the name was not finally abandoned until the Persian Empire conquered Babylon in the sixth century BCE. Eridu, the city, had identifiable, concrete, and conceptual status, and at the centre of life in the city was the temple.

Engur—the radiant site

Each city was home to its patron deity, and the deity (or at least the cult image of the god) lived in the temple.[16] The temples were at the centre of Sumerian city life, where large temple estates and complexes provided everything the god and their servants required, from meals and offerings to textiles and pottery.[17] As Schneider makes clear:

> the point of the temple was not so much a place where people could pray to the deities, but a place where the deity could live and have people take care of him, and so the temple also required the space and resources to produce all that the deity and his retinue needed.[18]

So the Sumerian temples were where the god lived, quite literally, with attendants, meals, and entertainment, but the temple itself also had its own character. In the Temple Hymns sequence, 'poems are addressed to the gods' houses themselves' and 'each house has a special character related to the deity and to the community for which it provides a centre'.[19] The 'radiant site' of the temple itself had a personality, and the temple hymns are praises to the place, rather than simply to the person of the god. So once again, the 'where' of Enki in terms of the character of his temple in Eridu is important in understanding the nature of the god himself.

Enki's temple at Eridu was called Engur which is variously translated as 'house watery deep',[20] or 'house of subterranean waters',[21] and sometimes left untranslated as *engur*. According to de Shong Meador, the cuneiform of the *engur* sign (which can also mean *abzu*, one of the those difficult-to-translate terms) carries implicit meaning—the star-symbol of divinity enclosed in a protected space,[22] and the collection of Sumerian temple-hymns compiled by the important priestess and poet, Enheduanna, begins with Engur, as the king list began with Eridu. De Shong Meador notes that is little strange because at that time the god Enlil (at Nippur) was the most prominent god in the pantheon, but then goes on to say that this emphasises once again the importance of Eridu as the first city and Enki as its resident god.

The hymn to Engur begins:

> Growing between,
> this first temple tower split heaven and earth
> whose roots reach Eridu's dark cella
> watery shrine built for a prince[23]

and it continues:

> O crowned Eridu shining crown
> sworn by your prince the great prince [...]
> where [the *abzu*] hits the Great Below
> and voices pour out to Utu[[24]]
> revered shrine stretching toward heaven.[25]

These two excerpts make it abundantly clear that this temple links all the Sumerian cosmological realms: heaven, earth, the *abzu* and even the Great Below (the underworld). It links the city of Enki, to heaven—the 'first temple tower' splits apart heaven and earth (the words *an* and *ki* also relate to the god An and Ki his wife, an earth goddess) and reaches down to the *abzu*, the realm of Enki in 'Eridu's dark cella', which also touches the Great Below, the Sumerian underworld and place of death. Black and Green note that the Sumerian underworld was not a place of happy repose, but is always described as 'as in complete darkness, dusty and unpleasant. All the dead, without exception, wander there, thirsting for water and having only dust to eat.'[26] Quite different to the *abzu* itself.

The Temple Hymn is not the only text which makes these links. *Enki and the World Order* describes how 'your great house is founded in the *abzu*, the great mooring post of heaven and earth'.[27] But the text *Enki's Journey to Nippur* is even more explicit.[28] At the start of the poem, Enki builds himself a splendid palace (or temple) of silver and lapis lazuli, which is praised at some length. Isimud, Enki's minister, directly addresses the temple and says:

> Enki's beloved Eridu, Engur whose inside is full of abundance! *Abzu*, life of the Land, beloved of Enki! Temple built on the edge, befitting the artful divine powers! [. . .] Engur, high citadel standing firm on the earth! Temple at the edge of the *engur*, a lion in the midst of the *abzu*; lofty temple of Enki, which bestows wisdom on the Land [. . .].[29]

The importance of the temple which links the cosmological regions to the city is repeated time and again so that the temple, the home of the god, which gives the city its purpose, provides the conceptual link between the concrete everyday world of the city and the 'other world' of the *abzu*.

Abzu—a cosmological region

The *abzu* is frequently mentioned in texts related to Enki and Eridu; indeed Enki is the king of the *abzu* and his palace is built there. As already suggested, however, *abzu* is a problematic term which often leads to it being left untranslated.

The *abzu* is not the underworld (the Great Below), but it is not in the everyday world either. It has been defined as 'sea, abyss; home of Enki' in one glossary,[30] as 'a freshwater ocean',[31] and elsewhere in the same book as a 'subterranean sweet water ocean'.[32] However, although the watery nature of the *abzu* certainly seems to be accepted by the time of Babylon's ascendancy, during the Sumerian period *per se*, it is not described as an ocean anywhere. As one scholar says the *abzu* is 'definitely described as an under-earth structure and it is certainly connected to clay [. . .] whether the early layers of Sumerian mythology considered that structure filled with water is [. . .] an open question', for 'no early text [. . .] describes *abzu* directly as an ocean, lake or sea'.[33]

One point on which the texts do agree, however, is that the *abzu* is the home of Enki. In *Inanna and Enki*, the goddess Inanna organises a visit to Enki, where he feasts with her, but Enki seems very relaxed in his own palace, and he gets drunk and gives away many *mē* to the goddess.[34] At the start of the text *Enki and Ninmah*, the *abzu* is also the space where Enki lies sleeping before being called into the action which results in the creation of humanity. At Enki's order, clay is taken from the roof of the *abzu* to fashion into humans. The description of the *abzu* in the text is brief but complex and the translations do not quite agree on how to untangle it. It has been translated as 'a well into which water seeped',[35] 'a deep hole that pours out the water',[36] 'the deep *engur* in the flowing water'.[37] It is also described as 'a place the inside of which no god whatever was laying eyes on',[38] 'the inside of which no other god knows',[39] and 'at the place where no god is/where no worship takes place'.[40]

To try to sum up, the *abzu* formed a significant part of the Sumerian concept of the cosmos and is a region that is not the earth and not the heavens, and not the underworld. The *abzu* has nothing to do with the dead—almost the opposite, in fact. It is a space that can be entered and left. It can be known, though it is not 'on earth' as such. The *abzu* lies between the everyday world and the underworld. It is beneath, perhaps interior. It seems to contain both earth (clay) and perhaps water. It is private. It is creative and fecund, but not chaotic—the *abzu* is not a place of chaos where there is no logic or sense. It is separate, but it is accessible. It is fertile and contains potential. The poem *Enki's Journey to Nippur* calls it the 'pure place, where fates are determined', emphasising its function rather than describing its nature.[41] Most often, however, it is simply stated that it is where Enki lives. His palace, his temple was both there *and* in Eridu, bearing in mind the cuneiform sign for the temple and the *abzu* is the same.[42] And it is where the *mē,* the attributes of civilisation (the 'artful divine powers' mentioned in *Enki's Journey to Nippur*) were stored ready to be dispensed by Enki.

Enki

Now is a good moment to turn to the god Enki himself, the god who is resident in the temple and king of the *abzu*. Modern academics have often tried to position Enki as a 'trickster' god, but I would argue this does not fit well with the texts and descriptions.[43] As noted above, Enki is not the most powerful of the Sumerian pantheon, but he is one of the most frequently mentioned and, unlike the distant An, he is generally well disposed towards humanity.[44] Eridu is his city, Engur is his temple, and he is king of the *abzu*, but he has another interesting title, which, like *abzu*, is difficult to translate. He is often called *Lord Nudimmud* which may mean something like 'image fashioner',[45] or 'shaper-creator'.[46] In *Enki and Ninmah*, he is also called *geštú dagal* which has been rendered as 'wise one',[47] 'the one with the cunning grasp',[48] 'he of the vast intelligence',[49] or 'the one of great wisdom',[50] but which others suggest is better rendered simply as 'understanding/knowledge personified'.[51]

So, Enki is not, and this is perhaps a key point, a creator *per se*. Enki does not create the world. He does in some stories bring it to life and shape it because he is the holder of the *mē* (the attributes/skills of civilisation which also craft the environment), which he hands out and shares. In *Enki and Ninmah*, he is directly equated with the *mē* themselves. The other gods praise him, saying 'like a form giving father who decides over the *mē-s*, you are the one who is the *mē*.' The *abzu* is where things are given form by Enki—'the wise and intelligent one, the prudent [. . .] of skills, the fashioner of the design of everything',[52] but he does not create the world as such. Instead, he is a god of technical skills, organised planning, abundance, and knowledge, and the multitude of *abzu*-shrines in Early Dynastic Sumer points to a prominent role.[53]

So Enki fashions humanity from the clay of the *abzu* (although Sauren believes this may belong to a later version of the text).[54] He has in his keeping the *mē*, the attributes of civilisation, which he dispenses. He is clever. He is skilful. He fashions things. He is 'at home' in the *abzu*. He is not a creator god, but he is a fashioner, an image maker: he is 'understanding and intelligence, the care-taker, the skilled one, fashioner of the form of all the things'.[55] Again, these descriptions of Enki and his role do not fit well with the idea of a trickster god whose role is to provoke and to upset the status quo, but in keeping with a Jungian perspective on the figure of Enki, a different proposition is thrown up.

In his essay 'The Transcendent Function' (written in 1916 but not published until 1957), Jung pointed out that 'directedness is absolutely necessary for the conscious process, but as we have seen it entails an unavoidable one-sidedness.' He argued that, 'since the psyche is a self regulating system, just as the body is, the regulating counteraction will always develop in the unconscious', adding that 'to this extent the psyche of the civilized man is no longer a self regulating system'.[56] For Jung, the key to redressing this imbalance lay in seeking to understand the images thrown up from the unconscious, in the form of dreams, visions, and mythology, through the process of amplification. The post-Jungian analyst James Hillman suggested that mythic tales and figures should be removed from the realm of story only and pulled down and in 'showing how a myth precisely works in the psyche, in its habits of mind and heart'. He went on to say that we 'seek to reflect back and forth between the two, myth and psyche, using them to provide insights for each other, preventing either from being taken on its own terms only'.[57]

Time and again, Jung wrote about the problems of our own era, noting that civilised life today demanded concentrated, directed conscious functioning, and this entailed the risk of considerable dissociation from the unconscious,[58] and much of Jung's writings on the self-regulation of the psyche relates to learning to listen to the promptings of the unconscious, whether through dreams or active imagination, which activates the transcendent function in order to rebalance the psyche. The correspondences between psyche and myth, between inner and outer worlds as noted at the beginning are also integral to a specifically Jungian analysis of myth.[59] Indeed, like the non-Jungian mythologists quoted at the beginning of this chapter, Jung suggested that myth *can* be viewed as a historical document, or at least up to a point. It is not a history *per se*, not an account of a specific, one-off event, but rather, he said, it is 'the product of an unconscious process in a particular social group, at a particular time, at a particular place'.[60] Therefore, he added, one can, broadly speaking, suggest that 'at a particular place, at a particular time, a particular social group was caught up in such a process'.[61] So a Jungian analysis of Enki at Eridu requires a consideration of the function of the mythic narratives at that historical moment insofar as such a thing might be possible, but there were two large-scale changes happening in the era immediately preceding and during Sumerian dominance that may help us to understand Enki's role.

Returning to the figure of Enki and his city Eridu, it is clear that they correlate closely with the rise of urban civilisation in the region. Enki is associated with the *first* city, the first temple tower, and he is the keeper of the *mē*, the attributes of civilisation, in fact specifically *urban* civilisation and as such, rather than a trickster, Enki could be characterised as the god of directed thinking. Now this 'directed thinking' is perhaps not of the same order as the diamond-tipped consciousness that we see from the sixth century BCE onwards in classical Greece. Sumerian culture is not generally credited with being capable of abstract thought to that degree, but rather Enki may represent a consciousness that remains in relatively close connection with the unconscious. His temple Engur connects the *abzu* with the city, thus when Enki's minister Isimud addresses the newly built temple, he describes it as 'Temple built on the edge, befitting the artful divine powers!' and notes that the 'foundation pegs are driven into the *abzu*'.[62] The *mē* tree is planted in the *abzu* but is described rather beautifully as 'a grove of vines extending over the Land',[63] and in *Enki and the World Order* the god travels in his boat assigning roles and responsibilities amongst the other gods.

Enki holds the *mē*, the skills and principles of urban civilisation itself, but they have their roots in the *abzu*, a region that, at least from a Jungian point of view seems to have an affinity with the unconscious. Enki's home is in the *abzu* and often times he is in a lowered state of awareness there. He is sleeping in the *abzu* when Nammu rouses him to deal with the complaints of the labouring gods. He gets drunk there with Ninmah and on another occasion with Inanna, leading on the one hand to a lengthy drunken debate with Ninmah and, on the other, fool-hardy gifts of *mē* to Inanna. It is a private interior space and one where directed thinking is not always to the fore, but where creativity germinates and which Enki and other gods can enter and leave at will. Enki may be the god of directed thinking, but he is not invincible or all powerful. His attention can wander and he must sometimes be reminded and cajoled to arise from the *abzu* (the unconscious) to carry out into his acts of creation and other activities. So Enki can be seen as the occasionally distracted god of consciousness and directed thinking, sometimes spreading the *mē*, the knowledge and crafts of urban civilisation, sometimes falling back into somnolence and dreams.

It is interesting to note that the Sumerian Enki is manifestly not a warrior god and does not normally resort to violence. Instead, he persuades and holds debates, and this is perhaps where the second large-scale shift in Sumerian society can be discerned. Many of Enki's stories that have survived seem to involve the god placating, debating, or soothing disgruntled goddesses. In *Enki and the World Order*, Inanna complains that Enki has not assigned her any special responsibilities. Enki reacts with surprise, taking time to praise her and enumerate her powers and abilities before asking 'What more could we add to you?',[64] although in *Inanna and Enki* the goddess seems to trick Enki out of some of the *mē* anyway.

The poem *Enki and Ninmah* begins with the creation of humanity, but it continues as a disputation between Enki and the goddess Ninmah, and is seen as difficult by many writers, especially as the ending is fragmentary. Yet its meaning may become less difficult (missing lines of text aside) if it is seen as an argument about the pre-eminence of the two sexes in creating new life. The poem ends by positioning Enki (the male) as the winner, but having to admit that the role of growing and nurturing the foetus (the female role) is a crucial one. In *Enki and Ninhursag*, Ninhursag brings Enki to heel by making him sick, and then curing him again. Ninmah is another name for Ninhursag, and it might be remembered, as noted above, that Enki seems to have ultimately gained power in the pantheon at her expense. There is an ongoing power struggle between these two gods.

Now it is tempting to link these stories of ill-tempered goddesses with the development of patriarchy, illustrated in the poem the *Exaltation of Inanna* where the exile of Inanna's high priestess is described in starkly gendered terms.[65] As the power of the goddesses was gradually undermined in physical as well as theological terms, male deities made a play for creativity and generative force, whilst Inanna in particular made a counter-play for the *mē* of civilisation. The dominance of patriarchy was not yet been fully established and, in part at least, Enki's role seems to have been to placate and reassure the goddesses, although in *Enki and Ninhursag*, there is also violence and rape. In this context, it is interesting that his chief minister or vizier, Isimud, mentioned by name in two of the poems, is depicted as two faced and referred to in both masculine and feminine forms.[66]

The decline of Enki's own power adds an intriguing epilogue to his mythology within this Jungian context. Jung suggested that the 'definiteness and directedness of the conscious mind are qualities that have been acquired relatively late in the history of the human race',[67] but in fact they might be even more recent than is usually thought. As masculinity began staking its claim to power, and to definiteness and directedness, indeed to civilisation itself, the nature of the conscious attitude evolved and changed the role of Enki. As Babylon rose to power, the god of directed thinking, flexible and creative, the negotiator, who moves between *abzu*, the city and the heavens, is himself displaced.

Vanstiphout observes that in *Enki and the World Order* there is a 'manifest absence of large cosmic issues', by which he means specifically 'the netherworld is completely absent: so are sickness and demonic dangers'.[68] It has been stated several times above that the *abzu* is not the underworld, and it is worth adding that the specific *mē* of the underworld did not fall under Enki's aegis, belonging instead to the goddess Ereshkigal, as demonstrated in *Inanna's Descent*, where Enki must resort to sleight of hand to allow Inanna to return.[69] Difficult as it was to persuade Ereshkigal to permit Inanna to leave the underworld, it is interesting that at this time the *abzu* does not contain monsters that must be bested by warrior heroes.

However, between the Akkadian period and the rise of Babylon, the character of the *abzu* itself undergoes a shift. Wallis-Budge described *apsu* (the Akkadian word) as a 'boundless, confused and disordered mass of watery matter'.[70] In the *Enuma Elish*, also known as the *Babylonian Creation*, Apsu and Tiamat are the progenitors of the gods. The gods, however, upset their father with their noise so Apsu plans to destroy them, until Ea (the Akkadian name of Enki) causes the waters to rise and drowns the sleeping Apsu. So by the Babylonian period, the *abzu* has undergone a transformation and contains a monster, or at least, like Kronos in the Greek cosmogony, a monstrous father; but Ea himself is quickly displaced by his son Marduk, whose exploits fill the rest of the narrative, to such an extent that Hallo thinks the text would be better called the *Exaltation of Marduk*.[71] This should not be surprising for, as Jung pointed out, 'one-sidedness is an unavoidable and necessary characteristic of the directed process, for direction implies one-sidedness', it is 'an advantage and a drawback at the same time', so that 'even when no outwardly visible drawback seems to be present, there is always an equally pronounced counter-position in the unconscious'.[72]

So as the Babylonian period came to an end, and with it the final traces of Sumerian civilisation, culture has shifted more definitively towards a directed conscious attitude, with all the one-sidedness implied. This can be seen in the representation of the *apsu* populated by monsters and requiring the very masculine hero Marduk to overcome its chaos to rule—a story which appears at the very foundation of Campbell's monomyth, but one still very much alive in contemporary times.[73]

As Sumerian culture fades away, classical Greek culture is rising and its cultivation of abstract thought leads to an unprecedented flowering of the arts, philosophy, and science which are still so central to contemporary Western culture. Discussions around the reasons for this shift have tended to revolve around alphabetic literacy and a *logos*-centred culture, but in his book *Money and the Early Greek Mind* (2004), Richard Seaford cogently argues that it was 'the monetisation of the Greek *polis*' which 'contributed to a radical transformation of thought'.[74] The ability to conceptualise the abstraction that is 'money' (as opposed to more general trade) led to a 'crucial and unprecedented *conceptual* transformation', and it might be suggested that the Greeks added the *mē* of money to the attributes and skills of civilisation established by the Sumerians millennia before and that money is still the dominant *mē* of the contemporary world.[75]

Sumerian literature and archaeology describe an urban culture where temples served as a unifying symbol at the centre of public and private life, linking both city and temple to the cosmological realms of the gods. As the political and cultural context of the region changed, the mythological stories maintained that unifying symbol for a time, but by the time of the Persians, it had lost its grip as a symbolic system and the Greek establishment of the *mē of* money as an abstract concept confirms the dominance of evermore directed thinking.

In considering 'Enki at Eridu'—the god and his specific location—we gain a tantalising glimpse into a era of a less differentiated consciousness, one not resident in the airy heights of heaven, but moving freely between the heavens, the city, and the *abzu*; an envoy of civilisation and practical skills, an image shaper and negotiator, intimately connected to the goddesses. This figure is gradually replaced by more violent male warrior gods battling to maintain a strict border between the conscious and the unconscious realms, between perceptions of order and chaos, but losing something of Enki's flexibility and creativity along the way.

Notes

1 J. Hillman, *The Dream and the Underworld,* New York: HarperCollins, 1979, p. 23.

2 C.G. Jung, *Nietzsche's 'Zarathustra': Notes of the Seminar Given in 1934–1939,* ed. J.L. Jarrett, Princeton, NJ: Princeton University Press, 1988, p. 24.

3 R. Hopcke, *A Guided Tour of the Collected Works of C. G. Jung,* Boulder, CO: Shambhala, 2013, p. 13.

4   B. Foster, 'Sumerian Mythology', in H. Crawford (ed.), *The Sumerian World*, Abingdon: Routledge, 2013, pp. 435–443, p. 436.
5   R. Averbeck, 'Myth, Ritual, and Order in "Enki and the World Order"', *Journal of the American Oriental Society* 123 (4), October–December 2003, 757–771, emphasis added.
6   W. Hallo, *The World's Oldest Literature: Studies in Sumerian Belles-Lettres*, Brill: Leiden, 2010, p. 718.
7   W. Hallo and W. Simpson, *The Ancient Near East*, New York: Harcourt Brace Jovanovich 1971, p. 157.
8   W. Hallo, 'Enki and the Theology of Eridu', *Journal of the American Oriental Society* 116 (2), April–June 1996, 231–234 (p. 233).
9   Hallo and Simpson, *The Ancient Near East*, pp. 170–171.
10 J. Black and A. Green, *Gods, Demons and Symbols of Ancient Mesopotamia: An Illustrated Dictionary*, London: British Museum Press, 1992, p. 30.
11 W. Hallo, 'Antediluvian Cities', *Journal of Cuneiform Studies* 23, 1970, 57–67, p. 58.
12 Available online from: http://etcsl.orinst.ox.ac.uk/section2/tr211.htm. Accessed 10 March 2017. J.A. Black, G. Cunningham, E. Flückiger-Hawker, E. Robson, and G. Zólyomi, *The Electronic Text Corpus of Sumerian Literature* (www-etcsl.orient.ox.ac.uk/), Oxford, 1998–. Copyright © J.A. Black, G. Cunningham, E. Robson, and G. Zólyomi, 1998, 1999, 2000; J.A. Black, G. Cunningham, E. Flückiger-Hawker, E. Robson, J. Taylor, and G. Zólyomi 2001. The authors have asserted their moral rights.
13 Hallo, 'Antediluvian Cities', pp. 57–67 (p. 66).
14 G. Leick, *Mesopotamia: The Invention of the City*, London: Penguin, 2002, p. 6.
15 A.R. George, *Babylonian Topographical Texts*, Louvain: Peeter, 1992, pp. 251–252.
16 M.V.D. van de Mieroop, *The Ancient Mesopotamian City*, Oxford: Clarendon Press, 1996, p. 46.
17 See, for example, van de Mieroop, *The Ancient Mesopotamian City*, and A.R. George, *House Most High: The Temples of Ancient Mesopotamia*, Ann Arbor, MI: Eisenbrauns, 1993.
18 T. Schneider, *An Introduction to Ancient Mesopotamian Religion*, Cambridge: Erdmans, 2011, p. 73.
19 B. de Shong Meador, *The Sumerian Temple Hymns of Enheduanna: Princess, Priestess, Poet*, Austin, TX: University of Texas Press, 2009, p. xii.
20 T. Jacobsen, *The Harps that Once . . . Sumerian Poetry in Translation*, New Haven, CT: Yale University Press, 1987, p. 154, fn. 4.
21 Available online from: http://etcsl.orinst.ox.ac.uk/section1/tr112.htm. Accessed 10 March 2017.
22 de Shong Meador, *The Sumerian Temple Hymns of Enheduanna*, p. 34.
23 de Shong Meador, *The Sumerian Temple Hymns of Enheduanna*, pp. 31–32.
24 That is, a sun god.
25 de Shong Meador, *The Sumerian Temple Hymns of Enheduanna*, pp. 31–32.
26 Black and Green, *Gods, Demons and Symbols of Ancient Mesopotamia*, p. 180.
27 Available online from: http://etcsl.orinst.ox.ac.uk/section1/tr113.htm. Accessed 9 March 2017.
28 Foster, 'Sumerian Mythology', in Crawford (ed.), *The Sumerian World*, pp. 441–443.
29 Available online from: http://etcsl.orinst.ox.ac.uk/section1/tr114.htm. Accessed 1 March 2017.
30 S. Kramer and J. Maier, *Myths of Enki, the Crafty God*, Oxford: Oxford University Press, 1989, p. 253.
31 Black and Green, *Gods, Demons and Symbols of Ancient Mesopotamia*, p. 27.
32 Black and Green, *Gods, Demons and Symbols of Ancient Mesopotamia*, p. 75.
33 P. Espak, 'The God Enki in Royal Sumerian Ideology and Mythology', unpublished Ph.D. thesis, University of Tartu, Estonia, 2010, p. 178.
34 The *mē* are another distinctly Sumerian concept which is difficult to translate, but can be described as the knowledge and accomplishments of civilisation. Enki is the keeper of the *mē*.
35 Jacobsen, *The Harps that Once . . . Sumerian Poetry in Translation*, p. 154.

36 P. Espak, 'Ancient Near Eastern Gods Enki and Ea', unpublished Masters thesis, University of Tartu, Estonia, 2006, p. 117. See also Espak, 'The God Enki in Royal Sumerian Ideology and Mythology', pp. 174–175, for a longer discussion of the nature of the *abzu*.

37 Available online from: http://etcsl.orinst.ox.ac.uk/section1/tr112.htm. Accessed 28 February 2017.

38 Jacobsen, *The Harps that Once . . . Sumerian Poetry in Translation*, p. 154.

39 Available online from: http://etcsl.orinst.ox.ac.uk/section1/tr112.htm. Accessed 10 March 2017

40 H. Sauren, 'Nammu and Enki' in M. Cohen, D. Snell and D. Weisberg (eds), *The Tablet and the Scroll: Near Eastern Studies in Honor of William W. Hallo*, Bethesda, MD: CDL Press, 1993, pp.198–208, p. 200.

41 Available online from: http://etcsl.orinst.ox.ac.uk/section1/tr114.htm. Accessed 10 March 2017.

42 de Shong Meador, *Sumerian Temple Hymns of Enheduanna*, p. 34.

43 See, for example, Kramer and Maier's interpretation of Enki across their book, *Myths of Enki, the Crafty God*.

44 Espak, *Ancient Near Eastern Gods Enki and Ea*, p. 111.

45 Espak, *Ancient Near Eastern Gods Enki and Ea*, p. 26.

46 H.D. Galter, 'The Mesopotamian God Enki/Ea', *Religion Compass* 9/3, 2015, 66–76.

47 Sauren, 'Nammu und Enki', in Cohen, Snell, and Weisberg (eds), *The Tablet and the Scroll*, p. 200.

48 Kramer and Maier, *Myths of Enki, the Crafty God*, p. 32.

49 Jacobsen, *The Harps that Once . . . Sumerian Poetry in Translation*, p. 154.

50 Available online from: http://etcsl.orinst.ox.ac.uk/section1/tr112.htm. Accessed 10 March 2017.

51 C. A. Benito, '"Enki and Ninmah" and "Enki and the World Order"', unpublished PhD thesis, University of Pennsylvania, 1969, p. 22, line 12, and commentary on p. 49; cited in Espak, 'Ancient Near Eastern Gods Enki and Ea', p. 117.

52 Available online from: http://etcsl.orinst.ox.ac.uk/section1/tr112.htm. Accessed 10 March 2017.

53 Galter, 'The Mesopotamian God Enki/Ea', pp. 66–76.

54 Sauren, 'Nammu und Enki', in Cohen, Snell, and Weisberg (eds), *The Tablet and the Scroll*, p. 204, fn. 17.

55 Benito, '"Enki and Ninmah" and "Enki and the World Order"', cited in Espak, 'Ancient Near Eastern Gods Enki and Ea', p. 117.

56 C. G. Jung, 'The Transcendent Function', in *Structure and Dynamics of the Psyche* [*Collected Works*, vol. 8], tr. R.F.C. Hull, London: Routledge and Kegan Paul, 1960, §131–§193 (§159).

57 Hillman, *The Dream and the Underworld*, p. 24.

58 Jung, 'The Transcendent Function', in *Collected Works*, vol. 8, §139.

59 S. Walker, *Jung and the Jungians on Myth*, New York: Routledge, 2002, p. 91.

60 Walker, *Jung and the Jungians on Myth*, p. 91, quoting from a seminar given at the Basel Psychology Club in 1958 reproduced in W. McGuire and R.F.C. Hull (eds), *C.G. Jung Speaking: Interviews and Encounters*, Princeton, NJ: Princeton University Press, 1977, pp. 370–391.

61 Walker, *Jung and the Jungians on Myth*, p. 91.

62 Available online from: http://etcsl.orinst.ox.ac.uk/section1/tr114.htm. Accessed 8 March 2017.

63 Available online from: http://etcsl.orinst.ox.ac.uk/section1/tr113.htm. Accessed 8 March 2017.

64 Kramer and Maier, *Myths of Enki, the Crafty God*, p. 55.

65 See B. de Shong Meador, *Inanna: Lady of Largest Heart*, Austin, TX: University of Texas, 2000, pp. 181–182.

66 Black and Green, *Gods, Demons and Symbols of Ancient Mesopotamia*, p. 110.

67 Jung, 'The Transcendent Function', in *Collected Works*, vol. 8, §134.

68 H. Vanstiphout, 'Why Did Enki Organize the World?', in M. Geller and I. Finkel (eds), *Sumerian Gods and Their Representations*, Groningen: Styx, 1997, pp. 117–134.

69 B. de Shong Meador, *Uncursing the Dark, Treasures from the Underworld*, Wilmette, IL: Chiron Publications, 1992, p.69.

70 E.A. Wallis Budge, *The Babylonian Legends of Creation: And the Fight Between Bel and the Dragon* [1925], New York: Cosimo, 2010, p. 12.

71 Hallo, 'Enki and the Theology of Eridu', pp. 231–234, p. 234.

72 Jung, 'The Transcendent Function', in *Collected Works*, vol. 8, §138.

73 J. Campbell, *The Hero with a Thousand Faces* [1948], Novato, CA: New World Library, 2008.

74 R. Seaford, *Money and the Early Greek Mind: Homer, Philosophy, Tragedy*, Cambridge: Cambridge University, 2004, Press, p. xi.

75 Seaford, *Money and the Early Greek Mind*, p. 6.

INDEX

For Product Safety Concerns and Information please contact our EU
representative GPSR@taylorandfrancis.com
Taylor & Francis Verlag GmbH, Kaufingerstraße 24, 80331 München, Germany

www.ingramcontent.com/pod-product-compliance
Lightning Source LLC
Chambersburg PA
CBHW050517280326
41932CB00014B/2352

*9 7 8 1 1 3 8 3 0 0 5 4 5 *